THE HUMAN BIRTH DEFECT:

On the Origins of Human Unhappiness, and It's Cure.

William J. Kelleher, Ph.D.

The Empathic Science Institute

Los Angeles, California

DEDICATION

Besides the works mentioned throughout this book, the author must also acknowledge the inestimable contribution of the Sunday Morning Meditators, hosted by Wade and Avery, and of Amy (co-host), who introduced me to the *Course.* This work is dedicated to all those who, like the Sunday Morning Meditators, are seeking a cure for the Human Birth Defect.

CONTENTS

PREFACE

Twentieth Century philosopher, Michael Polanyi, has written that centuries of critical thought have taught educated people to distrust their intuitive powers for comprehending themselves and their world. But, he prophesized, once people realize the crippling mutilations imposed on their self-understanding by the dominant objectivist framework, many fresh minds will strive for new ways of satisfying their need to know themselves.

To that end, Dr. Helen Schucman, while a professor of medical psychology at the Columbia University School of Medicine, compiled the results of her quest to understand the human mind and condition. However, lacking a scientific language adequate for expressing her insights, she used a poetic language that rejects and defies the pseudo-scientific jargon in the behavioralist's and cognitivist's mutilating paradigm of social science.

Empathic Science embraces the challenge of articulating a coherent paradigm that can satisfy both the desire for social scientific rationality and the recognition that knowing also entails intuition. Articulating Schucman's understanding within this new framework for social science, this book is a progress report.

The Philosophical Dictionary

In the natural state enjoyed by all quadrupeds, birds and reptiles, man would be as happy as they. Domination would then be a chimera, an absurdity of which no one would think; for why seek servants when you have no need of their services?

Voltaire (under "Equality")

***

Ode to Joy

Joy will nourish us forever,

Flowing forth from nature's breast.

Good or bad, we all endeavor

To find joy in endless quest.

Joy has brought us wine and kisses,

Friends still true where death has trod.

Lent the worm its lowly blisses,

Led the angle unto God.

Friedrich Schiller, Beethoven's 9th Symphony

Introduction

The Sources and Methods of Empathic Science

This book is an introduction to empathic science. Empathic science is the study of the invisible. Being invisible, however, does not mean that there is nothing to see. Whole worlds exist which have never been clearly seen by human eyes. Natural science knows that a vast invisible world exists in nature. There are more planets than the human eye has ever seen. Our universe may be made of waves of energy the eye cannot see. The world known to microbiologists is populated by more life forms than any lay person has ever known. There are tones we cannot hear, and shades of color we cannot see.

The mind is no more visible than any of these other things. Yet, there is an amazing amount to be known, and which can be known. All one needs are the proper tools. We present these instruments for knowing the mind in this book. If "technology" consists of "techniques," then we present here a truly revolutionary technology for acquiring both self-knowledge and the knowledge of others. The causes of human unhappiness, and a way to cure it, as we will show, can be known with the certainty of science.

The methods of empathic science consist of four major elements. These are: i.) introspection; ii.) empathic observation; iii.) intersubjective consultation; and, iv.) our knowledge of the natural sciences, such as physiology, biology, and neurology. The natural sciences help to set the boundaries of the invisible. Neurologists can observe the growing brain knitting together billions of neurons, dendrites, and axons, magically communicating across trillions of tiny synapses. Some of the functions of specific areas of the brain can be determined by observing the consequences of brain injuries, or by probing in the brain during surgery. Highly sophisticated electronic scanners can view shifts in brain energy as the organ engages in mental activity.

The two speech areas in the left hemisphere (at least for right-handed people), Broca's and Wernicke's areas, were discovered over a century ago as a result of observing how injuries to the brain affected the injured person's speech. Injuries to the prefrontal cortex have resulted in personality changes, suggesting that self-image and self-control are located, at least in part, in this area. Surgery, which cut the connections between the right and left hemispheres to help epileptics, has incidentally shown that each side has its own specialized functions. Thus, while our study is of the invisible mind, we will make numerous references to the findings of those sciences which observe the visible. We are interested in exploring where our subject ends, and theirs begins, and vise versa. In Chapters One and Two we present the initial results of our research into how mind and brain interact. Our concern with these relationships is a recurring theme throughout this book.

Unlike the natural sciences, which look outward from the observer to the thing observed, emphatic science begins by looking inward. Introspection and empathic observation are the primary means by which emphatic science can contribute to human knowledge. But, without introspection, there could be no empathic science. Introspection is not difficult to understand. Everybody does it. But we raise it to the level of a research technique, with the clarity of a microscope. After we elaborate on this point, we will return to the roles of emphatic observation and of intersubjective agreement.

Let us ask, then, "what is introspection?" A variety of metaphors, analogies, and similes are used to refer to this mental act. People often talk about "looking within," or using "the mind's eye," or the "third eye." These are visual metaphors. Some people talk about getting "in touch" with their feelings. This would make introspection analogous to the tactile sense. Others say that introspection is like "going within" oneself. That is a spatial simile. There are many other metaphors; for example, the shopkeeper's model of "taking an inventory." Or, the Sherlock Holmes model of "self-investigation." There is a more studious model of "reading" the "text" of one's feelings. And, there is the "self-examination" model evoking the nobility of Socrates.

One common problem here is an implied dualism. Each model suggests an observer and a thing observed. If introspection is "looking within," who is doing the "looking," and what is he or she looking at? This purely verbal problem can distract one's attention from the actual mental processes the words are meant to refer to – if one lets it. In the next chapter, we will show that there is no "duality," but rather two dimensions of each individual's self-reflective consciousness.

The tacit assumption that introspection is a form of perception is the main culprit causing this particular confusion. Introspection is a distinct mental act, which is very different from sense perception. In sense perception, attention is directed outwardly, and is dependent upon sense data. There is very little awareness of oneself in the act of perceiving, because attention is focused on the

3

objects of perception. For introspection, attention is directed inwardly, and is independent of sense data. Whereas in perception the self is *implied*, for introspection the self is at the center of attention. Hence, the two ways of acquiring knowledge and understanding are not at all the same.

Perception is a far more familiar process, and our vocabulary for it is mature and rich with metaphors. We also have a wealth of scientific knowledge about how the senses interact with the brain during perception. But, as yet, neuroscience knows very little about what the brain does during introspection. As we apply our methods of introspection in novel ways throughout this book, the reader will come to understand that we have poured new wine into the old bottles of the perception metaphors. We are developing a new vocabulary, which is better suited to the unique phenomena to which it refers.

Introspection is a process of self-reflection. While perception may be understood on a linear model of sense stimuli going to the brain, introspection is more of a circular process. We understand it as a method of decoding meaningful messages, which can be either called into consciousness by the desire to know oneself, or allowed into consciousness by lowering barriers. In this sense of meaning arising from within, introspection is more like the recall of a memory than it is like any form of perception.

The simile of "recall" suggests one's understanding of such left hemispheric remembering as one does for names and events, both in the long term and short term. But we broaden the familiar meaning of memory to include nonverbal, preconceptual memories of the sort neurologists say are located in the right hemisphere. That is, holistic memories of meanings and feelings.

Perception understands the world as being based on the logic of causation. Sun light, for example, refracted from the Earth's surface and setting off a chain reaction from eyes to brain to consciousness, explains visual perception. But because introspection is a process of attending to oneself, the explanatory logic is that of "inclusion," rather than causation. One introspects to discover what is *included* in oneself. The process involves interpreting what one means to oneself. As the reader will see, this process entails some self-image making as well as some self-image discovery.

A quick glance at the history of introspection may help to clarify what we mean by that term. The kind of introspection with which we are concerned only entered into widespread awareness in the 20th Century. Freud's "sexy" writings about unconscious motivations mark the first systematic usage of introspection. The familiar saying by Socrates that "the unexamined life is not worth living," referred to the analysis of conventional wisdom about such conceptions as "love," "justice," "beauty," and so forth, rather than to psychological motivations. Saint Augustine's *Confessions* confined introspection to the very limited function of conducting a kind of auto-inquisition for "sin." This notion has prevailed in Christendom ever since. Eastern philosophers have developed theories of universal spirituality, but not an individual psychology.

While Viennese Freud initiated the interest in noninquisitorial introspection, Americans began pursuing the practice with a fervor exceeding even the Great Awakening of the 19th Century. Clever entrepreneurs have made millions selling the public "mirrors" into which they can gaze to see themselves. The marketing technique of "pop psychology" is to present "psychological portraits" made of traits which large numbers of the book-buying public can see in themselves. Although little more precise than astrology, pop psychology has provided a valuable service. That is, it has been helping to create a culture of acceptance for the secular practice of introspection. Few people are looking for sin now when they introspect. Rather, they are trying to find-out what makes them, and those they know, tick.

Amidst all the rage over pop psychology, there is also some serious effort to understand this newly discovered human ability to introspect. Humanistic psychologists such as Maslow, May, Fromm, and Frankel have attempted to dig deeper with introspection than have the fortune makers in pop psychology. But the most methodical efforts to date can be found in the client-centered therapy of Carl Rogers. For Rogers, psychotherapy is not a process of the know-it-all psychologist telling a "patient" what is wrong with him or her. Instead, it is a process of encouraging self-discovery and the development of self-understanding by cultivating a "sense of self." His clients report having "breakthroughs" of self-understanding as false notions about themselves are shattered, or as areas of ignorance are illuminated. Gradually they develop a sense of themselves, which they describe as feeling "organic;" that is, a self which is an authentic expression of their very organic being. In Chapter Two we will further discuss this "organic," or end-of-the-line, feeling.

Of course, there are numerous writings on the lessons learned from psychological introspection. The line in Wordsworth's poem, "My Heart Leaps Up," that "the child is father of the man" is now an established principle in psychology. First steps at introspection can be guided in therapy by encouraging a client to talk about his or her relationship with his or her parents. Not only traumas, but also normal interactions in these relationships go a long way towards shaping one's personality.

Empathic science has taken the methods of introspection developed in psychotherapy, and applied them to lines of feeling other than those stemming from the parent-child relationship. As the reader will see, our new applications of this method of self-understanding have already led to some astonishing discoveries, and will surely lead to many more.

In Chapter Three, for example, we will present our empathic understanding of how the very first human beings felt as children being socialized into hominid society, roughly 150,000 years ago. Chapter Four will show how humanity coped with life by cultivating love for over 100,000 years. Chapter Five will explain how and why this practice was abandoned, between 30,000 to 35,000 years ago, as humans began their current pursuit of "power-pleasures." In Chapter Six we will see how the techniques of both ancient and modern wisdom can be used to liberate humanity from its age-old addiction to power-pleasure, and find a fountain of love within.

In therapy one learns to call into consciousness latent "feelings;" i.e., previously unconscious meanings or motivations. These can often be traced to their sources, or origins. Depth psychology, as we have said, often focuses on those feelings stemming from the parent-child relationship. In this, and in a broader sense, feelings as objects of introspection, are configurations of meaning which often have not been fully understood. To "feel one's feelings" is to call into consciousness, and then to receive into consciousness, ill-defined emotions in their raw form. Decoding, or deciphering, the meaning contained within feelings is a separate step in the process of introspection.

Introspection, then, entails the interpretive process of trying to understand the meaning included within one's thoughts and feelings. For example, suppose Joe finally goes in for therapy after losing six jobs in a row for arguing with his bosses. He tells the therapist "I hate all my bosses, but I don't know exactly why. They're just all jerks!" After a few sessions Joe begins to understand that he was transferring his suppressed resentments against his father on to his bosses. Joe's father had died when he was a boy, and his mother never remarried. Joe felt abandoned and robbed of a father-son relationship. The only way he could express his undeciphered resentful feelings was by arguing with these "father figures." After a few cathartic experiences during therapy, Joe resolved his painful internal conflicts, and forgave his father. He went on to become the manger of a large factory, and was well respected by his employees and employers. He also had three sons of his own who are now A-students in college (or, so it would be if this were a book on pop psychology!). Joe was able to improve his condition because he came to understand the meaning of his uncomfortable feelings, and re-parent them with reason.

Introspective interpretation, just like perception, can be mistaken. One can look at a picture of two opposed faces and think, at first, that one sees a vase. Likewise, one can "look within" and see that this time it really is "true love," unlike the ten times before! Of course, this is one reason why professional therapists can perform a useful function. Every therapist knows that false self-understandings can, eventually, and sometimes painfully, be seen through. Because introspection is a central element in the method of empathic science, we must rely on a system of "checks" as security against the hazard of making mistakes. We will discuss this further in a moment.

Introspection is vital to the next methodological step in empathic science, which is empathic observation. It is so important because all empathic observations are based on the assumption of mutuality between observer and observed. So, developing a clear sense of self through introspection is a prerequisite for making empathic observations because one must be able to distinguish oneself from the self of the other.

In Chapter One we will discuss how Paul MacLean's theory of the "triune brain" enables people to empathetically understand one another, and, in a measured way, all other sentient creatures. We will discuss what distinguishes humans from animals. That distinction will enable all who grasp it to see themselves and others with a clarity heretofore unimagined, if not avoided. The elements of mutuality upon which empathic science relies will be discussed openly throughout this book for all to consider, and to accept, reject, or criticize.

The empathic scientist must be on guard against projection. One must strive to distinguish oneself from that which one is observing. In general, one can ask "what does a person know when he thinks he knows another person?" Our answer is that empathic science observation, like introspection, is a continuing process of consciously critical image formation. Besides being subject to error, empathic science knowledge, like that in the natural sciences, is never complete. One can only know parts, and not the whole, of another. Also, people are always growing, learning, maturing, aging, and in many ways changing. Empathic science must present its findings as probabilities rather than certainties, and as tentative rather than eternal. Our quest is for synthetic rather than analytic truths.

Empathic observation entails a large measure of nonverbal communication. Chapters Three and Four will explain how humanity had once developed its full potential for such communication. How and why this cultural treasure was ejected from man's mind, by the "Great Shift" of awareness to verbal communication, will be explained in Chapter Five.

With a full understanding of the elements of mutuality we develop herein, an aspiring empathic observer can learn to read the minds of others like a radiologist can read an x-ray. Indeed for the accomplished empathic scientist, the mind of another becomes more visible than the body to which that mind belongs. The empathic scientist can see that everyone is always "open." That is why an empathic observer can sometimes understand more clearly than another person what that person's immediate mental state is. Take, for example, our old friend Joe. One night he raised his eyebrows and gritted his teeth because his wife was late in having his dinner ready. She said, "there's no reason to get so upset." And Joe shouted back "I'm not upset!" Later he realized that he was upset over a trifle, and that he was in denial about it. So, he had the courage and the courtesy to go to her, confess, and apologize. His feelings were a part of him, which he did not recognize in that moment. However, his wife saw those feelings before he did. She was acting as an empathic observer.

That instance of momentary lack of self-awareness can stand as a paradigm for a whole host of feelings of which humanity itself is not aware, but which an astute empathic observer can clearly see. Indeed, a talented empathic observer can lead people to see what they had no idea, and would completely deny, was in them.

This book is a tribute to the greatest empathic observer of whom we know. Her name is Dr. Helen Schucman. Before she died in the 1970's she was a professor of medical psychology at the Columbia School of Medicine in New York. Her writings show that her x-ray vision penetrated into the deepest recesses of the human mind to illuminate all of its darkest secrets. She had the courage to empathically delve into humanity's worst fears and greatest pain, and then to dwell in them while her eyes adjusted to the darkness. Enduring the agony, she described with precision the hellish landscape she observed. Such self-sacrifice is surely the most honorable act of human courage known to man. Then she offered a program for remediation. Although her descriptions of humanity's ills and her therapeutic prescriptions are presented in the poetic language of her book, *A Course in Miracles,* we have translated her presentation into the secular language of science, empathic science. Two philosophers of science who have made this translation possible by their re-definitions of "science," are Robert S. Hartman, *The Structure of Value*, and Michael Polanyi, *Personal Knowledge*. (Abraham Maslow's, *The Psychology of Science*, was also an important influence on the development of empathic science.)

These towering minds were part of a cultural milieu. They drew from it, clarified its themes, and synthesized them into a unity that no one else could imagine. They wrote in the milieu of the 1950s and 1960s. Here was a time when anti-materialist and more humane and spiritual values were being expressed. These sentiments are well represented in such works as *The Greening of America* by Charles A. Reich, and Marilyn Ferguson's *The Aquarian Conspiracy.* In this period began the movement towards more emotional openness, the criticism of the a-morality of science, the desire to find some way of making humanity more humane, and the belief that oneness with nature, and with each other, plus happiness for all, are achievable goals – ideals to which our society has been paying tribute, at least since that time.

For those who feel intuitively that we are living at the Dawn of a New Age, herein are the facts which will validate that feeling. Empathic science is the science that can make these dreams come true. Man's level of civilization can be both measured and raised by science. This book will show how. Guided by Hartman's formal logic of value, and the understanding of the aims, methods, and knowledge of science provided by Polanyi, we have culled from Schucman's spiritual writings numerous concepts, principles, and discoveries, gained by her introspection and empathy. She has shown us where to look. We have looked, and we will present here what we have seen. Our empathic observations can be checked within oneself by introspection. These understandings can then be cross-checked through the process of intersubjective consultation. Agreed findings can become the basis for new discoveries. Hence, empathic science knowledge is cumulative. Its claims are subject to validation, as well as falsification, by the relevant community of informed participants.

As Polanyi shows in *Personal Knowledge*, all fields of science, in both natural and empathic science, depend upon intersubjective consultation and agreement to establish what knowledge claims will be acceptable for each field. This process consists of several elements. These include the participation of interested parties who understand and agree upon the methods used, and who work together in the good faith desire to advance human knowledge. Participants may compete for discoveries, and all will use their independent judgment and skills for critical thinking. The intersubjective agreement of Hartman, Polanyi, and Schucman, along with a score of other insightful writers, to be mentioned in our narrative, provides the foundation of empathic science. While the fields of natural science are lead by certified experts, because it is new, empathic science is open to everyone, and all are invited to participate in it by agreeing with or criticizing its claims, especially the readers of this book.

Illustrations of the necessity of intersubjective agreement for the progress of science are easy to find. The history of natural science is full of stories about how progress was stalled because lesser minds failed to appreciate, or refused even to consider, the claims of genius. Gregor Mendel's contribution to genetics was unrecognized for decades, because the people who should have known better failed to appreciate his findings. Belated intersubjective agreement raised Mendel to his current status in natural science. The story of Galileo and his telescope is a classic. By a tradition begun in the Dark Ages, the power elite of the Catholic Church were the guardians of what their "flock" could believe as "true." Because Galileo saw planets which, according to their reading of the Bible, the Church Fathers said could not exist, they refused to take a look through his new fangled instrument. They forced the 70 year old Galileo to recant, by threatening to burn him as a heretic. As with Mendel, belated intersubjective agreement raised Galileo to his current status in natural science. Without a change of intersubjective agreement, the work of these men would still be unknown.

Today's Dominant Paradigm

Empathic science largely relies upon introspection and empathic observation as its "new fangled instrument." There will be "experts" and "authorities" who will also refuse to take a look through these instruments of knowledge. Chief among these will be the high priests of behavioral psychology, and the Grand Dragons of its campy derivative, the so-called "cognitive sciences." In *The Rediscovery of the Mind*, by the University of California, Berkeley, professor of philosophy John R.

Searle, the aims and methods of behavioralism and cognitive science are stated, and then criticized. In this, Searle anticipates and articulates the main philosophical criticisms that empathic science sees in the dogmas of these "empirical" approaches to human understanding. They doubt, and sometimes deny, the existence of consciousness in the human mind. We accept the obvious fact of consciousness. The reader can test the behavioralist's doubt right now by asking "am I conscious?" If not, how do you know that you asked this question? In Chapter One we will discuss what consciousness is, how it works, and its relationship to the brain.

As if to doubt the existence of consciousness was not nonsense enough, they are extremely skeptical about the existence of sentience in both humans and animals. That is, they do not recognize the existence of feelings as anything more than products of the ill informed, unscientific imagination. Their "empirical science" only sees visible bodies. These bodies move, they say, simply because the brains in them have been programmed in evolution to make the calculations needed for the organism's survival. In their view, humans and animals are no more than organic robots with no more feeling than a machine.

Empathic science accepts the existence of sentience, and the capacity to choose, as essential elements of both man and animals. The mutuality of our biochemistry, physiology, and neurology enables us as humans to understand one another and to relate to all other sentient creatures. In Chapter Two we will discuss what we humans can learn from the animals about living a life much richer in sentience than we now experience.

The empathic scientist cannot help but feel ire when considering the role of behavioral science in contemporary society. Polanyi scoffs at the stubborn obtuseness of behavioralism and dismisses it as "a fit subject for ridicule," in *The Study of Man*.[i] Searle repeatedly challenges the proponents of those "mindless" theories to confront their own "fear of the subjective." We go a step further and deem those schools of thought, in all their variations, "the cowardly sciences." We have seen courage, and what courage can show us, and they have none of it. One aim of the cowardly sciences is to ape the methods of natural science, so as to appear to be "scientifically" producing knowledge about human behavior. Behind their façade of great learning is their real "fear of the subjective." That is, they are trying to hide the terror they feel of looking within. Their self-deception would not be worthy of notice, if it was confined to their own mutual admiration societies. Unfortunately, they are the dominant paradigm in nearly all of the universities in the United States today.

In our view, their dominance does not rest upon the contribution they make to human self-understanding. For, what they teach is not self-understanding, but self-loathing. They reduce the awesome marvel of the freethinking, deep feeling mind to the level of a machine, like the ones that mind creates. They suck-out the intrinsic value appropriate to humanity, and leave for study nothing more than bodies moving along a causal chain. They mimic the methods of 19th Century physics, which have long been disregarded by modern physics, and teach trusting students that they are "doing science."

No, the dominance of the behavioral/cognitivist paradigm throughout the social sciences is not due to the knowledge it imparts, but to the services it provides to its powerful patrons, the American ruling elites. It is often corporate money that pays for the university "chairs," the prestigious "think tanks," owns the textbook publishing companies, and provides most of the lucrative "research grants" that the cowardly scientists crave. Many of them are knowing sycophants, driven by greed.

The connections between behavioralism and the superrich corporations and individuals, which rule America from outside the government, are well known. Through billion dollar foundations, like those owned by the Rockefellers, Fords, and others even larger, huge endowments are given to those universities that propagate the "Big Lies" of behavioral science. These schools get fancy laboratories with all the latest equipment needed to house small animals for testing with electric shocks and surgery to see how they learn, and if they have consciousness or sentience. New libraries are built to store all the books and journals the behavioralists write for one another. These items give the schools, their administrators, and alumnus prestige and bragging rights. The propagators of the behavioral paradigm receive "genius grants" with no strings attached. The "star" grant-getters receive so much money that they can live well for years on "sabbatical leaves." But, of course, the foundations must first approve of their research proposals.

In addition, the foundations fund "professional societies," so that the behavioralists can meet in Las Vegas and other resort areas to hold conventions and give each other awards. The critics of that paradigm, by comparison, receive far less in the way of grant money and honors. As might be expected, all this glitter is gold attracting young scholars to learn the art of propagating behavioral science. Behavioralism and cognitivism, then, are less "sciences" than they are professions of beggars and performers bent upon their own self-enrichment.

Anyone with a mind for math might start adding up all the money the foundations are giving to the behavioralists and ask what the rich are receiving in return. The key service, perhaps the one and only service, which behavioralism must provide for its generous pay, is to desensitize students to, and discourage them from, introspection.

Since behavior is a "learned response," say the behavioralists, there is no need to ask such questions as "who am I?" or "what am I living for?" or "why am I, and people generally, so discontented?" or "what can make life more worth living?" Behavioralism teaches that such thinking is irrelevant to scientific knowledge. Every "well adjusted" person has learned "the meaning of life" through socialization. Thus behavioralism teaches students that "mental health" consists of uncritical conformity to the social order.

The American socio-economic order could not survive in its present form without behavioral propaganda. Its doctrines have become the conventional wisdom, which keeps everyone singing from the same page. For cover, behavioralists permit students to hang posters in the school hallways that say "Think Critically" or "Question Authority." But in the lecture hall, all the answers are given. These lectures often include the "scientific" finding that the students have no minds with which to perform the acts promoted by the posters. The behavioralists know, without being told, that the American ruling elites need unthinking, unfeeling, self-loathing automatons to keep the economy growing. Unless everyone unquestioningly accepts his or her "conditioning" to live for the making and spending of money, the economy could suffer, and the superrich would lose opportunities to increase their wealth.

Behavioralism saves the economy from this "disaster" by teaching students that they have nothing to "introspect" into; therefore, introspection, and all that it could reveal, never becomes a problem. It's not that behavioralists forbid introspection, like God at the Gates of Eden. They are too crafty for that. They simply herd students into an intellectual corral in which introspection does not make sense, and has no adult support. Then the students graduate from school, thinking that they have been "educated," and go out to find their position as functionaries in the economy.

Obviously, empathic science is at odds with behavioralism. Without hyperbole, and without apology, we regard that paradigm as "the enemy of the people," and seek its destruction. Their corporate patrons be damned! This book is the statement of our case. Like Thomas Jefferson, and the Founding Generation of the United States, we declare our reasons and intentions out of "a decent respect for the opinions of mankind." We want empathic science to be as open as a Townhall Meeting. We claim no access to special knowledge, which must be taken on faith. We state our methods and our findings as openly as we know how. Let "a candid world" be our judge.

Chapter One

Our Model of Mind

Defining Our Terms

Empathic science studies the mind in relation to its source, the brain. In our view, the mind only exists in relation to the brain. There can be no mind without an organic base. Those who feel a strong intuition that they exist at the behest of a "higher power" are experiencing a true self-awareness. However, the verbal expression of that self-awareness, as evidence of "God's existence," is, from the scientific point of view, misplaced. That "power" is not "higher" in the sense of being outside and above the mind; rather, like body heat from the body, the mind emanates from the brain that produces it. The experience of a "higher power" to which one's self owes its existence is, in large part, the experience of the mind/brain relation.

The mind, as Searle writes, is the product of the brain. One of the functions of the brain is to produce its own consciousness, and then to give that consciousness content. Because this is its own consciousness, and its own contents, the brain is a self-reflective organ. This is one of the fundamental premises upon which empathic science rests. Through introspection one can learn to sense, at first, and then, with effort, to see clearly that one's own brain produces self-reflection. Just as the proper combination of hydrogen and oxygen produces water, the brain has its special production. This is an awesome and powerful magic, but one we take, like Searle, as fact. We agree with Hartman that consciousness is essentially "pure self-reflection." Therefore, the main aim of this chapter is to explain our understanding of "consciousness," its "content," and the relationship between these and the collection of organs called *the* brain.

We understand the term "mind" to include consciousness, its content, and a tacit supporting subsystem, which is in part accessible to consciousness, and in part inaccessible to consciousness. By defining our terms in this chapter, we will also be explaining our model of mind. The rest of this book is premised upon that model.

Let us begin by asking, "what is consciousness?" Consciousness, in our understanding, is the field of awareness created by the brain's self-reflection. As the brain produces self-reflection, its other products emerge as objects in the field of self-reflection. We call these objects the contents of consciousness. Consciousness is always the brain's awareness of its own productions. Because, as we will see, the brain produces mental activity, we may say that consciousness is always of, and only of, mental activity.

We envision five dimensions of mental activity. These are: i.) consciousness itself; ii.) sense data; iii.) internal organ messaging; iv.) thoughts (or cognitions); and, v.) feelings (or affectations). Following Edmund Husserl, the founder of phenomenology, psychologist Franz Brentano distinguishes consciousness from its content, and further observes that consciousness is always intentional. That is, consciousness is always (at least in the normal waking state) "of" something. Normally, consciousness is not of itself, but rather it is of the other four kinds of mental activity. For example, sounds pass in raw form as waves through the air. The waves strike one's ears. This sensation is sent through the nerves to the brain. There, the signals from the nerves are sent into consciousness and translated into music, noise, a friendly voice, etc. In this causal chain, consciousness is of the brain's product rather than of the sound itself.

Likewise, messages are sent from a full bladder, or an empty stomach, along nerves into the brain. These get translated into meaningful feelings and passed on to consciousness, where decisions can be made as to what course of action to take. "Should I continue reading, or get up and go to the bathroom, or go make a sandwich?" Asking oneself that question constitutes thinking, or what psychologists technically term "cognition." Each person has a continuing internal (some would say "infernal") dialogue as a major part of the mental activity of which one is normally conscious. Feelings, emotions, or technically "affectations," also occupy a large measure of a person's consciousness.

Such mental activities are expressions of one's personality. What goes on in each head, so to speak, is different because each personality is unique. Thus, consciousness is always *of* something from any one, or a mix, of the last four categories of content. Our amazing brain coordinates and screens these four sources of content so that they do not come pouring into consciousness all at once and drive us crazy. We call this function of the brain "the screen of meaning," and we will return to it later in this chapter.

Empathic science draws from many sources in developing its understanding of the mind. However, the process by which consciousness can be of itself is not well understood by psychologists and neurologists, although, as we will see in Chapter Two, they are searching for answers. Indeed, *the single most important message that empathic science has to deliver is that, and how, consciousness can be of itself.* In Chapter Two, we will offer our explanation of this uniquely human capacity of consciousness.

The brain produces self-awareness, as we have said, and consciousness is the field of "awareness" in that self-awareness. Thus, we call our understanding of consciousness "the field theory of consciousness." As a field, distinct from the aforesaid elements of content, consciousness itself has several constituent properties. Among these are: i.) boundaries; ii.) luminosity; iii.) flow; iv.) focus; v.) unity; and, vi.) self-reflective plasticity. Those brain and neurological processes that never enter consciousness set its boundaries. For example, the movement of sense data through the nerves and into the brain is not felt, but one is only aware of the information allowed into consciousness by the screen of meaning. In this way, neurological processes set some limits on what information will cross the border and enter consciousness from the senses or the internal organs.

There is even a specialized gate within the screen of meaning that monitors the thoughts and feelings of which one is socially allowed be aware. Thus, the brain can learn to develop a conscience. Every society has taboo thoughts and feelings, such as incest, infanticide, parenticide, and so on, which children are taught are too terrible to allow to enter consciousness. While these taboos do not succeed with everyone, the exceptions prove the rule. The brains of most people do not allow prohibited thoughts and feelings into consciousness. Some people struggle in varying degrees to keep them out. A small number experience such forbidden mental fruits, and a much smaller number act upon them.

Such borderline skirmishes with temptations suggest that the boundaries of consciousness are not clear-cut, but phase into a less conscious, or even a subconscious, realm. Psychotherapy shows that subconscious suppressed thoughts and feelings can exert influence on behavior and the quality of one's life. When these are brought up into consciousness, they can often be reasoned, or reparented, away. Unwanted behavior can be changed, and the quality of one's life improved. Also, everyone has had the experience of a word, name, or fact in memory, but just on the tip of the tongue, yet too out of reach to say. This is also an experience of the borderline of consciousness.

Consciousness has the quality of luminosity. For example, when first awakening from sleep one's field of awareness may be vague and limited, content indistinct. Each person experiences a peak of clarity during a typical day, as well as a daily norm of awareness. This may decline with fatigue into drowsiness. Having too much to drink, or receiving a sock on the jaw, may also reduce luminosity.

The dynamics of the rise and decline of luminosity, plus the orderly manner in which content parades through consciousness over time, creates the quality of flow.

The focus of consciousness consists in degrees of concentration. Concentration puts a focus upon that which will enter consciousness. It can also determine what consciousness will be of. Concentration is an act of will, but it can be triggered by surprise, such as a knock on the door, or the ring of the phone. It can also be relaxed or intensified. One may be in a relaxed and restful state of unfocused daydreaming – until the boss comes in! Then one suddenly focuses on one's work in a grand display of concentration. Attention deficit disorder is largely a problem of an inability to control focus through one's will.

Focus generally entails a peripheral awareness. For example, while reading this book one may also be somewhat aware of the music playing on one's radio, while also monitoring the stomach/bladder situation mentioned earlier.

The individual experiences consciousness as a unity. Indeed, the use of one word for it implies a singular object of reference. But whether there is actually only one consciousness, or many, is not a scientific certainty. Following the work of neurologist Paul McLean, many scientists divide the brain into three evolutionary layers. These are the reptilian, the mammalian, and the human. Each represents a stage in the development of the brain. Our brain also has two large hemispheres, each with several areas of specialization. How these parts, and the numerous organs contained within the brain contribute to the individual's experience of a unitary consciousness is not fully understood by science. There may be distinct "consciousnesses," or fields of awareness, the confluence of which each person experiences as his or her singular consciousness.

This potential complexity of consciousness is especially important to keep in mind when tempted to wax poetic about the analogy of consciousness to light. Light is properly the subject of physics, because it has physical properties. Consciousness is properly the subject of empathic science, because its properties are invisible, yet commonly experienced. Part of scientific training is to learn that descriptions are never the thing described, but are always abstractions and at least one step removed from the real thing. Metaphors and similes are even further removed from the thing referred to than is a direct description. To say facilely "consciousness is like light" may actually convey no more hard information than to say, "Mary is a peach of a lady." Empathic science tries to do better than that. So, any easy analogy of consciousness to light should be made with this warning on the label.

The final quality of consciousness on our list is also the least understood outside empathic science. This is the capacity of consciousness for self-reflective plasticity. In other words, as mentioned above, consciousness has the flexibility to turn away altogether from everyday content, and to reflect exclusively upon itself. We call this "the consciousness of consciousness." The next chapter, and the rest of this book thereafter, will be devoted to illuminating the various aspects of this most human, but least understood, quality of consciousness. But before we examine the consciousness of consciousness, and how it can be achieved, let us consider further how consciousness came about. Because consciousness is an element of the mind/brain relationship, it evolved in conjunction with the evolution of the brain. We will see that the direction of this evolution is one of increasing complexity in both structure and function. Gradually, the stage was set for the appearance of the human brain with its unique cognitive capacities and forms of feeling.

The Origins of Mind

Contrary to creationist dogma, the complex system called "the brain" did not just "pop" into existence. As Polanyi explains, in *Personal Knowledge*, the mind/brain relationship and its functions have been shaped, tested, and honed by hundreds of millions of years of evolution. Evolutionary biologists speculate that perhaps two billion years ago, there were single-cell protozoa attracted to the surface of the sea by the light and warmth of the sun. This "attraction" theory presupposes a microscopic element of sentience and self-awareness, in a tiny mind/brain relationship, which likely evolved out of plant tropism. Some of those protozoa that were more attracted to the

25

surface of the sea than to its darker, colder depths by the sun's rays evolved into a species of larger, more complex organisms. They did not plan it that way, they were simply sentient organisms that felt more comfortable in the light and warmer water. An additional unintended consequence of this protozoa behavior was to establish a novel principle on Earth, which would hold true in various forms for billions of years, and even now. That is, that sentient creatures tend to seek some level of comfort, and to avoid discomfort.

After about one billion years of evolution, marine invertebrates had developed the mental capacity to distinguish between "food" and "nonfood," and the ability to seek the former. There also developed creatures that ate other creatures. Some of them became vertebrates. Those "prey" that evolved the capacity to recognize "predators," and flee, outlasted the standpatters. Those predators that devised new ways of catching prey, such as larger, stronger, faster bodies, flourished, while those which could not catch fleeing prey vanished into extinction.

Thus, seeking warmth and avoiding cold gradually evolved into the more complex motivations of seeking on the bases of hunger and food recognition, and avoiding on the bases of fear and the recognition of predators. These were the contents in the consciousness of those early self-reflective organisms. Among the first affectations, then, was the desire for food; that is, the desire to satisfy hunger. Also, with "recognition," a cognitive element was added to the mind/brain relationship of organisms at an early stage in evolution. To be sure, this was a very simple form of "cognition." The capacity to recognize food and nonfood has been observed in earthworms. They also show a preference for moist soil over the dry stuff. Indeed, Polanyi makes the empathic observation that the contemporary "amoeba hunts for food."[ii] "Hunting," of course is an intentional activity, implying the basic elements of a complex mind/brain relationship.

Over a billion and a half years of evolution passed before the sentience of protozoa evolved into the sentience and cognitive capacity of such simple organisms as the earthworm. But in the interim, numerous organizational revolutions were required to produce this result. Such revolutions entailed reconfigurations in the structure of the nervous system in organisms, and in the functions which those nervous systems performed. The structures and functions of less complex systems were subsumed and reconfigured in the more complex systems into which the lower forms had evolved. Each reconfiguration entailed a minute creative leap beyond its original base, so that each new organism was not identical to its predecessor. Natural selection then sorted-out which of these new combinations of characteristics would survive and reproduce.

Early in evolution, both prey and predator needed ever more complex systems of limbs and muscles connected to nerves, which were connected to a central decision-making agency and information-receiving center called "the brain." Through the competition for survival, these increasingly complex systems of bodies capped by self-reflective brains evolved into millions of different life forms. There were fish and primitive amphibians 350,000,000 years ago. By this time the basic elements of the reptilian brain had begun to emerge in the forerunner of the reptiles. The reptilian mind/brain relationship went on to rule the world until, by chance, its reign was violently ended about 65,000,000 years ago.

Long before then, some small reptiles had mutated into mouse-size mammals, which bore their young, rather than laying eggs, and which had mammary glands for nurturing their off-spring. Their brains grew a string of tissue layered over the reptilian elements of the brain, which intensified their instinct for nurturing and other forms of social behavior. That addition to the old brain evolved into what is now called "the limbic system."

Scientists generally agree that one of the basic differences in behavior between reptiles and mammals is that the latter tend to be more maternal in the treatment of their young, and more political in their social organization. That is, reptiles lay eggs, and do some, but comparatively little, nurturing of their young. Turtles, crocodiles, and lizards may not even recognize their own hatchlings. While reptiles may congregate in groups, they have very little social organization. Crocs, for example, will fight over a kill, but not organize or cooperate in a hunt. Reptiles generally lack complex group behavior, like male-female food sharing, the protection of each other's offspring, or a common understanding of group leadership. The development in the mammalian brain of the limbic system, and additional cortical tissue around the brain, is generally regarded as the seat of the more nurturing and more complex social behavior of mammals.

One of the unintended consequences of this creative process of evolution is what McLean calls "the triune brain." That is, the three-layer brain. The most complex development of this brain is the human brain, with its comparatively large complement of cortical tissue – the neo-cortex. In this understanding, the human brain subsumes structures and functions of both the reptilian brain and the mammalian brain, and reconfigures them into what we humans understand as "ours," even though they entail the contributions of millions of ancestors going back to the protozoa.

Empathic science depends upon, and extends, this theory of the triune brain's evolution. We rely on it, for example, to explain our own conception of "mutuality," which is the basis of empathy. "Mutuality" refers to our common ground in biochemistry, physiology, and neurology with other sentient creatures. This common ground enables humans to understand quite a bit about each other's mental experience, and that of other forms of animal life.

Consider, for example, how humanity's "practical judgment" came about. It began with tiny worm-like organisms in the sea that could choose between food and nonfood, and recognize predators and wiggle away. They survived to produce offspring. Gradually, a reptilian brain evolved that could manage the complex internal organs of huge dinosaurs as well as perform the judgments required for survival. For such meaty creatures to survive they would have had to exercise a practical judgment as to whether fight or flight would be the best response to a threat. Predatory dinosaurs would need sufficient reasoning skills to hunt, and to make such judgments as whether to attack now, stalk, or stay away. To make all these survival judgments and decisions, the mind of the dinosaur would have to be conscious of its needs, its options in a particular circumstance, and its abilities to undertake a course of action. Natural selection would soon take care of all those would-be predators that were foolish enough to attack tougher "prey." Their dead bodies would become fertilizer, while more prudent predators produced offspring. These dinosaurs were the benefactors of trends which had begun long before the great reptiles emerged. Thus, early in evolution, natural selection favored the mind/brain relationship that could successfully engage in practical judgment.

So, before the first mammals appeared, complex creatures walked the Earth with a brain, an intricate nervous system, and sufficient consciousness to evaluate circumstances and make judgments and decisions necessary to survive. This also required a filtering mechanism in the brain to monitor and screen the information flowing into consciousness in favor of the organism's survival. Minds full of irrelevant information would be unable to make the quick decisions needed for survival. In other words, ancient animals had minds with many characteristics like those of the human mind.

At this point, one may challenge us to prove our point. If there are behavioral scientists today who stare at one another in the laboratory, each doubting that the other has consciousness, because each cannot see it in the other, then how can one claim with any degree of confidence that dinosaurs had practical judgment, or even consciousness at all?

Our answer is that we exercise an informed and measured empathy. We can know from our own experience what is required for a successful hunt. We can observe lions in the jungle, wolves in the forest, sharks in the sea, and eagles in the air. Not much empathy is needed to determine with reasonable certainty what elements of mind we share with these animals to succeed at the same endeavors. Even the pet cat is a living demonstration of the animal mind/brain relationship. To jump on its owner's writing table, Felix must first be aware of that option, and then judge the difficulty of the task, and his ability to accomplish it. Finally, he takes his decision, crouches, and leaps. Its possible he will slip on the paper covering the table, and fall off. Or, he could undershoot and miss the table. Or, his owner could catch him in the air and tell him "no." Or, he may decide that he has gotten too fat, or too old, and stroll over to a much easier target, like the couch.

Accepting the proposition that animal consciousness exists is different in kind from accepting the existence of Leprechauns, evil spirits, angles, souls, or gods. While all are ostensibly invisible to the naked eye, the degree of belief required is far less for animal consciousness because of the quality of evidence available. One can observe the animal body, which houses the brain. One can observe that body's movements. From there, one can infer, with no great leap of empathy, the consciousness, and the mental activity, needed for decision-making prior to action. Of course, it is precisely this tiny empathic inference that the cowardly sciences are terrified of making. By acknowledging the existence of any consciousness, they would come perilously close to admitting that their own consciousness exists – then, watch out! The next step would be the terrifying act of introspection. (Help!)

The Animal and Human Mind/Brain Relation

Once the principle of animal consciousness is accepted as a reasonable certainty, if not beyond a reasonable doubt, then one can apply it beyond the immediate evidence. One need not observe dinosaurs to make reasonable inferences about their brains and minds. Their bones show that they had brain cases, and backbones to house a central nervous system. Their teeth show that some were carnivorous and some herbivorous. We know that the carnivores must hunt to eat. We know that herbivores must make fight or flight choices when a carnivore approaches. If one accepts that consciousness is required for effective decision-making in humans, then there is little reason not to apply that principle to animals. A somnambulist animal is no better at decision-making than is a man in that condition. Thus, we may infer that an alert mind, which has an automatic filter to block unnecessary input, is as essential for animal survival as it is for human survival. Consciousness, as we understand it, then, evolved early in the history of life, first as a simple preference for comfort, and later as an instrument for survival decision-making.

Empathic science, then, holds that the field theory of consciousness applies to animals as well as to humans. We further state that the reptilian brain is sufficient to produce the self-reflective field of awareness that is consciousness. The reptilian brain, as well as the mammalian brain, has a filtering function which monitors the amount and kind of data that enters consciousness. Decision-making for survival has top priority in this filtering system. Like the reptile, the brains of both animal and man perform a filtering function in the service of consciousness. These mechanisms were gradually built-in by natural selection. For example, neither man nor animal needs to experience electro-chemical impulses rocketing through their nervous systems on the way to the brain. That would only be a distraction from the business of watching for predators, or looking for food. We need not experience the process of our stomach separating nutrients from waste, nor our immune system battling germs. The human "screen of meaning" has resulted from the creative subsumption and adaptation of these animal functions.

The capacity to create new knowledge highlights one of the differences between man and animals. While animal memories work as well as human memories, nature limits what they can know about the world around them largely to what their senses are able to perceive. Man's learning capacity goes well beyond the limits of his senses into an infinite capacity for abstract knowledge. Natural selection has molded animal species to fit into a particular niche. Animal learning merely enables individual members of a species to fine-tune their adaptation to their environment. A lion can learn to hunt a variety of prey, from wildebeests to wild boar, but it cannot learn to farm. Nature has set limits to learning, which the lion, or any other animal, cannot go beyond.

Domestic cats are another example of how evolution has minimized the need and ability for learning in animals. Pet cats have retained vestiges of their hunting instinct, but they must learn to recognize what is prey, and how to capture and kill it. However, the amount of learning necessary for this is so limited that a kitten raised in a house without a feline mother can learn to capture and kill prey simply through trial and error, propelled by instinct. One episode of the program "Nature" on TV showed how two orphaned cheetah cubs learned to survive through trial and error. The instinct to hunt guided their behavior, and learning merely honed their inherited abilities to survive in their niche.[iii] Human history shows that we are not tied to any particular niche. We can create all sorts of ways of life from farming to finance. But one price we pay for this great learning capacity is the long childhood dependence we have compared to any animal. For our species to survive, human parents have the responsibility to nurture and protect their off-spring for many years, rather than simply attend to their own needs. Even the children of contemporary hunter-gatherers must spend far more time learning survival skills and social cooperation than any animal.

As Polanyi shows, the human capacity for immense abstract learning evolved out of its precursor function in the animal brain. Human learning is of a different order than animal learning because, as a part of the reconfiguration of the animal brain functions, humans can make highly complex meanings. This ability originated in the reconfiguration of functions that were regulated and limited by instinct in the animal brain. Such characteristics as animal learning ability, problem solving skills, practical judgment, and awareness of needs, pleasures, and pains are subsumed, recombined, and extended by a creative leap into the marvels of abstract thinking and a fertile meaning making imagination in mankind. "Meaning," for empathic science, consists of abstract presuppositions about facts and values, which are woven together in the context of our self-reflective minds. We will discuss the nature of meaning further in this and later chapters. Whether meaning making follows its own binary logic, combining fact and value, remains a research question.

This capacity for complex meaning making is one of the largest differences between the mind/brain relation in the animal, and that in man. While both man and animal have self-reflective brains, the "self" of which animal and human are aware is made different in kind, not merely in degree, by its abstract complexity. Let us consider some of the similarities, which contribute to this "self," before looking at the differences.

Each individual human and animal is unique. While similarities in the building materials exist within a species, the way these materials are organized to produce the nervous system, bodies, and brains are unique for each individual. This organizational uniqueness accounts for differences in temperament, behavior, and intelligence among individuals within the same species. Both man and animal have needs, and must make calculations as to how to satisfy their needs. Each makes decisions for action based on their awareness of options. Like man, the animal self has an ego that performs the executive function of gathering information in one place, and making decisions based upon what is known. Animal need-awareness, their processing of information, and their decision-making are governed by the species instincts provided them through natural selection. But man's self, and his parallel functions, are mediated more by meaning. The elements of instinct and meaning account for the two different kinds of self.

An animal can be aware of its needs, options for action, and its abilities, but only humans can meaningfully employ the concept of "myself." For example, orangutans, chimpanzees, and gorillas have been taught to communicate in sign language. But in every instance, these animals refer to themselves in the context of the third person. "Koko want banana, hurry," signs the famous gorilla. When her pet kitten was run-over by a car, the big ape signed "Koko sad, no kitty." This third person self-referencing shows that the experience of both needs and emotions enters into animal consciousness, but that they appear to lack the capacity for understanding the first person meaning of "I."

A man can write a multi-volume autobiography elaborating the meaning of "I" to him. An animal just cannot get it. Koko uses her name as a label for the organism that experiences needs and emotions, but not as the title of an autobiography. Likewise, a dog responds to the call "here Fido," both because it has been bred to obey, and because it has learned that rewards follow the appropriate response to the command (such as favorable attention from its master, a hug, and a biscuit). But no matter how clever he is, Fido will never write his autobiography. Not only because he cannot write, but also because he has no meaning of "I" to write about. Animals have a consciousness of "self" as a center of needs, desires, and the physical abilities to satisfy those needs and desires, but these awarenesses do not occur within the context of an identification of a personality, that is, a personal identity. Self-awareness and self-conception are not the same.

The animal self is defined almost entirely by inherited behavioral predisposition. Each animal is unique, and can engage in some learning, but its range of behavior is set and limited genetically. Humans also have inherited limitations, but as we have seen, the capacity for meaning making lifts all the limits which instinct put on the animal's ability to learn, invent, and create. Within the context set by physiology and neurology, each human creates himself or herself by exercising the meaning making function. The self-made element of the human self explains why human self-awareness is in the first person, and animal self-awareness is in the third person. Because humans have a self-made self-conception, a human can say "May I have a banana, please?" or, in some cases, "I wanna banana!" But no normal adult human says, for example, "George want banana, hurry!"

The Self-Created Self

The making of this self-conception begins at birth. There is much debate among the professionals about the psychological significance, if any, of birth. Behavioralists, of course, see nothing but one bag of skin dropping out of another. There are other psychologists who see birth as one of the most, if not the most, profound experiences of life. Empathic science, once again, finds the behavioral point of view not only devoid of insight, wisdom, and feeling, but an offensive diminishment of humanity. We draw from that long tradition in psychology that sees birth as a major turning point in the experience of the human individual. Birth marks the beginning, among other things, of the self-created self, and, as we will suggest, of human unhappiness.

In our view, consciousness emerges in the normal fetus as the brain reaches its ability to produce it. As consciousness is always *of* something, in the fetus it is of the experience of a living system of organs that are perfectly nurtured by a placenta. The little body is one with its environment. The needs of all its internal organs are anticipated and satisfied automatically, before they reach consciousness. Temperature is perfectly controlled, and the senses are free from irritation. We agree with the renowned psychoanalyst, Otto Rank, that the feeling of which consciousness is aware in this condition can only be described as "bliss." All systems are humming. Fear is unknown. All is right with the world. At the very worst, for the normal growing fetus, there may seem to be a little less legroom than there used to be. The prenatal mind/brain relationship consists in consciousness of the contentment produced by the harmoniously functioning organism.

Suddenly pushing and squeezing motions jolt the fetus. Discomfort violates bliss consciousness. The tiny body is pushed through a narrow passage without its consent, and beyond its control. For the first time it is exposed to dry air, cooling its skin unpleasantly. It may then be held in the air, smacked on the butt, with fingers shoved in its mouth and nostrils. Strange sounds and bright lights penetrate its virgin senses. Then it is wrapped in dry cloth to contemplate its shocking experience.

Every infant is unique, and will respond in its own way to birth. Some may seem to take it calmly. Others may seem to withhold judgment. While still others, may scream in protest. But, for all of them, during this dramatic moment, the brain goes to work as it had never done before. In its own little way, it attempts, in the words of psychologist William James, to make sense of all the "blooming, buzzing confusion." Baby's first efforts to think are likely tiny mental lunges in the direction of demanding to know "what is going on here?!" These little efforts to make sense are exhausting, and baby needs plenty of sleep.

As baby tries to make sense of the birth trauma, it is engaging in a process that will have huge consequences for the rest of his or her life. Baby is defining who he or she is, the nature of the world that he or she is living in, and also arranging the neuropathways in his or her brain so that all future sense experience, internal organ messaging, thought, and feeling will be understood in the self-reflective self-conception which baby is now making. This is a big job for someone with so little worldly experience!

We concur with Schucman's suggestion that there is no "I," as a self-conception, before birth. "I" requires a prior separation to sustain it. This separation comes with birth. The sense of "I" begins to develop as birth and the people and the environment around baby act upon the baby's body. Thus, "I" is initially defined by the experience of the body. Baby's mind begins to create a body image as a result of its experiences. The skin becomes the outer boundary. Bumps and bruises reinforce the lesson that this body is a vulnerable thing in a hazardous environment. Messaging from internal organs define the body as having an interior. Messages from the stomach come first, but bowels and bladder soon gain attention. Attention itself emerges as a product of birth. Nothing can get the attention of a person in bliss consciousness faster than birth!

Innocent, helpless, little baby is engaging in the business of formulating his or her first, and for most people, final, answer to the big question "who am I?" At first, "I" is defined as the physical center of experience. Later, that premise is enveloped in an expanding definition of "I" as a personality with numerous social roles, such as football player, cheerleader, father, mother, doctor, retired behavioral psychologist, etc. The constant self-definition underlying the rest is the one first formed as "I - the physical center of experience," or what Schucman calls "the body identity." The body identity and the body image are significantly different conceptions, but baby commingles them. We will discuss the consequences of this error later.

Someone may ask, at this point, how baby could formulate such a complex self-definition so long before he or she has learned any language or developed the rational faculties that such meaning making would seem to require. Our answer is that there are two kinds of meaning entailed in the mind/brain relationship. The one that gets all the attention from sophisticated speakers is the linguistic, conceptual meaning. This meaning is largely the product of the language centers in the left hemisphere of the brain (at least for right-handed people).

However, the right hemispheric meaning making ability is the first to go to work, with only some distinction-making assistance from the left. Both left and right side meanings consist of fact and value presuppositions woven together in a self-reflective context. But right hemispheric meanings are nonverbal, preconceptual, and more emotional and holistic in nature than are the literal, analytic, and specific meanings made on the left. Stanford University psychology professor Robert Ornstein specializes in studying right and left hemispheric similarities and differences. In *The Right Mind*, he observes that this analytic-left, holistic-right difference between the two hemispheres originates in the animal brain, and is so primitive that it has been observed in the behavior of laboratory rats. According to Ornstein, neurologists have found that as the human brain is developing, it parcels-out functions for specific areas to specialize in. At birth, the left prefrontal lobe has not learned any conceptions with which to work, and it is slightly less developed than its counterpart on the right. Thus, the meaning making which defines who one is, and what kind of world one lives in, is done primarily on the holistic, intuitive right side of the brain. The human function of meaning making subsumes its precursor in the limited learning ability of the mammalian brain, and reconfigures that function into something altogether new – an instrument for *imaging* oneself and the surrounding world. We call these pre-conceptual images "semblances;" self-created configurations of meaning.

By empathic inference, we hypothesize that from its emergence on the stage of evolution, and for at least its first 100,000 years, humanity had devoted nearly all its attention and intelligence to the use and development of its right hemispheric capacities for meaning making, feeling, and nonverbal communication. In later chapters we will suggest that the dominance of the right hemisphere in mental activity was not limited to the period of infancy, but continued throughout human life, until the modern era. In Chapter Five we will suggest that only after man's encounter with Neanderthal, some 35,000 to 40,000 years ago did humanity begin to turn its attention from the right to the literal/analytic centers on the left.

Our World of Semblances

For empathic science, the self-created self consists of "semblances," which are configurations of meaning made from nonverbal, preconceptual presuppositions of fact and value. These are woven together by right hemispheric processes, beginning, as we have said, from birth. As a semblance, the self-created self is like an invisible self-portrait. This self-reflective meaning of whom one is to oneself has a corresponding physical existence in the patterns of electro-chemical signals running along neuropathways in one's brain. These self-initiated connections are established during the creative process of self-making. Like a fingerprint, each person's arrangement of personality-carrying neuropathways is unique, one time only, and never to be repeated. These neuropathways, like electrical wiring, are the "memory" that holds the self in place. This process of self-wiring is replicated as baby fashions his or her understanding of the nature of the world within his or her immediate reach. As baby grows, he or she also fashions a broader conception to include the world outside of arm's reach. Also a semblance, this conception is like an invisible landscape painting. Some babies color it darkly, others brightly, depending upon temperament, experience, and other factors. To get some idea of the emotional, or valuational, element in such semblances, think of the word "home." For some it brings up a warm and fuzzy feeling, for others it might be a "yucky" feeling due to bad experiences, and everything in between. Baby becomes "father to the man" as his unconscious process of semblance making ever expands beyond his reach, to include the wider world, and beyond that, the heavens.

Empathic science has found, then, that there are at least three major categories of semblances. These are: i. the self-created self, which consists in a fusion of the body image and the body identity; ii. the image baby fashions of his or her immediate surroundings, including his or her emotional appraisal thereof; and, iii. the expanded semblance of the human condition one develops as one grows into childhood, and which one continues to develop into adulthood. In the chapters to follow, we will discuss that third semblance as the "first philosophy of life."

The postpartum mind/brain relation begins with semblance making. Here, mind and brain start to relate through semblances. Semblances are the stuff dreams are made of. If there is a code by which semblances are translated into neuro-connections, it has yet to be discovered. Semblances contain a "language" with which to communicate to consciousness. While there is much to be learned about this language, empathic science does know that it operates as a "private language" for each person. Unlike verbal and nonverbal communication, which are forms of inter-communication, this private language is a form of intra-communication. We will also discuss these forms of communication further in later chapters.

The History of Sentience

Sentience, as we have mentioned, began with the simplest form of attraction imaginable. What may appear in hindsight to be a slight shading of plant tropism into a tiny speck of self-awareness in ancient protozoa actually entails a succession of micro-evolutionary revolutions. According to Polanyi, the common ancestor to plant and animal evolved by a series of creative leaps advancing the complexity and sophistication of the lower form from which it came. A flower turning its petals towards the sun entails at least the possibility of sentience; indeed, there is even a hint of effort, or intention, in the action. The idea of sentience in protozoa entails the notion that it *sought* the warmer waters and engaged in some form of primitive self-propulsion to reach those waters. The behavioralist's inept and inapt philosophy of science has desensitized biologists to the role of will, or intention, in the evolution of sentient creatures.

That microscopic particle of gelatin with only a speck of self-awareness, seeking warmer waters, contained within itself the potential out of which future animals, some the size of the brontosaurus, and others with the speed of a cheetah would grow. Besides the potential for physical growth, that minute creature, which first transcended plant life, contained the potential out of which the full spectrum of animal and human sentience would take shape. Animal sentience, then, which led to human feeling, has as long and complex an evolutionary history as does the evolution of animal physicality. By taking introspection seriously, the way will be opened for empathic scientists to write a history of sentience as rich as that of the physical forms of life. Our writing here is only a primer.

Sentience, then, includes, among other things, feelings of attraction and repulsion, the rage that enables man and animal to fight in self-defense or to attack, the fear which can give rise to flight, and pain and pleasure. Sentience is always experienced in self-reflection. It entails evanescent feelings as well as moods of various duration. It acts as a self-monitoring device in both man and animals. It is produced by the operation of processes that go on within the organism, but outside of consciousness. When all is well, the mood of consciousness is that of contentment. When some dysfunction occurs, a warning device like worry, fear, or pain may override contentment. Hence, sentience is a continuing element of the content of consciousness.

Picture, for example, the brontosaurus we mentioned grazing in a lush primitive jungle. There are no threats in sight. Streaming through its nervous system is data concerning sights, sounds, smells, tastes, air temperature, and so forth, as well as internal organ messaging about hunger, bowels, bladder, etc. Because all is well, this data is largely filtered from consciousness. Continuing contentment would be its primary sentient experience.

Of course, objections can be raised to our claim that dinosaurs felt contentment. But we base our claim on reasonable evidence. The reptilian brain can be seen in operation in contemporary reptiles. Sentience is essential for their survival. Reptiles with no fear, for example, would not flee an approaching predator. With no feeling, they would not avoid painful situations, such as a forest fire. However, reptile behavior clearly reveals sentience. Being cold-blooded, reptiles prefer, and seem to enjoy, sitting on a rock in the warm sunshine. In the Western United States, where small reptiles thrive, people may witness this drama: a lizard is sunning itself on a rock. Meanwhile, Felix is slowly and stealthily creeping up to it. Suddenly the cat springs into the air, and the lizard darts away, just in the knick of time. Its wits sharpened by its life in the wild, the lizard is likely to escape nine out of ten house cat attacks. Without fear to prompt an instant reaction to a predator's charge, the lizard population would soon decline into extinction.

Only a small empathic step is necessary to understand the feelings of our lizard friend. Before climbing up onto the rock, he felt uncomfortably chilly. He had knowledge in his memory, which he had learned from other lizards, or which he had discovered by trial and error, that sitting on a rock in the sunlight is a pleasurable experience. Hence, desire moved him to search out the rock. His enjoyment of the warming sun satisfied that desire, and enhanced his contentment. That is, until certain sense data set-off the survival alarm in his reptilian brain. Then fear, perhaps terror, overrode contentment. When the danger had passed, relief and a return to contentment would follow. He could then resume his place on the rock, that is, until hunger, Felix, or the sight of a sexy lady lizard moved him from it.

Such is the emotional life of a lizard. Because his reptilian brain shared many of the organs and functions of that in the dinosaur brain, no great leap of inference is needed to conclude that the emotional life of the dinosaur was much the same.

Consider the African crocodile. They enjoy sunning themselves just like our lizard. They are carnivorous hunters. Crocodiles know how to lie in wait on the shore of a drinking pond, or a river. From a distance they can judge when an animal small enough to eat is approaching for a drink. With precision timing, a croc can slip into the water, propel itself towards the target as swiftly as a shark, burst out of the water, grab the prey by the head, shake it violently to break its neck, and leisurely enjoy its feast.

One can imagine the feeling of anticipation as the croc sped through the water executing its strategy. Imagine, too, the murderous rage it felt as it grabbed the head of the hapless prey, perhaps a small gazelle, and shook with all its might to break that neck. The reptilian brain was molded by natural selection to engage in all the sophisticated processes required for the croc's survival. This includes short term planning, such as lying in wait. Also included would be the ability to make a judgment as to its likelihood of success. For example, our croc would probably hurry past an elephant or a hippo wading in the water, having prudently judged that his time and efforts are better spent on the gazelle. Such judgments would be included in the general procedure of forming a strategy as to approach and method of kill while still on the far shore. Our croc likely started his day in contentment while sunning himself on the shore, but when he spotted the prey his adrenaline began to flow. Then his brain sped through the aforesaid cognitive and affective steps, which led to his meal. Instinct would soon return him to his state of contentment on the shore (perhaps to snooze on his full stomach).

Humans, as we have said, have a reptilian brain. It includes the brain stem, which is connected to the central nervous system at its lower end, and to other parts of the brain at its upper part. Neurologists (as well as many women observing men) have found that human sentience and behavior is affected by the reptilian brain. Such feelings as sexual desire, joy, anger, rage, fear, terror, and contentment can be sent into consciousness from the reptilian sector of the human brain. Of course, because the reptilian part is but the base, which is overlaid by two other sectors, our emotional life is far more complex than that of the reptiles. Even mammals probably have a more complex emotional life than reptiles, especially the highly social mammals.

Given all this evidence, empathic science may reasonably conclude that dinosaurs had an emotional life, which they consciously experienced. Their general mood was that of contentment. This would be overridden in consciousness by such negative feelings as fear, hunger, or pain, and enhanced by such positive feelings as those from mating, eating, or resting in the sun. Empathic science can arrive at these conclusions by a process of critical observation and empathizing with the behavior of contemporary sentient creatures, including ourselves. This is not a wishy-washy personification of everything on Earth. It is a method, which is wide open for public scrutiny, especially that of a community of trained professionals. Our observations are combined with the findings of neurologists about the common elements in reptilian, mammalian, and human brains and nervous systems. For example, these scientists have found that emotions are associated with specific brain chemicals, and that across the spectrum of species, brains share a common chemistry. They know, for instance, that earthworms have a rudimentary brain that produces chemicals, which are also produced in the human brain.

To reach these conclusions, we add up knowledge from a variety of sources. For example, paleontologists have shown us that dinosaurs had a brain case with two eye sockets, and backbones with four limbs, assembled on a pattern like that seen in contemporary birds, reptiles, mammals, and man. Combining facts from different sources, we may fairly conclude that even though dinosaurs have been extinct for sixty-five million years, they had brains which produced consciousness, filtered the data input to that consciousness, had practical judgment, need awareness, reasoning skills for problem solving, and sentience, all not unlike the reptiles of today.

Of course, we do NOT claim that dinosaur minds were "just like ours." Their brains, as we have noted, likely lacked, among other things, the mammalian limbic system, and surrounding cortical tissue of mammals. Like ours, their brains screened and greatly limited the range of experience that could enter their consciousness. Nevertheless, they had an experience with which we can empathize, and of which we can have a measured understanding.

This discussion of reptilian sentience, and especially of dinosaur feeling, demonstrates, to some extent, the method of empathic science. We believe that our method is the most powerful tool ever invented for illuminating the life experience of all sentient creatures. If we can explain and understand the life experience of creatures as distant as dinosaurs, then we can understand and explain the life experience of far less remote beings, like the first humans on Earth. Indeed, that is precisely what we shall do in the next two chapters. From there we shall explain how the human sentience which connects us to our first human predecessors evolved to its present state. But first there is a little more groundwork to be laid.

Animal and Human Buddha-nature

Following Buddha, the Dalai Lama has made the empathic observation that "animals with their limited intelligence, are happier and more peaceful than we are." This seems to us like a sound observation. Thus, the major part of the time in which animals are awake is spent in contentment. We know of no natural species on Earth the observation of which does not confirm this claim. Even in seemingly ill tempered animals like badgers, weasels, or the Tasmanian Devil, angry behavior occurs in only a fraction of the time during their daily routines. The same may be said of large predators. For most of the time that they are conscious, such animals are in contentment. Listlessness or boredom due to lack of mental stimulation may diminish the natural contentment of animals in zoos, but working animals, like elephants in Asia, or big cats in circuses, or carriage drawing horses seem to be contented, if well treated. As we have noted, contentment is the mode of being in consciousness when all of its supporting subsystems are working well; in other words, contentment is the sentient organism's experience of equilibrium.

Hypothetically, contentment could be measured from the production of the brain chemicals thought to cause that feeling. In his pioneering work *Zen and the Brain*, Dr. James H. Austin reviews hundreds of neurological studies pertaining to the problem of how the brain produces contentment. Some parts of the brain produce chemicals, which inhibit fear and anxiety, while other parts secrete chemicals, which result in relaxation, and in increasing amounts, euphoria. No one knows exactly how as yet, but somehow the amazing brain coordinates the secretions of anxiety inhibitors and calming chemicals in diverse areas of itself. Contentment can be observed as the normal condition in animals, because that is the state created by their normally functioning brains. Austin notes that even the brains of rats in laboratories produce such chemicals. In the long stretch of evolution, natural selection and nature's creativity have molded an animal brain that naturally regulates just the right mix of chemicals to make contentment the normal state of being for these sentient creatures.

Contrary to the "wisdom" of the dominant behavioral paradigm, empathic science concurs with Buddha, and finds that animals not only have feelings, but that they are naturally happier than are we humans. Of course, we do not use the word "happy" in the frivolous sense of birthday party jubilance. Rather, we mean it in the serene sense that all is well with life and nothing more is wanted than this moment. Thus, animals appear to live much more in the moment than do humans. In that sense, happiness is living in a continuous moment of contentment. An EKG shows high and low spikes in measuring one's heartbeat, but one can see from the graph that the heart has a regular rhythm. Animal contentment likely follows much the same pattern. Their consciousness will experience highs and lows in the flow of contentment, but normally the feeling returns to its own homeostasis.

Behavioralism also blinds humanity to the startling fact of its *inferior quality of life*. But empathic science takes the position that progress can only be made from a realistic assessment of its starting condition. We measure the quality of life, not from the number of cars, houses, or TVs one has, but one's contentment. Now, apply that standard to humans. Does humanity appear to be living up to its full potential for contentment? We suggest that the painful truth is too obvious to belabor the proof. Not only

Fido, Felix, Elsie, and Polly, but all animals in the wild live at a level of contentment unmatched by man.

We suggest that there are few humans alive today who can honestly and convincingly claim to be living at their full potential for contentment. In the next chapter we will discuss what that full potential is; at this point, however, we will simply postulate, with the main evidence to follow, that humanity today is living far below its potential level for happiness. Some evidence can be found in the reports of psychotherapists. Individuals may explain their discontent with a wide variety of reasons. For example, "my parents were abusive and incompetent," "my boss is mean and stingy," "my spouse is cheating on me," "I'm helplessly addicted to … " (you name it!), "my luck has run out," "God hates me," and so on.

Empathic science recognizes that there are numerous secondary causes of individual unhappiness. However, in the neurologically and physiologically normal person, we find that there are two primary causes of human unhappiness. These are the trauma of birth, and what we call "the human birth defect." These causes of unhappiness relate to each other developmentally. That is, one emerges very early in life, and the other emerges in the transitional period between childhood and adulthood. The first cause will be addressed here, and the second in following chapters.

In our view, no one has understood the birth trauma and its consequences more fully than Otto Rank. In *The Trauma of Birth*, he recognized, as we have said, that the sentience of a normal fetus is bliss. At one with its environment, no feeling of need, no fear, no wanting or desire of any sort, no "I," just complete satisfaction. With birth, as we saw earlier, all of this is lost. In the growing embryo, bliss consciousness probably emerges in the transition from the second to the third trimester of mom's pregnancy. This is the time when the brain has matured enough to begin recording memories. Thus, says Rank, both bliss and the trauma of birth are indelibly recorded in every human's memory.

As baby grows, its attention is constantly being called to its physical experience; that is, internal organ messaging, and learning about the people and the world around it. The condition of all systems humming, which once gave rise to prenatal bliss, has changed. In the early years of childhood, the contented mood in consciousness is a carry-over of the bliss of the fetus. But as attention is trained to focus on physical matters, and the body and the personality emerging within the body define the self, the feelings of bliss recede. Feelings created by worldly desires, joys, pleasures, and frustrations begin to replace whatever remained of prenatal bliss. Thus, one of the patterns of human development, and we believe cross-culturally, can be seen as that of declining contentment in childhood, and the increasing need to manage discontent with age.

Post-partum anxiety is an additional corrosive for contentment. Rank identifies this anxiety as a form of fear which is specifically related to the birth trauma. A fetus has no knowledge of danger. Considerable experience is necessary before a mind can form that idea. But natural selection has developed a fear response to change in one's environment. That fear response is initiated at birth, which is a direct attack on bliss. Because memory begins recording long before birth, the record of prenatal bliss is overlaid with the emotional response to the birth trauma. This is when the first fear was felt. Babies have no control over their emotions. Thus, like a nightmare, the memory of the first fear may erupt into consciousness and overwhelm it at any time, making baby cry. Baby is then soothed by mom, and taught to calm down and to contain, or suppress, his or her fear. But fear suppressed is not fear resolved. Hence, the anxiety initiated by birth haunts consciousness like a phantom in the night. Fear of attack and the infantile feelings of vulnerability and helplessness erode contentment. Unless and until these feelings are brought up into the light of reason, and resolved, they never go away. That process, for Rank, is the main purpose of psychotherapy.

Baby's unhappy experience of helplessness during birth, recorded in memory, is a key element in sustaining that life-long anxiety. Truly, "the child is father of the man." Fear and the feeling of helplessness, deep in our earliest memories, undermine contentment. Cultures vary as to how this situation is dealt with, but none have found a way to overcome it. As Rank shows, humanity devotes much mental effort to wrestling with this daemon, never understanding the problem, and therefore failing to resolve the conflict. That conflict lies in the absurd and futile longing to return to the lost state of fetal bliss, which never leaves memory, but remains to mock and torment man. Because adult humans are both physically and emotionally unable to return to the womb, they feel compelled to vainly search for compensatory substitutes, usually unto death.

Animals do not have this unhappy experience. They, too, know bliss as their prenatal sentience. But birth is far less traumatic for them than it is for us. Their brains naturally regulate the production of fear inhibiting and contentment enhancing chemicals, so that the birth trauma does not haunt them as it does us. Their attention is turned to the demands of their bodies, but their normal brain functions prevent the corrosion of their contentment. They experience fear, to be sure, but not as an unresolved gnawing at the edges of consciousness. Their fear is situation appropriate. For example, when senses warn of an approaching predator, or when drinking at a water hole where crocodiles have been known to burst from under the calm surface. In man's mind, fear is suppressed, but still runs amuck beneath the surface of consciousness.

While psychoanalysis may or may not result in the restoration of fetal bliss, as Rank hypothesizes, his thesis fails to account for the natural contentment of animals. Why don't they need psychoanalysis to restore their pre-birth bliss? As we have suggested, their brains naturally take care of that problem. So, why don't ours? That is the question which has led empathic science to the discovery of the human birth defect. The human brain fails to do what the animal brain does naturally. In the rest of this book, we will explain both why this failure occurs, and how to correct the malfunction.

Chapter Two

The Contentment Module and the Natural Order of Values

The Mind/Brain Misalignment

What is a healthy mind? This has been a central question in modern psychology since its beginnings in the early 20th Century. Various writers and schools of thought have propounded a variety of propositions and theories. Behavioralism questions the existence of "mind," and defines "health" in the objective terms of "social adjustment." Like the characters in the 1956 novel *The Man in the Gray Flannel Suit*, by Sloan Wilson, the well-adjusted person busies himself or herself with making and spending money, and raising children who will do the same. They simply suppress and ignore their emptiness.

Empathic science rephrases the question, which has been central to psychology for over a century. Because we study not the mind alone, but the mind in relation to the brain, our central question is "what is the good mind/brain relation?" We ask the question this way using Hartman's definition of "good." Hartman, building upon the conceptual analyses done in ethics by the philosopher G.E. Moore, has defined "good" as the fulfillment of a conception. This is not a moralistic notion of "good," but one based on the relationship between a thing and the definition of it.

For example, every cardiologist has in mind an idea of a healthy heart. They have learned in medical school to think of a heart, for instance, as a muscle with four chambers that receives blood from veins and pumps it out through arteries in a regular rhythm. The description of the general properties of a heart enable the experts to form an idea of a properly functioning heart. Of course, the cardiologist's conception of a good heart is far more complex than this simple illustration. But if a patient presents himself to a doctor with a heart that pumps too slow, or too fast, or has problems with the valves between chambers, then the cardiologist has the cognitive framework needed to recognize that, and why, this is not a "good heart." The patient may be a very charitable person, but that is another meaning of the expression.

In cases where a heart is pumping with an irregular rhythm, or abnormally fast, or slow, the likely treatment would be prescription drugs; but, the cause could be psychological. Everyone knows that the heart has a relationship with the mind/brain. For example, when one merely thinks that one may be in danger, that thought triggers a fear response in the brain which causes the heart to pump faster than its normal rate. This happens to millions of moviegoers during chase scenes, or when the hero is about to be grabbed by "the Green Monster." Some fans scream with excitement as their favorite "heart throb" appears on the screen. Semblances in the mind can produce physiological responses.

The relationship of the heart to the mind/brain is one of the new frontiers in neurology. They have traditionally regarded this relationship as strictly involuntary. Yet, recent experiences with biofeedback experiments show that ordinary people can learn to relax their own heart rate intentionally, by attending inwardly. Yogis from India have long known how to control their own heart rate intentionally, but until the biofeedback experiments they were not taken seriously. Now scientists recognize that the relationship of the heart to the mind/brain is far more complex than doctors had previously thought. Clearly, there is a latent volitional element in that relationship. The possibility of people with arrhythmic heart beats learning to adjust their pulse through introspection flies in the face of traditional Western medicine, and threatens the profit margins of drug companies. Yet, introspection may lead to new forms of self-healing as more is learned about the relationship between the heart and the mind/brain. As of now, neither cardiologists nor neurologists know enough about the relationship to form a textbook description that would define the "good" relationship between heart and mind/brain.

We may learn one day that the "good relationship" here is one in which the mind of the individual is fully involved with the workings of the heart. Heart disease is one of the major causes of death today. One may ask whether the alienation of heart from the mind/brain is not a contributing condition to heart disease. Once the possibility is raised that introspection can connect mind, brain, and heart, new questions about the elements of a healthy heart can be raised. Research could show that establishing a connection between mind, brain, and heart may help to prevent heart disease.

Introspection can be used to integrate mind, brain, and body to a degree far beyond what is now being done, or even now thought possible. Out of social necessity, children learn to control bladder and bowels. But all the possible relationships between mind and particular organs are not now even minimally understood. Perhaps there are elements of health, and possibilities for self-healing, to which our ignorance and self-alienation blind us. Intentional self-healing is today an unknown science. Yet, doctors have always known that some sort of relationship between mind and health exists. They often witness patients doggedly fight an illness and overcome it, or "give up the ghost." There is evidence in the growing number of spectacular recoveries from cancer and other illnesses that the *attitudes* the afflicted take towards their illness is an important factor in their recovery.

Clearly, there is an element of self-reflection in good health. Those who take proper care of themselves tend to have better health than those who do not. The key seems to be to infuse care, or positive regard, into one's body image. It may be that internal organs have a need to feel cared for, or attended to, by the mind.

Psychologists have traditionally ignored the process by which baby forms his or her body image. But in a more caring world, guidance in forming the body image would be standard fare in public education. Self-caring can be taught. There is no reason why a person's body image cannot include caring for each specific part that it encompasses. Also, there is no reason why one's body image could not be as clear, precise, and inclusive as a three-dimensional computer model. Through introspection, the process by which the body image is made could be educated so that an individual could choose to be as aware of his immune system, respiratory system, and circulatory system, for example, as he now is of his digestive and elimination systems. This heightened degree of self-awareness could lead to a kind of friendship with one's internal systems. It could also lead to new knowledge in the techniques of self-healing. This integration of internal systems and the positive regard of the mind, learned through public education, could also result in raising the general level of public health and longevity.

We raise these points only to illustrate the wide range of applications for physical health which are made possible by introspection. Unlike Western scientists, who gawk at the body from the outside like a puzzling piece of machinery, the Yogis have shown us that the wondrous human organism can be more subtlety understood from the inside.

As one might expect, empathic science has learned a great deal about the healthy, or "good," mind/brain relation from Dr. Schucman's writings. As a professor of medical psychology, the interplay of mind and body, as that relates to health, happiness, and self-healing, was of special interest to her. One of the inferences we draw from her writings is that happiness is an essential requirement if people are to realize their full potential for good health. In Chapter One we noted that we equate happiness with contentment. We will define more precisely what we mean by these terms in this chapter. In the course of describing the elements of the mind/brain relationship, we will define what is a "good" such relationship, and we will show that the key measure of a good mind/brain relationship is contentment.

Discontent is, in large part, the product of alienation, or misalignment, of mind and brain. To put it another way, dissatisfaction with one's life experience is largely due to discord in the fit between mind and brain. One central characteristic of the mind/brain relationship is that it will remain out of accord for each individual until he or she brings it into line by an intentional effort; i.e., as far as we know now, unhappiness can be, and can only be, self-healed. In this chapter we will explain how and why man's mind is out of sync with his brain, until each individual sets it aright. We will touch briefly in this chapter on how mind and brain can be brought into alignment, but Chapter Six will present a complete program for self-healing.

How, then, does the human mind become misaligned with its life-sustaining brain, and why does this happen?

The Contentment Module

In the previous chapter we stated our view, supported by a long tradition in psychology, that a third term fetus's prenatal experience is normally consciousness of bliss. No needs are known, and all systems are humming. But, birth throws bliss into chaos. Each unique individual responds to this event in his or her own way. However, there are general patterns. In the absence of pathology, every baby begins to form a self-image at birth. Little incomplete efforts to formulate answers to some of the major questions of life exhaust baby's brain, and send him or her to sleep. When baby awakens, he or she tries again to make sense of "the blooming, buzzing confusion." Empathy suggests that long before words and concepts have been acquired, baby makes a halting mental effort in the direction of asking such questions as "what is happening to me?" and "who am I?" and "where is my peace?" and "how can I get it back?"

Rudiments of the body image begin to take shape at birth. Then, as the stomach, for example, experiences emptiness, distress signals are sent to consciousness as hunger pangs. Gradually, baby learns to identify portions of the body's interior. Baby also forms an image of the world outside the skin. Thus begins the life-long process of defining the image of oneself as a body in relation to a larger world. Pleasures, including the joy of using the body, add to this image formation. Early on, baby also learns that the body is vulnerable to pain in an environment which can be hazardous.

Through this nonverbal, preconceptual, yet cognitive response to birth, baby builds his or her self-understanding from the materials of experienced events and his or her emotional responses to them. These creations are woven together in memory as tiny threads of meaning. In this way, body image becomes background as baby learns to suppress birth-initiated anxiety, and to disregard his or her longing to return to "paradise lost." Each unique self is created on these common themes. The personality is a text of meanings, which each baby one-day learns to call "I."

In our view, every aspect of mind has an organic base in the connections between neurons in the brain. Brain produces mind, but mind has a hand in arranging the neuro-connections in the brain. Empathic science agrees with those existentialist writers who say that man creates himself by his own choices, and that each person makes his or her own meaning. But we reject the notion that "self" is all construct. Baby's self-creation is the product of choices, which are partially influenced by genetically determined characteristics, such as temperament and health. These choices are later influenced by the values of family and culture. The phenomena of twins, separated from birth, creating similar personalities and interests, suggests that inherited predispositions are a major factor in arranging the neuro-connections in the brain which make a person who he or she is. Empathic science has found that the human burden of each person having the responsibility for realizing, maintaining, and enhancing his or her own happiness is among humanity's genetically inherited characteristics. Our reasons for this claim will be given in the next chapter.

Recently, the project of decoding the basic elements of the human genome was completed. Geneticists have found that a precise formula exists for each part of the human body. The skeletal pattern of backbone, four limbs, tail bone, neck bone, and skull are the products of a genetic formula, which may be shared by many creatures going back hundreds of million of years. Some scientists have suggested that the sequence for producing a head may be uniform for every form of life from a fruit fly to a man. Whether that is so or not, the existence in man of this common skeletal pattern, plus skin, muscles, internal organs, nervous systems, and brain, all of similar bio-chemistry, strongly suggests that humans and animals share many gene sequences. In Chapter Three we will discuss the implications for human happiness of that enormous decoding achievement.

Neurology is nowhere near the precision of genetics in understanding the sequences between the trillions of neural connections, which produce mind, and the particular characteristics which constitute a personality. Probing the brain during surgery, and examining the effects of injuries, only enables neurologists to speculate as to the functions of general areas. Brain imaging techniques are a blunt instrument for the task of tracing the neuro-pathways that precisely correspond to distinct aspects of mind and personality. Some of this work of tracing the links between brain and personality might be done better from the inside. That is, through introspection one may be able to explore these neuro-connections. Future experts in introspection could focus upon specific sources in the brain for particular aspects of mental activity. With education, perhaps anyone could learn to visualize one's mind/brain connections, and to follow their operations. Then one could learn to "feel" one's way into brain regions. If neurologists could over-come the inhibiting influences of the cowardly sciences, and learn to attend inwardly, with their knowledge of how the human brain is constructed and how it functions, a new era of brain science could be started.

Our method of introspection has enabled empathic science to make the discoveries, which will be presented in this and the following chapters. These chapters will show that, although still in its infancy, introspection is already a more precise instrument for exploring the mind/brain relation than any multi-million dollar machine on the market.

Introspection follows the logic of inclusion. One seeks to know what is included within oneself. This requires unflinching honesty. Through the empathic observation of others, one can learn to distinguish those elements of one's mind/brain relation which are general to the species, from those which are particular to oneself. One can also "see" that some of the neuro-connections in one's brain are self-made, while others are structural; that is, the result of genetic inheritance. These structural neuro-pathways are like organs in the brain, because they have their own special functions to fulfill, and their own physical locations.

The process of psychotherapy described by Rogers, in *Client Centered Therapy*,[iv] and later in *On Becoming A Person*,[v] is one of a person struggling to reintegrate self-made and inherited neuro-connections. Those clients who report feeling organically based within themselves are touching upon their own unique mind/brain relation. Through therapy, they have learned to improve the alignment between mind and brain within themselves. Empathic science can contribute to the understanding of this process of realignment and integration by identifying the key structural elements in the brain to which alignment ultimately aims. Thus, scientific guidance can give a focus to the therapy of Rogers which can save clients years of frustrated groping in the dark. We will return to this point later in this chapter.

The self-created self, for most people, is largely out of alignment with its natural neurological base. That with which it is misaligned most importantly, the very polestar of the mind, we call "the Schucman Corridor." The Schucman Corridor is a structured neuro-pathway in the brain, which is produced by genetic inheritance. We hypothesize that it is the "contentment module" of the brain. For at least a century, neurologists have speculated about the neuro-basis for intense religious experiences, episodes of ecstasy, and visions of Jesus, Mary, and several saints. Some noteworthy examples of their writings include *Zen and the Brain,*[vi] by James H. Austin, *Phantoms in the Brain,*[vii] by V. S. Ramachandran, and *Why God Won't Go Away,*[viii] by Andrew Newberg. In the spirit of these scientific explorations, the next chapter will provide a precise anatomical description of the Schucman Corridor and its location in the brain, taken from a popular medical school text. We assign Schucman's name to this neuro-circuit because her writings enable us to describe its functions to perfection.

Our brain contains roughly three trillion synapses, which are the connections between neurons. Throughout the complex interconnected systems of nerve tissues in the brain, there are areas which specialize in the production of fear inhibiting and contentment producing chemicals. In the good mind/brain relationship, the Schucman Corridor regulates this chemical production so that the normal mood of consciousness is contentment. In this way, the Schucman Corridor is the functional equivalent of similar neuro-pathways in the animal brain. While their neuro-pathways produce contentment naturally in animals, humans must "retune" the Schucman Corridor, or it will not work up to par. This resetting burden is the key symptom of the human birth defect. We will discuss the genetic basis of our birth defect in the next chapter. In this chapter, we will discuss both what the Schucman Corridor does, and how it can be properly adjusted.

We concurred with the Buddhist observation that animals are more contented than humans in the last chapter. Neurologists have found that the experience in consciousness of contentment, for both man and animal, is, at least in part, a result of a mix of chemicals produced within the brain. Animal contentment is, in part, a signal to animal consciousness that all is well, both within its internal systems and with its immediate environment. We attribute this regulation of contentment to an inherited process in the animal brain.

Empathic observation leads us to the conclusion that humans everywhere lack the natural contentment of animals, but this lack of contentment is not an immutable part of being human. It is a condition, which can be corrected. We base this claim on the intersubjective agreement of Schucman with Buddha's teachings, and a long line of writings on human spirituality from ascetic Stoicism to modern Zen. There is also widespread agreement among these writers that humans can find contentment. This agreement includes the point that an informed intentional act is a prerequisite to realizing one's potential for life-long contentment. While many of these writings are couched in scientifically unpalatable religious rhetoric, metaphysical speculations, and mysticism, within the dirty bathwater there sits a baby. The *fact* is that some people have found a deep and abiding joy in life, which many others crave but cannot find. Science is always concerned with facts, and these are the facts with which empathic science is concerned.

The Composition of Contentment

As we have said, the functioning Schucman Corridor produces contentment, or happiness. We have defined "happiness" as more like serenity than jubilance. But empathic science can turn its introspective microscope on contentment, and more exactly describe its constituent elements and their relations to one another. For the neurologist, conscious experience is the unified product of numerous subsystems within the brain. Each of these subsystems has its own characteristics, and involves the production of different types of brain chemicals. Thus, the experience of a unified or singular consciousness is like that of listening to a symphony. There may be fifty or more instruments contributing to a unified piece of orchestral music. While the average listener experiences a unity of sound, a skilled conductor can focus his attention on each instrument as a score is played. Likewise, future neurologists who have developed their ability for introspection will try to trace all the single elements, which lead into the experience of consciousness as a unity.

Contentment, too, has a wide variety of analytically single items, which converge to form a unified experience in consciousness. That symphony metaphor also applies to contentment. But an art simile works just as well. Contentment, one may say, is like a beautiful painting, which consists of numerous colors, in a variety of shades, taking several different forms, and producing a pleasing totality. One could use the analogy of a meal full of various flavorful foods. Or, a glass of wine, with a bouquet of fine aromas and tastes. While the focus of the neurologist is on electro-chemical processes in the brain, our focus is on the feeling, or experience, of contentment in consciousness.

Our first observation is that the experience of contentment is totally personal. That adds to the difficulty of discussing it. The situation is like that of a room full of people each of whom speaks a language which is foreign to the others. No one can experience another person's self-experience. But people can understand one another substantially through empathy. This is how some measure of the communication of feeling can take place. Based on the intersubjective agreement of those giants, upon whose shoulders empathic science stands, a basic model of contentment can be formulated.

The general elements of contentment appear first of all to include a sense of personal completion, and of having found what once was missing. There is also a feeling of species unity, or brotherhood with all other people. There is a distinct sense of belonging to, or of fitting in with, of being a part of, or at one with, nature. Then there is a surety, or confidence, in these feelings which is not contingent upon belief in some philosophy, or the word of some authority, but wholly upon personal experience and understanding. Included is a calmness, or serenity, which seems to follow from that surety. There is also a continuing joy in the experience of this understanding. There is no sense of "oh hum, I'm happy again today." Rather, a child-like sense of delight at the novelty of every moment seems to weave in with the other feelings.

These themes often combine to produce in consciousness an experience of "love." But this is not an object-dependent love, like the love of some possession, or the romantic love of another (especially the sort that entails lust, or a desperate neediness). This is an objectless love, which gently flows through consciousness like a stream.

The feelings of oneness with other people and with nature seem to produce a strong sense of respect, even honor, for the former, and of reverence for the latter. Individuals are seen as too precious to use, and compassion, or brotherly love, are the natural attitude toward others. Reverence for nature seems to be related to a heightened sense of its charm, beauty, and majesty. The awareness that other living things have sentience is also enhanced. One begins to value oneself, others, and the world around one as precious parts of a whole. A new dimension of values opens up, which Hartman calls "intrinsic values." Rather than being a rare occurrence, intrinsic valuing becomes one's approach to life.

All these feelings, in various tones and combinations, and which may be expressed in different words, telescope in consciousness to appear in a unity as "contentment." Once this contentment is experienced, one sees it as the meaning that one had long felt to have been missing from one's life. This adult experience is reminiscent of bliss consciousness in the fetus, but with the addition of cognitive maturity, including education, language, and years of lessons in the school of hard knocks. Contentment, then, is like the aura of a special meaning, which consists of factual and valuational presuppositions that emerge together in a whole. The central fact felt is unity. The main value felt is love.

Turing up the power of our introspective microscope, we have found that these two themes of fact and value are interconnected. Each theme entails three identifiable sets of feelings, which are cross-related. The sense of unity as factual has three dimensions. These are: i.) the feeling of being whole and complete within oneself; ii.) the feeling of oneness with all other humans; and, iii.) the experience that man and nature are one.

In conjunction with this new sense of the factual comes a new awareness of values. The value of love has three corresponding dimensions. These are: i.) the personal experience of child-like delight and joy in daily life, the serenity of surety in the fact of unity, and the feeling of objectless love; ii.) the sense of brotherly love, that oneself and others are too precious to be used, and of compassion for others, especially those who may still be out of contentment; and, iii.) a sense of the awe inspiring mystery, majesty, and beauty of nature, the world, and the universe. The table below reflects the relationships of the elements of contentment.

FACTS	VALUES
1.unity within oneself	surety and serenity
2.specieshood of man	honor and compassion
3.oneness with nature	awe and reverence

We have learned from Dr. Schucman that the achievement of the consciousness of consciousness causes a *change in perception*, so that facts are no longer empty bits of data. The inward perception that one's internal unity is a fact produces the feeling of joy and serenity. The new perception that one is, in fact, a part of a whole species brings out the positive regard for others. And, the actual perception of oneness with nature generates one's high regard for it. The brain, of course, is the source of both factual and valuational experience. In short, this new perception experiences oneness as both a description of one's condition, and as a cause for its celebration. The factual perceptions produce the feelings, and the feelings reward and encourage the generation of those factual perceptions in a self-sustaining process, which can last for life.

The contentment module competes with other organs in the body for the attention of consciousness. It is different in that its communication does not pass through the central nervous system up into the brain, because it is a part of the brain itself. Its neurological lines of communication are as yet unknown. We may be certain, however, from our knowledge of its function, that it generates electro-chemical impulses in the brain which enter the screen of meaning. These impulses, like those of other organs, are then translated into meaningful feelings, which one can understand.

This module probably begins to communicate its messages to consciousness in early adolescence. The contentment module communicates a very exact message to consciousness. The message contains only three elements. These are: i.) that it is ready to function fully, but its operation is being constrained; ii.) that its work is to provide life-long contentment; and, iii.) that it can only be freed from constraint by the deliberate release of the self-created self. For one who has learned to receive this message, it is as clear as a communication from one's stomach that it is starving.

This homing message is sent across thousands of synapses, in the form of electro-chemical impulses. If the message is clearly translated for consciousness, then the individual will have a personal understanding both that he or she can have life-long contentment, and what to do to achieve that end. For anyone who clearly receives that message, the next step is a "no brainier"— you find your way of getting what you need. One of the problems that plague humanity in this process, however, is that the clear, simple, and exact message, which is sent by the Schucman Corridor, becomes so muddled before reaching consciousness that, for people by the billions, it fails to register.

Empathic science, impelled by the momentum of our founders, seeks to clarify this problem in scientific terms. We hope that our science can do for human happiness in the coming years, what natural science has done for human health in the past couple of centuries. To more clearly understand the good mind/brain relation, we must look again at the process by which baby responds to the birth trauma by creating a self to give some order to experience.

Baby's Error

Each person has a creative memory at the core of their mind/brain relation. It is the agent that began the process of self-creation in response to birth. That memory intentionally holds its contents in place throughout a person's life. This is more than a passive remembering. While mind continuously knits together new patterns of neuro-connections in the process of personality development, it holds on to its basic pattern, first created by baby, and integrates new patterns into these. This "holding on" element accounts, in part, for what consistency there is in personality from baby to senior. Baby's self-understanding builds upon the image of being a body at the center of sense experience. Then baby blends into this image an awareness of internal organs, followed by the integration of thoughts, feelings, and social roles. All of these come into the picture seen by conscious self-reflection.

This body-oriented understanding created by baby becomes, in baby's mind, the complete answer to the question "who am I?" Baby is not sophisticated enough to make the left hemispheric distinction between "an" answer and "the" answer. Each innocent babe uncritically accepts the initial, right hemispheric holistic response as "the" answer. This nonverbal, preconceptual configuration of meaning soon calcifies into what Dr. Schucman calls "the body identity."

Unfortunately, baby errs. The most human element of all, as we mentioned in Chapter One, is the capacity for consciousness to become fully and exclusively conscious of itself. But baby leaves this out of the self-portrait! Because baby defines himself, or herself, without recognizing the capacity for the consciousness of consciousness, the awareness of the potential, and any reason for realizing it, never enters the mind of the adult that baby becomes. Hence, baby's error is rarely corrected because it is so seldom seen. Yet, this error renders one's baby-made self-understanding woefully under inclusive.

This under inclusion of one's self-understanding is the central factor in the mind/brain misalignment. Mind is out of alignment with the self-reflecting brain simply because mind does not include that key element within its self-image. This is a problem because achieving the consciousness of consciousness is the one and only way to initiate the full operation of the Schucman Corridor. To correct baby's error, one must let go of this constricted self-understanding, and allow the mind/brain relation to reintegrate the excluded part. But, one may ask, how can this be done if the necessary awareness of the problem is barred by one's self-image? To answer this question, let us revisit the notion of Schucman Corridor signaling.

By blinding a person to all of whom one is, the body identity desensitizes a person to the natural feelings of oneness within, with others, and with nature. It creates an illusion of separation, and feelings of isolation, aloneness, and encapsulation in a kind of physical shell. Baby's confusion of his or her body image with his or her identity as a person becomes the basis for the vacuous infantile materialism that most people live by in their daily lives.

Baby's assumption that "I am a body, and only a body," leads the adult to seek happiness through pleasures. While sex is one such pleasure, we will contend in Chapter Six the penultimate pleasure people strive for over and over again is that which comes from the exercise of power, whether in reality or in imagination.

The body identity, then, becomes integrated into the developing screen of meaning, as that is filled-in by the self-created self. This causes havoc when the Schucman Corridor, or contentment module, begins to signal its need for attention. The part of the message which says that the self-created self must be released becomes distorted into a *death threat*, which sets off the self-preservation alarm. The reason for this is understandable given the premises which baby has established. If the self-created self must be released, and the body identity is a central part of that self, and the body is one's life itself, the Schucman Corridor appears to be calling for the release of life itself!

Ironically, the benign signal, which would lead the way to life-long contentment, winds-up triggering the self-preservation response in the lower brain. The anxiety, which this sets off, makes life worse instead of better! The reptilian brain has no faculty for scrutinizing the semblances which are set before it. In the theater of the mind, the ancient brain responds to unreal death threats, like that car chase in the movie, just as it does to real ones. Since the Schucman Corridor is constantly sending its signals of readiness, the screen of meaning is constantly presenting death threats to the fear-making part of the brain. Because the source of such threats is not understood, due to self-ignorance, the threats, and the intense fear they cause, must be kept suppressed from awareness, or one would be unable to function in daily life. This is the fear which wreaks havoc just outside the boundaries of consciousness. In response to that fear, the subsystem of the mind/brain relation, which holds on to the self-created self, clings all the more tightly to its organic base, rather than doing the releasing of which it is capable. Thus do people live in a high state of nervous readiness to protect the "fortress" of the self from that attack, which they feel sure is imminent.

The Right Intention

The creative memory, which holds our self-set neuro-connections in place, can be influenced, like other internal organs, by an informed introspective intention. We call this "the right intention." By forming the right intention, one can signal one's unconsciously held grip to let go. This task has two parts. The first is to deliberately release one's hold on the neuro-base of the self-created self. The second is to do this with the consciously formed intention that by doing so mind and brain will reintegrate, and expand one's self-understanding sufficiently to include an indubitable awareness that "self" includes the consciousness of consciousness. As Swami Vivekananda writes, in his insightful essays on Yogi, the word "I" includes a "small self" and a "Big Self." Once one experiences the consciousness of consciousness as one's Big Self, mind comes into full alignment with its producing brain, and thereby sets the Schucman Corridor into full operation.

The Schucman Corridor cannot be set in motion directly, but only by this rather circuitous route of letting go of the self-created self and trusting the mind/brain relation to re-align and heal itself. No command issued from consciousness to this unconscious process will succeed. One must accept this genetically inherited condition, and work with it. One must learn the distinction between willingness and willfulness, if one is to achieve life-long contentment.

The chief obstacle to grasping this distinction on something deeper than the mere literal level is the fear, as we have said, that letting go means "death." One can truly say, "I fear the death of who I think I am now, although I do not know who I am really." Even though built on shifting sands, this is a powerful fear. However, one can learn to hear the beckoning of the Schucman Corridor through the noise and static of that fear. While one's contentment module is out of order, it acts as an inner guidance system, like loaded bowls. Once the signal is heard, it can be followed. But before it can be heard, one must be willing to listen.

This listening requires the clear acknowledgment of at least two factors. First, that one's life is empty, or painfully incomplete. Second, that one is unable to make the pain go away, or to fill the emptiness, by one's own actions or willfulness. These admissions will help to reduce defensiveness in the screen of meaning. Then it will be more receptive to the Schucman Corridor signals. Unfortunately, generating the willingness to listen inwardly, and to be guided, is not as easy as it sounds. This requires practice. Like many Zen Masters, Schucman calls this practice "mind training." As each mind becomes willing to listen inwardly, it will develop its own language both for interpreting these homing signals, and for responding by communicating the signal of release back to the brain.

Our Private Languages

Every mind uses private languages. That is, methods for translating electro-chemical impulses from internal systems into a form of meaning with which consciousness can work so as to make decisions for action. This is a function of the screen of meaning. For example, baby learns by the time he or she is a tot to interpret electro-chemical impulses from the stomach, through the nerves, to the brain, and into consciousness, as meaning "I'm hungry." This is not an infallible system of communication. The experience of hunger may come from worry, or a disorder in the central nervous system, or in a faulty link between that system and the stomach lining, or otherwise be a form of miscommunication. Many obese people feel hungry so often because they are actually suffering from one of these types of internal communication disorders. For a variety of reasons, people can fail to properly fashion a coherent private language between their consciousness and a subsystem within their body.

A private language can be used for two-way communication; that is, from an internal system to consciousness, and from consciousness to an internal system. The Yogis in the East who can relax their respiratory and circulatory systems use a private language to communicate their intentions inwardly to those systems. There are Buddhist monks in Tibet who can raise their body temperature so high that each can put a wet sheet over his head and dry it! While we are not suggesting that people give up their dryers, we do contend that those who have learned to understand their body from the inside have mastered aspects of their own private languages which Westerners never imagined existed. The age-old concern with dream interpretation is yet another angle on the function of one's private languages.

The formation of a private language requires education. The tot must learn what it means to him personally to say, "I'm hungry." Those monks learned to turn up their inner thermostat, in part, by visualizing a warm fire during meditation. Each monk learned to integrate his own take on a common private language between his consciousness and his hypothalamus – the organ in the brain that controls body temperature, among many other things. The monks also learned to keep the fire going, so to speak, during sleep. After each dries his sheet, they climb to a Himalayan mountaintop and sleep outdoors with only that sheet for cover!

Many cases of self-healing may be further instances of a person using a private language. That is, the afflicted may have learned to "speak" with their affliction, or their afflicted part, and persuaded it to heal itself. Each person can form a relationship between his or her consciousness and any part of the body to which nerve tissue allows access. This intra-personal connection, through a meaningful feeling, is a private language. "Prayer" may be a means by which some people cultivate a private language which can ease their worries, or even help in self-healing. "Faith healing" may result from one person, with a gift for teaching, showing another person how to develop the private language needed to self-heal. When tots learn to control bladder and bowels, they first learn to introspect sufficiently to identify the source of the pressure in their body image. Then, having learned to correctly understand this communication from organ to brain to consciousness, they reverse the communication and signal bowels and bladder to "hold on" until the tot can get to the toilet. Once safely in the bathroom, consciousness gives the awaited release signal. There is nothing special in this. Dogs and cats do it too. Indeed, the human private language is simply the human version of an ancient animal capacity. (There is even a "hold and release" communication channel between brain and penis, which could make some men better lovers, if they understood it.)

Just as lines of communication exist between the digestive and eliminatory systems and consciousness, so a line of communication exists between consciousness and the Schucman Corridor. Yet another line exists between consciousness and that part of the brain which holds on to the self-created self. The big difference is that no one today is socialized to form the private language needed to find happiness. If happiness is ever to be achieved on a wide scale among humanity, then socialization must include lessons for the youth about how to form the right intention when they become old enough to feel the need to do so. Every tot learns to distinguish clearly between "number one," "number two," and being hungry. Except for fear and ignorance, there is no reason why that clarity of understanding cannot be achieved in the adult, so that he or she can say with full awareness, "I'm unhappy, I need to let go of my self-created self."

Implied here, then, is yet another fault in the much criticized curriculum of public education. Where the lesson plan for learning how to become happy should be, there is only behavioralism teaching trusting students to doubt the existence of their own sentience. In our view, not only is the existence of sentience a certainty, but so is the capacity of sentience for life-long contentment. Empathic science has given us "the science," next we need to put it to use in society. Were it not for the domination of the behavioral paradigm, more people would see the monumental gap in the public education curriculum. We will suggest at the conclusion of this chapter how that fault in public education's curriculum can be corrected.

Clearly, throughout the vast stretches of world culture ignorance prevails where techniques are needed to prepare youths during socialization to develop a way to hear, understand, and respond to the calls of their contentment module. In this matter, the left brain does not know how to communicate with the right brain, where the mechanism for releasing the self-created self is likely located. Yet, some sort of dim awareness exists in most, if not all, self-reflecting brains, that one is not receiving one's full measure of life satisfaction.

Intersubjective Validation

Only a shallow look within will alert one to the presence of this unsatisfied need to find life's deeper meaning. Library shelves are full of books that attest to this need. But these *words*, whether religious, spiritual, philosophical, or scientific, can never be more than a signpost on the road. What gives these sign posts significance, if any, is the "ring of truth" which resounds in the right hemisphere. Some people find in such language an intuitive "pull." That feeling comes from the communication link between consciousness and the Schucman Corridor. It is that *feeling*, rather than the *words* which elicit it, that must be attended to, dwelt in, and followed. To dwell on the literal interpretation of words is to remain in left hemispheric processes. Houston Smith says that in Zen this is called "the Philosopher's Disease."[ix] It consists of compulsively hanging on the literal meanings of words, when an intuitive leap is needed from the ever-analyzing left into the right hemispheric nonverbal, preconceptual understanding that "all is one."

Also, one's mind can easily confuse words and "Truth." Words can create an illusion of "knowing" what only personal experience can really know. In the worst form of the Philosopher's Disease, a person comes to believe that he or she has found "salvation" in the illusion of words. Religious organizations create dogmas that work this magic. The illusion of "Truth" can seem to fill one's emptiness, and make the powerless feel powerful. Adherents then team-up around rival dogmas, and fight to prove which is Right.

Empathic science recognizes this sickness of the mind as avoidance behavior. It stems from the fear of letting go of the self-created self, which thinks it knows that "words are Truth." Our hope is that we can reduce the power of fear by replacing ignorance with scientific knowledge. Those readers who experience an intuitive pull by our words are already participating in this educational process. But to avoid the errors of the past, we stress that this pull does not come from our words; rather, it comes from the yearnings to be heard by a neglected organ in the reader's own brain. Our words can only direct the reader's attention to the channels of communication within, which suffer atrophy, and which long to be fully used. The best course for any reader to take is to leave our words behind, and to attend to the subtleties of his or her own feeling.

Empathic science, like every other science, is built upon the intersubjective agreement of its founding giants. Besides those we have mentioned, we find further support for our claims about the function of the Schucman Corridor from a wide variety of sources, some from far outside the scientific orientation of Western culture. Yoga from India, Taoism from China, and especially Zen Buddhism from Japan validate our views. Indeed, when the history of Zen's entry into the United States and Europe is written, one man will stand head and shoulders above all others as the source from whom the popularizers of Zen have drawn. No one deserves more credit for bringing authentic Zen to the attention of the Western mind than D. T. Suzuki. As Huston Smith writes, "[D. T.] Suzuki brought Zen to the West single-handed."x

Suzuki's statement of Zen represents principles that have attracted spiritual seekers in Japan for over 800 years. Travelers brought these teachings there from China. The pragmatic Chinese had distilled these notions from the Buddhism that had been brought in from India, but which had acquired inessential dogmas and rituals. Buddhism itself originated from Buddha's efforts to simplify the message in the numerous sacred books of Hinduism, and the Vedanta Sutras. These writings, in turn, surely derived their message from an oral tradition in the East that taught about the connection of mental discipline, meditation, and the entering into of Nirvana. Those old oral teachings reach back in time far beyond any written records, and even beyond writing itself. Empathic science, through its founders, links that ancient wisdom to the methods of modern science.

The consciousness of consciousness, i.e., the release of the self-created self, is our term for what in Zen is called "satori." D. T. Suzuki writes, in *An Introduction to Zen*,[xi] that satori "is the raison d'être of Zen without which Zen is no Zen. ... It is acquiring a new point of view for looking at things."[xii] Satori, or "enlightenment," is not an intellectual doctrine, but "the awakening of a new sense which will review the old things from a hitherto undreamed of angle."[xiii] When the mind which has prepared well "is ready for some reasons or others, a bird flies, or a bell rings, and you at once return to your original home."[xiv] Indeed, the "ultimate destination of satori is towards the Self; it has no other end but to be back within oneself."[xv] Having this "thoroughgoing and clear-cut [experience] generally marks a turning point in one's life ... which will be more satisfying, more peaceful, and fuller of joy than anything you ever experienced before."[xvi] But life after satori is not an exceptional condition to be examined by "abnormal psychology ... it is a perfectly normal state of mind."[xvii]

First, then, among the principles of Zen is that enlightenment is not a paranormal condition, but "a perfectly normal state of mind," and for that reason, any normal person may have it. Secondly, satori can only be attained by an intense and sustained mental striving for it. Thirdly, words or ideas about it are not to be confused with one's personal experience of it. Finally, the experience of life-long contentment, according to D. T. Suzuki, comes suddenly and thoroughly to the mind that is prepared for the realization of this "new point of view."

Empathic science regards these four points as axiomatic. An informed, intentional effort must be made to realize one's full potential for contentment; that is, one must form the right intention. Contentment, itself, as we have defined it, is the experience of this "new point of view," or change in perception. A new experience of everyday perception results from the integration of the self-created self with the personal knowledge of one's consciousness of consciousness. This is the correction of baby's error. Reinvigorating the Schucman Corridor, or achieving satori, is not an end, but the beginning of a new life. It is the elevation of the mind/brain relation to its normal, or healthy, condition. It is the cure of the human birth defect.

At the conclusion of this chapter we will return to our considerations about Zen, both for more lessons to be learned from it, and to offer some criticisms of its ways. There is much to be learned from the writings of D. T. Suzuki. One can truly say of him what he said about the ancient Asian Avatamsaka Sutra. He wrote that it embodies "the essential fountain of life from which no religious mind will turn back athirst or only partially satisfied."[xviii] Empathic science shares the aims of Zen, but rather than appeal to the "religious mind," we offer to the scientific minded our own social psychology of enlightenment.

The Natural Source of Values

We find that the body, interacting with the brain, produces its own values. Values are the instruments by which a person arranges his or her agenda for action. For example, when the body requires nutrition, signals understood as "hunger" enter into consciousness. Then one can arrange one's action agenda accordingly. One who was struck by hunger early in Chapter One has probably made and eaten that sandwich. Hopefully, after that, the importance of returning to this book rose again in the reader's hierarchy of values. If so, one would be acting in accordance with Abraham Maslow's theory of motivation. His view, in brief, is that once the satisfaction of bodily needs has been secured, the mind seems to turn naturally to such "higher" values as creativity, education, and the pursuit of deeper meaning in life. In this connection, we find it noteworthy that in *Toward a Psychology of Being*,[xix] and in other writings, Maslow acknowledges Hartman's influence on his theory of a natural hierarchy of values.

Maslow came very close to understanding what we call the polestar of the mind. His idea about the natural turning of the mind towards "higher values" falls just short of describing the process of Schucman Corridor signaling. The very idea of "higher values" derives its intuitive pull from the beckoning of the contentment module. Indeed, once the mind has come into full alignment with the brain, whole new vistas of understanding open up. One sees that this is what one has always wanted. One understands then that one had misunderstood all the signals from the Schucman Corridor, which had been so obscured by ignorance and fear.

Seeking wisdom from books, like finding the right job for one's "self-actualization," or the "perfect" mate for one's completion, are examples of *false happiness conditionals*, or illusions, which obscure the mind/brain's ultimate desire. With the hindsight of satori, one also sees that one's urgency and determination to achieve illusory goals was a misdirection of the natural desire to retune the Schucman Corridor. One further sees that Maslow's intuition hit the mark; that is, a natural order of values does exist within oneself, which has always been a part of oneself, but not recognized.

This natural order of values is produced in the mind/brain relationship. It has two parts. One is the pre-consciousness of consciousness dimension. The other is the post-consciousness of consciousness dimension. The first part can only be fully understood after realizing the second part. In the pre-consciousness of consciousness state, achieving the consciousness of consciousness is one's most urgent need. Unfortunately, this is not understood because one's values are vague, arbitrary, and whimsical due to fear and ignorance. In this needy state, illusions command actions. D. T. Suzuki understood the duality of pre- and post-consciousness of consciousness values. He writes, with scholarly understatement, that when "life becomes more enjoyable and its expanse broadens to include the universe itself, there must be something in satori that is quite precious and well worth one's striving after."[xx] In *Zen and the Brain*, Dr. Austin tells the story of a more passionate Zen Master who was asked by a beginner "is seeking enlightenment really important?" Keeping in Zen character, the Master replied, "is it important to put out a fire on the top of your head?"

Only after achieving the consciousness of consciousness can one realize how urgently one had needed it. One can then begin to see that this value came from a distressed organ in the brain. Gearing up the Schucman Corridor opens to consciousness a completely new experience of values which had been dormant in the brain, and blocked from self-reflective awareness while mind and brain were out of alignment. We stated what these values are earlier in this chapter, in our definition of "contentment." Let us return once again to an outside expert who can help to validate our claims. D. T. Suzuki writes,

> Generally, we are blind to [the fact] that we are in possession of all the necessary faculties that will make us happy and loving toward one another. All the struggles that we see around us come from this ignorance. Zen, therefore, wants us to open a 'third eye' as Buddhists call it, to the hitherto undreamed of region shut away from us through our own ignorance. When the cloud of ignorance disappears, the infinity of the heavens is manifested where we see for the first time into the nature of our own being. [xxi]

What he means by "the nature of our own being," we mean by the natural order of values and the consciousness of consciousness. That is, that the normal healthy condition of the human brain, when mind and brain are in alignment, is to feel oneness within, with others, and with the world around one. It is to see others with compassion for their suffering, and to see each person as too precious to use.

This potential condition of the normal human mind/brain is the result of evolution. As we said earlier, scientists agree that mammals care for and nurture their young far more so than reptiles, and feel a greater sense of community, largely because their brains have developed the limbic system, and surrounding cortical tissue. As selective mating behavior stimulated the growth of this brain tissue, the brain, in turn, prompted the selective behavior that led to the growth of more such tissue, in a self-producing cycle of evolution. In the next chapter, we will see that, and why, the human mind/brain has expanded its sense of community to include all members of the species in its feelings of care and membership. Hence, the natural order of values is an inherited value system produced by genetically structured electro-chemical pathways in the brain. Unfortunately, our defective self-awareness is out of touch with these values during the pre-consciousness of consciousness state.

The natural order of values is not a doctrine, nor a philosophy. It also has very little influence over behavior. Each person remains free to make his or her own decisions for action. While one may value others as too precious to use, self-defense is also an in-born value. Thus, there is nothing in the natural order of values to deter one from taking decisive action against an attacker for one's self-defense, or the defense of another. The natural order of values in the post-consciousness of consciousness state is a clear feeling, to be distinguished from articulated ethical principles. Such principles may be necessary for social order; however, one may or may not intellectually agree with how they are formulated or applied. But the natural order of values is only *felt*. This distinction between feeling and principles formulated in words will be addressed again, and hopefully clarified, in the next chapter. We will also explain at length both how the human mind/brain evolved the natural order of values from its animal predecessors, and how the human birth defect came about.

Zen Practice and Public Education

Before concluding this chapter, however, let us consider for a moment what can be learned from the practice of Zen so as to correct the faults of public education mentioned a few paragraphs above. Zen is an established institution in Japanese society. Western societies can borrow some of the elements of Zen-as-an-institution to facilitate the efforts of their people to heal. However, Zen's program for preparing the mind to achieve satori has elements in it which are a peculiarity of its history, and not, in our view, necessary or even appropriate for Westerners to follow. As the religion of the Samurai in its early days in Japan, Zen has developed a very strict system of military-like order and discipline. The aim is to instill hardness to pain and fear so that the novitiate would cultivate the courage to let go of the self-created self with a warrior's indifference to death. Zen Masters have even used corporal punishment in question and answer periods on monks who "didn't get it." Such tactics won't fly in the West. Westerners demand scientific explanations, and less threatening, more humane, methods of teaching. That is why we present, in Chapter Six, a program for healing developed by American writers with Western values.

Besides its obsession with strict discipline, Zen's militaristic origins have produced a penchant for hero worship. Zen writings are full of praise for the heroic "patriarchs" who attained enlightenment and became Masters in their monasteries, or who went on to found new monasteries. Indeed, in Zen literature enlightenment seems to be a condition which only "spiritual heroes" can claim to have achieved. But if D. T. Suzuki is correct, and enlightenment is a normal state of mind, then we believe that society should strive to make enlightenment the normal condition for its members. The institution of public education is ideally suited to help realize this social goal. Public education has the potential to be the primary institution in society for preparing youths to heal their unhappiness.

Institutional reformers who see the potential in public education to help people to find happiness can learn much from the practice of Zen-as-an-institution. For all its faults, Zen remains the only institutionalized practice that aims directly at healing the human birth defect, rejects distracting ideologies, and has had some success. But before we discuss the social organization of Zen, let us consider what Zen does in its practice. Earlier in this chapter we examined the role of private languages in the human mind/brain relationship. A private language is formed when electro-chemical impulses within a person's brain and nervous system are translated into meanings, and vice versa. We saw, for example, that Tibetan monks have learned to control their body temperature by visualizing a warm fire. This metaphorical image translates for them into a message carried by electro-chemical impulses to the hypothalamus to turn-up the internal heat.

We also noted that forming a private language is not so unusual that only trained monks can do it. Everyday all over the world there are mothers teaching a private language to their tots. Consider those moments when mommy puts little Jimmy on the potty each day at 8 am and exhorts him to "pooh-pooh!" She is positioning Jimmy so that he will fashion his own private language for bowel control. She is not conveying to him her private language, for that cannot be done. She is creating a situation in which he will eventually get the idea, and make his own inner connection between bowels and consciousness. Once he has learned the technique, he will have mastered that hold-and-release mechanism for life.

Zen practice is like toilet training. The Zen Master instructs the novitiates under his charge to sit and meditate every day, at appointed times. This is analogous to mommy putting Jimmy on the potty. The Master's ability to control his own hold-and-release mechanism for the self-created self cannot be conveyed directly to the beginners. But they can be positioned in circumstances which suggest to them what the Master wants them to do. From this set of circumstances some novices get the message and form the private language they need to convey the right intention to the brain.

Just as mommy need say no more than "pooh-pooh" for Jimmy to eventually catch on, so the Zen Master need say no more than a puzzling Koan to get the novice to understand that each must form his or her own private language. Once that point gets across, a successful communication takes place from the student's mind-made meaning into effective electro-chemical impulses. Satori occurs in that moment of understanding.

Over the centuries, many stories have accumulated about monks who "got it." One monk was sweeping a walkway when a pebble hit a wall. He had heard that noise a thousand times before, but in this moment it became his metaphor for release, and the whole universe took on a new meaning! Another monk was taking a break from his chores when he heard a crow caw – as he had never heard it before! A monk was passing time reading the biography under a portrait hanging on a wall, when suddenly he understood everything! Not those words, but grasping an ineffable understanding in itself became his signal for release. Yet another monk attained enlightenment as he accidentally fell into a well!

Clearly there is no formula here for instructing people as to how they may formulate their own private language for releasing the self-created self. Millions of people could practice falling into wells ten times a day, and not one of them would obtain the results had by that one unique person. A private language cannot be copied. But these monks did have something important in common. *They had been purposefully prepared for attaining enlightenment in an organized social institution.* And, that institution had the full support of its society. When understood in this "holistic context," Zen practice in Japan can be a guide for reform in other societies.

The practice of Zen does not consist of an individual acting alone. Zen is practiced as a sanctioned sub-system of a society. Its traditions are the products of Masters who lived in monasteries. These monasteries are, even today, institutions with a special meaning in the society of which they are a part. While some individuals may go to monasteries voluntarily, Zen monasteries, and Buddhist monasteries in general, are places where parents send a son or a daughter for the purpose of studying to become enlightened. The monastery is a special place in which the novitiate is given permission and encouragement by the supporting society to achieve Nirvana. Having the pursuit of healing sanctioned by social institutions, as occurs in the practice of Zen in Japan, can make a crucial difference in facilitating the efforts of an individual. A social institution that conveys approval and encouragement for healing may help one to overcome other discouraging and distracting messages.

But these practices need not be limited to Buddhist cultures. The same dynamic of parents sending their sons and daughters to a place where they may study to become enlightened can be replicated, de-religionized, and democratized in any society with a system of public education. This end could be accomplished in the United States, for example, simply by adding a couple of classes to the daily routine in existing public schools.

One of the classes we envision would show students not only that society believes they are worthy of happiness, but also how it can be attained. This would include learning techniques of meditation, the regular practice of meditation, and a discussion period following meditation. Students would have an opportunity to discuss their meditation experience, including problems as well as bright moments. The goal of this class would be to guide students towards achieving the consciousness of consciousness by learning best practices and forming the right intention.

As to what sort of progress teachers ought to expect from students in these classes, the advice of "the other Suzuki," also a renowned expert on Zen, may be the best practice. That is, Shunryu Suzuki cautions that enlightenment is more likely to come in gradual increments than all at once, contrary to D. T. Suzuki's dramatic characterization of attaining enlightenment suddenly, through the Grand Satori.[xxii]

The other class we propose involves the same goal of personal happiness, but by the development of emotional maturity. Students would also meet in small groups for this class. They would be encouraged to become aware of, and to share, feelings, as distinct from ideas, opinions, or stories. This would be a self-discovery support group for young lives in the transition into adulthood. One aim of this class would be to encourage students to develop a strong sense of self, and to be self-regarding in their selection of values. Besides enhancing self-awareness, this class would also provide an opportunity to practice foregoing judgmentalism and cultivating compassion, as these are discussed in Chapter Six.

Conclusion

We began this chapter by rephrasing the question "What is a healthy mind?" and asking instead, "What is a good mind/brain relationship?" We have shown that to have a healthy mind one must have a mind in alignment with its life-giving brain. Bringing mind into alignment with its organic base, i.e., healing the human birth defect, is humanity's life-task. Thus far, humanity has not done so well. But there is light ahead, especially for societies with an established system of public education. That institution can be reformed so as to be the primary place where the young are prepared to heal the unhappiness they are sure to experience as adults. Once such reforms are up and running, we will be well on the way towards our goal of all humanity happy. But before the need for these reforms can be fully appreciated, we will explain the origins of the human birth defect some 150,000 years ago, and how humanity has dealt with it from then to now.

Chapter Three

The Human Genome and the Origins of Human Unhappiness

The Recipe for Humanity

The focus of this book is on how to realign the mind/brain relation in man. Empathic science attempts to look at this relationship from the inside; that is, using the methods of introspection, empathic observation, and intersubjective consultation. However, empathic science would not be possible without the knowledge of the natural sciences. We are especially reliant upon the field of evolutionary biology, and the sub-disciplines that feed into it, such as genetics, neurology, anthropology, and paleontology. The findings in these fields help form a base upon which empathic science can build.

In this chapter we will continue our discussion of how the Schucman Corridor and the natural order of values fit into the human mind/brain relation. Here we will present our theory of the origins of that relation. How did the human mind/brain relation evolve out of its predecessor hominid version? How does the human mind/brain relation differ from that of its hominid parents? Why do humans have the burden of needing to intentionally initiate the flow of contentment causing chemicals in their brain, while animals seem to enjoy that flow naturally? How did the natural order of values emerge in the human mind/brain relationship? If the natural order of values is a structural element of that relationship, why is mind so unaware of it? These and other issues will be addressed here.

The human mind/brain relationship is one of the products of the human genome. Without the human genome, there would be no human mind/brain relationship. Yet, the human mind/brain relationship is, above all else, what makes the human genome "human." Thus, our inquiry into the origins of the human mind/brain relationship necessarily entails a look into the nature and beginnings of the human genome.

On June 26, 2000, in a White House ceremony, a special announcement was made. Combining the resources of both private industry and government, scientists representing The Human Genome Project announced that they had completed "the first draft" of the human genome's "sequence." The genetic information that accounts for all the physical, and many of the psychological, traits and characteristics of each member in a given species is carried in the individual's DNA (deoxyribonucleic acid). The structure of DNA is symbolized by the famous double helix model made by Watson and Clark, the one that looks like steps on a spiral staircase. Each step represents a connected pair of nucleic acids. The way in which these nucleic acids are combined eventually determines the make-up of an organism, including a human being. There are four nucleic acids that can be paired. These are "adenine," "thymine," "cytosine," and "guanine." They are symbolized respectively as A, T, C, and G.

To sequence these base pairs, a sample of DNA is heated, given a fluorescent dye, dipped in a gel, and electronically scanned by a highly sophisticated computer. The machine then prints-out the sequence of A's, T's, C's, and G's for that particular sample. By taking a variety of samples from one species, the DNA sequence, which is unique to that species can be spelled-out. These high-speed computers took over ten years to decode and to spell-out the three billion base pairs that constitute the human genome.[xxiii]

A genome, then, is a highly complex sequence of base pairs out of which each unique member of a species is formed. In other words, the genetic sequence of a genome is the formula, or recipe, for making a member of a species. Genetically speaking, a human being is little more than a pinch of A's, a dash of T's, and a sprinkling of C's and G's. Of course, each "pinch" and "dash" is made up of hundreds of millions of pairs in a precise mix. Although highly complex, there is nevertheless a basic recipe for humanity.

The very discovery that a human genome exists means that all humans are products of the same basic formula. Furthermore, there are sub-formulas within the general recipe for the various parts of the body and their functions. Scientists are now at work trying to identify the sub-formula for the heart, lungs, kidneys, and other organs. Once these are known, abnormal variations in the sequences of a person's DNA may be "red flags" warning of potential diseases or dysfunctions which can be corrected before the problem starts.

Now that the Genie is out of the bottle, thoughtful people are beginning to wonder what the ethical implications are. Some predict a miraculous revolution in medicine, others predict a catastrophic violation of the Will of God! Can the genetic codes of dreaded diseases be identified in sperm cells or eggs and removed or treated before fertilization occurs? Can laboratories use this information to grow and harvest "perfect" organs for sale? Are we at the Dawn of the Age of Designer Babies?

While others ponder such important questions as to the future uses of this new knowledge, our concern here will be to suggest what it means for understanding human nature in the context of the past and present. Armed with the new insight that there is a distinct human genome, we can recombine established principles in evolutionary biology, and the sub-fields we mentioned, to formulate a novel theory of both our origins and our nature.

Unlike neo-creationists, evolutionary biologists do not take the position that the genome of a species simply "pops" into existence upon the command of some Higher Power in the sky. Each genome is a tapestry of fine threads drawn from pre-existing fabrics. Unless there is an unusual event, evolution takes place on a micro-level long before its macro-level expression can be observed. However, the Darwinian theory that new species always evolve gradually and smoothly along a continuous line has been readjusted to better fit the facts now known. As Steven J. Gould and Niles Eldredge pointed out in the early 1970's gaps exist between species. These gaps suggest that a smooth, linear evolution did not take place. Instead, there must have been a creative leap by members of one species into a new species. This would involve a period of rapid change, in which some members of a species rather suddenly metamorphosized into a new form of life. In this way, some unicellular creatures branched out to become multicellular creatures. One type of fish mutated into walking amphibians, some of which gave rise to the reptiles. A small prosimian-like mammal lived for millions of years almost unchanged. Then the dinosaurs died out sixty-five million years ago. Some descendants of the little mammals grew into giants, some of which, like the wooly mammoth and the great elk, roamed Europe until only ten thousand years ago. Other mouse-size mammals became the ancestors of primates, hominids, and humans.

The pattern of evolution, then is not an unbroken line of one form of life emerging out of another, but of a period of normal existence for a species interrupted by an abnormal period of rapid change in some of its members. These changes can result from several different causes. Suppose, for example, that some members of a species migrate into a new environment; or, the environmental conditions for a stable population changes. In either case, as the organisms adapt to the new conditions some traits may be more successful for adaptation than others. By natural selection, those without the needed traits in the new environment die off, and those with them live to reproduce. Geneticists Elrod and Stansfield write that such conditions, "could yield a new species very rapidly,"[xxiv] especially where members of a species become geographically, and therefore reproductively, isolated.

Also, mutations and recombinations of genetic material occur randomly in nature. Sometimes, by chance, one characteristic, such as size, can emerge and become a dominant trait in a breeding community. Large size in males could become an advantage for driving off reproductive rivals, or could become favored by females in mate selection. Then, a new species of large creatures could evolve out of a former species of smaller ones.

The theory of "punctuated equilibrium" proposed by Gould and Eldredge is given strong support by the Hardy-Weinberg rule in genetics.[xxv] They found that under stable conditions the characteristics of the individuals in a large breeding population will stay within a normal range of variation unless some extraordinary event causes them to change. Such an event could include an environmental crisis, like a change in climate, or in the sudden scarcity of food and water, or an invasion of disease or predators. And, as we have said, the migration of a small group into a condition of reproductive isolation from the larger group, can also lead to the making of a new species.

From these principles of evolutionary biology we can reasonably conclude, then, that the unparalleled human species and its genome could only have come into existence under a set of extraordinary circumstances. Although these circumstances occurred long ago, and no witnesses remain, we will hazard guesses as to what they were from what science now knows. Because genomes tend to emerge out of one another, rather than to spring up out of nowhere, scientists can sort out the common elements of related species to determine what's new in a particular genome. Considering the current knowledge of early humanity and its hominid ancestors, we can sort through the commonalties to try to isolate humanity's distinctive features. The question to guide our inquiry is, then, "what makes man different from his animal ancestors;" or, "what makes the human genome *human*?"

An additional point to consider is that the human genome defines the human species, and provides the evidence as to how our species differs from any other. This development in the science of genetics now enables taxonomists to clarify the meaning of the terms "Hominid" and "Homo sapiens." The precursors of us Homo sapiens were Hominids. All organisms that are expressions of the human genome are "humans." All organisms that are not expressions of the human genome, but express different genomes, are not human, but animal, insect, etc. Hence, the class of "Hominidae" consists of animals, as distinct from our species of humans, and the term "hominid" will be used here to refer to a particular type of animal. We will follow this more precise understanding of classification throughout this book.

Our Animal Ancestors

Paleontologists now know that the human body differs very little from the hominid body out of which humans evolved. That is, the skeletons show the same bone structure needed for upright walking creatures. The tilt of the pelvis, the balance of the skull on the neck bones and spinal column, the shape and size of the feet and hand bones show that the basic formula for the human body is, to a large extent, a carry-over from the hominid genome. That genome and the genome of the apes may have split from a common ancestor over six million years ago. "Lucy" is a famous example of the type of hominid that evolved long after that split. She was a three and a half feet tall, upright walking creature from about 3.5 million years ago. Her body would have resembled a petit modern woman's, except for her head, because her brain was about half the human size. Few paleontologists would disagree that humans and hominids share the same types of internal organs, muscles, and nervous system, all made from the same bio-chemical material. The recipe for these, too, carried-over almost intact from the hominid genome to ours. In fact, put a hat on the last hominid, before he became a human, to cover the size and shape of his head, and you would not be able to tell him, or her, from a human. All of our significant differences are from the neck up.

We humans pride ourselves on our ability to speak. However, Richard Leakey, member of the great paleo-anthropological Leakey family, has observed from the old hominid bones found in Africa that the anatomical conditions in the skull, jaw, and throat necessary for speech were present long before modern man, with his large brain, emerged. Thus, it is not the formula for these parts, which made the human genome "human."[xxvi] Leakey also suggests that our human ancestors likely came from a breed of hominids which had slight, or *gracile*, skeletal features that distinguish them from other sorts of hominids with thicker, sturdier bones. Indeed, in his opinion, there may have been as many as 16 different breeds of hominid over the past several million years.[xxvii] Some of them, such as the famous, or infamous, Neanderthal, were once contemporaries of humans. We will discuss the Neanderthal, and its fate, in Chapter Five.

Some of the gracile hominids evolved skeletons, jaws, and teeth, which are almost indistinguishable from those of humans, because they fall within the human range of size and shape. The main reason paleontologists can say they are not human parts is because the associated skulls are narrower, with less of a crown and forehead which shows that their brain was smaller and shaped differently than the human average.

The human genome, then, is "human," in part, because of the brain's size and shape, and because of the large dome-shaped skull needed to accommodate and protect the brain. But the human brain is not different in every part from its hominid predecessor. The size, shape and function of the brainstem, or reptilian sector, for example, were no doubt the same for the hominids as it is for us humans. With one exception to be discussed shortly, it is unlikely that the hominid limbic system, or mammalian sector, was in any significant way different than ours. They needed a system of circuits to monitor, interpret, and coordinate for consciousness the information coming into the brain from the internal organs and from the senses. Their cerebellum, used for motor control, was no doubt just like ours.

They needed a specialized nervous system to regulate vital functions, such as heart rate, breathing, body temperature, and digestion. They needed a fight or flight mechanism for survival in the wild. And, they needed a visual and tactile system, which was well coordinated with their reproductive parts to sustain their species. Our assumption here that similar functions were fulfilled by similar structures is given substantial support by impressions found on the insides of hominid skulls. These markings suggest that their brains were wrapped in a two-sided cerebral cortex, with four lobes on each side, just as is our brain.

By the process of elimination, then, we can conclude, with Leakey, that the chief physical differences between the human brain and that of its hominid ancestor is in the thickness of the cortical tissue around the sides, the top, and especially the front, "in apelike brains these areas are much smaller."[xxviii] Indeed, their occipital lobe, the rear part of the brain, which processes visual information, was probably the same size and shape as ours. The expanded, or swollen, part of the human cerebral hemispheres is called the "neocortex." This is one of the key distinguishing features of humanity. In our view, the expanded neocortex caused a revolutionary reconfiguration of the prior hominid mind/brain relationship. We will show that both empirical and empathic evidence combine to compel this conclusion.

Hominid artifacts can support several inferences about their creativity and problem solving ability. In the roughly three and a half million year period from Lucy's breed to the first human, hominids displayed very little inventiveness. While numerous pieces of broken and chipped rock have been found along with hominid bones, only a trained paleontologist would know how to recognize those "tools" from among ordinary pieces of stone. These were undecorated stones, which were never attached to a wooden handle or a spear. Hominids never made an arrowhead or a spear point. Compare their "inventiveness" to what humans have done. In just the last three hundred years we have rocketed from the catapult to the satellite, from horse and buggy to the Ferrari, and from bleeding the sick to penicillin. Even by twenty thousand years ago, humans had invented cave paintings, fired ceramic statuettes, carved fine jewelry, invented the wooden axe handle, a spear with a sharp stone point, a spear thrower, shelters constructed of stone, bone, and wood, plus numerous other items that the hominids had never even dreamed of. Thus, there are many reasons to distinguish sharply between hominid, or animal, culture, and human culture. In Chapters Four and Five, we will discuss other differences between the two cultures, and further argue that hominid culture was animal, not human, culture.

Their limited problem solving ability and lack of imagination followed from the thinner cortical tissue of their animal brain. For example, while the cerebral hemisphere can constitute as much as 85% of the volume of the human brain, it only takes up about 65% of the chimpanzee brain.[xxix] The last in the line of gracile hominids had average brain sizes of about 1200 cc. Compare this to the human average of at least 1500 cc, and we can infer that their cerebral cortex, at the sides, top, and front, was roughly 20% less than ours is. That is the variable to measure because all the other hominid brain organs were likely the same size as their human counterpart.

This 20% expansion is what caused the revolution in the hominid mind/brain relationship. The prior animal limitations on meaning making, abstract problem solving and creative imagination were exploded. The organic base for human creativity was established. Human culture was made possible by the growth of the neocortex. That's the good news; or, at least since Aristotle, humans have thought that news to be "good." Aristotle's proclamation that "man is the rational animal" expresses the main premise upon which many humans base their claim to "exceptionalism" among other life forms. However, all the news is not so good. One of the chief characteristics of the animal mind/brain relationship, as we have said, is that contentment comes naturally to their minds, from naturally occurring brain chemical production. A hypothesis that we will explore further is that the swelling of the human neocortex appears to have cut-off, or greatly restricted, that production of contentment causing chemicals in our mind/brain relationship.

From this discussion we can conclude, at least in part, that the human essence, that which is our key distinguishing feature, has two intertwined parts. These are the physical and the mental; or, the visible and the invisible. Our essential physical characteristic is our very large cerebral cortex. It is, as we have said, a much larger portion of the brain, on average, than that of our closest living relative, the chimpanzee. Our defining mental characteristics include our huge capacity for abstract thinking, as Aristotle and others have observed, and our chronic discontent, as observed by Buddha and others.

The formula for the human essence is contained in the human genome. Drawing from the current knowledge of evolutionary biology, and its sub-fields, we can reconstruct the process by which our special combination of A's, T's, C's, and G's was concocted. The story of the human genome's origins is also the story of how man's unhappiness began.

Hominid Politics and The Culture of Rap

In our explanation of how the human mind/brain relationship came into existence, we will trace those factors which caused the growth of the neocortex and made us who we are. Our ability for creative abstract thinking is one element to be explained. Our discontent is another. That discontent, as we discussed in Chapter Two, comes chiefly from the failure of the Schucman Corridor to operate naturally, as it likely did for our hominid ancestors. As we have said, ours can only be put into operation by an intentional effort, which each person must make on his or her own. Another feature of human discontent is the general lack of awareness of the natural order of values. We will explain how the natural order of values became a part of the brain in this chapter. In later chapters we will discuss further why so many people are so dimly, if at all, aware of their inherited values.

What caused the human brain to grow into the size and shape which is now preserved and replicated by the human genome? There are numerous factors, which may have fed into this process. One is that a genetic formula for gradual brain growth existed in the hominid genome that gave rise to humans. The brain case of the bones called "Lucy," thought to be about 3.5 million years old, shows that the brain was slightly larger than a modern chimp's. The cranium of Homo habilis, who may have lived about 2 to 2.5 million years ago, shows that he had a brain slightly larger than did his distant cousin Lucy's. The human brain, then, resulted from a creative leap out of the slight growth momentum established by the hominid brain over the past few million years.

The hominid brain underwent a growth spurt in Homo erectus, who lived about one million years ago. He, too, was likely a cousin, rather than a descendant of Homo habilis. His brain size was also due, in part, to having a larger body than his hominid ancestors. Humans are probably not direct descendants from Homo erectus, but we likely share a common ancestor. Whether or not

Neanderthal is a direct descendant or a cousin of Homo erectus has not been settled conclusively by paleontologists. (We will discuss how the Neanderthal brain differed from ours in Chapter Five.) The continuing, albeit slow, growth of the hominid brain may be due, in some part, to a genetic formula not shared with the primate genome. Perhaps when the hominid line branched off from its common ancestor with the primates, roughly six million years ago, one of the distinguishing genetic features of the hominids was this tendency for brain growth.

An additional, and perhaps more substantial, cause of hominid brain growth would have been selective breeding. That is, the addition of cortical tissue may have enhanced important adaptive traits which enabled their carriers to move to the front of the line in mate selection. Suppose, for example, that additional gray matter in the areas of the brain, which coordinate vision and finger dexterity enabled some hominids to chip a sharper stone blade than their rivals in their breeding community. This instrument would have given its possessor the champion's advantage in a fight, and thus helped lift him to Alpha status in his group. Because the males with the more deadly weapons could both ward-off rivals and impress the ladies with their power, their genes would move to a more dominant position in the gene pool. Furthermore, the guy who could chip more than one type of tool may also have had special reproductive privileges. The more intelligent females would likely have favored the handier males. This would explain, in part, why there seems to be a rough parallel between the increase in the variety and quality of tool production, and the growth of the hominid brain.

Perhaps the most important factor in the growth of the hominid brain was the gradual streamlining of its vocal apparatus, particularly in the gracile hominids. They developed a smaller jaw and teeth than did the more robust hominids. This may have given their bite less power, but it likely would have improved their vocalizing prowess. Lighter jaws can move more fluidly, more rapidly, and can sustain movement for a longer time before tiring. When combined with other factors, such as an agile "voice box" in the throat, the ability of some hominids to formulate a wide range of vocalizations would have greatly exceeded those, like Neanderthal, with heavy jaws and a poorly developed vocal apparatus. As the jaw muscles of the gracile hominids thinned, their brow ridges, once used to anchor heavy facial muscles, shrunk from disuse. Their faces then began to take on a more human-like appearance. Vanity inclines us to speculate that this change in the shape of the face may also have played a role in mate selection. But the larger factor in causing brain growth would have been in how their capacity for articulation changed their politics.

The politics of the gracile hominid set the stage for human speech long before it was actually developed. In Chapter Five we will explain our theory that speech, which rose above the level of animal calls, was not developed until between 40 and 30 thousand years ago. Leakey notes that "we have 50 phonemes; the ape has about a dozen."[xxx] In our view, that capacity for phoneme making developed over several generations of hominid politics. Thus, the organic apparatus necessary for human speech was put in place tens of thousands of years before language began. Bones, artifacts, and what biologists know of animal behavior offer many clues about how our hominid forefathers selectively bred in a way that had the unintended consequence of making human speech possible.

Two hundred thousand years ago, there were breeds of gracile hominids living throughout east central and southern Africa. Robust hominids, particularly Homo erectus, lived in northern and southern Africa, Asia, and Europe.[xxxi] Leakey is in accord with the widely accepted view of anthropologists that hominids likely lived in loosely connected large breeding communities of roughly 500 individuals. This extended group consisted of politically independent clans or families of from 25 to 50 members, which shared economic responsibilities.[xxxii] We will discuss the gracile hominid's politics here, and Neanderthal's different sort of politics in Chapter Five.

Like all intensely social animals, gracile hominids would have had their own means of competing for Alpha status. Of course, they would not have butted heads, like some antelopes and goats do, because their skulls were too thin. But neither would they have regularly relied on the use of their stone weapons, or wooden clubs and spears to fight for the top spot. Given the deadly nature of these weapons, there would not have been any males left to mate with the ladies if their politics had been limited to a fight to the finish.

Also, as Leakey points out, the *interdependency* of the hominid way of life "may have encouraged more subtle cerebral forms of competition rather than overt confrontation."[xxxiii] Therefore, we can reasonably assume that the gracile hominid's politics (that is, the means by which Alpha positions and privileges are distributed in a group) were similar to primate politics, which rely mostly on chest pounding, bluff, and bluster. Fights ending in fatalities as a means of determining who's who were surely a rare occurrence. These hominids would have cultivated their agile speech apparatus by awarding breeding privileges to those who, among other things, used that apparatus well.

As with nearly all animals, competition for Alpha status would have employed standard procedures of ritualized combat. The hominids in east central Africa, from whom humans emerged, likely followed a pattern of verbal competition. This form of competition may have been devised to offset the deadly dangers of the hand held stone blades, which were in use from at least two million years ago. As blade technology improved, the use of oral confrontations in the place of actual fighting likely increased.

In the initial steps of the competition, a healthy young male of respectable size and physical stature (perhaps 5'9" and 160 lbs.) would likely have made known his intent to challenge the established power holder with shouts of bravado, jumping, and dancing. Because power holding is a public office, challengers would want the public to be aware that a change of office was about to occur – that is, if fortune favored him!

As the Alpha male confidently squared-off with his agitated, adrenaline-charged rival, the two may have glared into one another's eyes, perhaps snarling. The challenger may have flailed his arms in the air, to appear bigger, and roared like a lion. If the Alpha male was a courageous guy, he may have laughed like a hyena at the ridiculous posturing of the young upstart. Then the verbal aggression would shift into high gear. We can imagine the challenger taking large sideways steps around the power holder, the challenger might have ominously cluck a subdued "click, click, click," then leapt into the air screaming "yada, yada, yada," and without a pause twist his face into the most ferocious expression he could imagine, stretch out his fingers like giant claws, and yell in a deep powerful voice "**ahhhhh**!"

The Alpha male, never moving his eyes from those of his opponent's, may have fired back in rapid succession, "whoop, whoop, **arrrr**, yak, yak, yak, **opa**, **opa**!" Having never heard such a creative variety of phonemes before, the less experienced youth may have become dazzled, confused, and frightened. Seeing this collapse of confidence, the seasoned fighter would have sent the youth packing with a guttural, mean "boogely, boogely, **shoo**!"

To a human observer, this hominid phoneme fight would be much like watching two naked men in a shouting match using a strange and foreign language. Such an observer may try to understand the words, but they would have no meaning to him. Those hominid "words" would have no meaning because they were not words. Hominids had no language because they lacked the gray matter needed to conceive of such high level abstractions as parts of speech, grammar, and syntax. Those combatants would have concentrated on producing a series of carefully shaped sounds. Their strings of vocalizations would have been designed to signify superior power, but not to have any specific meaning. Each contestant would have aimed at creating the most intimidating display of verbal virtuosity. Over time these "rapping" hominids would have developed conventions, by tacit understanding, to determine which verbal displays would signify greater power.

The victor's impressive display of vocal prowess would have won him the spoils of office. He was likely the first to eat at the common meal. Being healthy and strong, he was sexually active. As chief stud, his genes would have been prevalent in the gene pool. Mothers likely taught the winning lines to their sons, so that they could grow-up to be power holders some day. Women likely had their own style of sorting out status phonetically. Surely, children played verbal games in imitation of their elders. The growth of the lithe jaw, and the development of verbal politics, surely fed-off each other in the evolution of these hominids.

The culture of "rap" would have very profound genetic consequences. Both competitors would have strained their brains to the max. The frontal lobes, in which self-serving planning and reasoning take place, would be used to work out a vocal strategy that would be more intimidating than any yet heard. Efforts at innovation were, thus, encouraged in this culture. Broca's area, which controls speech muscles, would have been pushed to the limits of its ability to move and coordinate lips, tongue, jaw, lungs, and throat. Wernicke's area, which analyzes sounds for significant patterns, would have been stretched to full capacity, as it strained to find any signs of superior power in the opponent's vocalizations. In the course of the contests, each would have learned new sound patterns from the others. All ambitious individuals would have frequently exercised the brain tissue involved in the recall and analysis of those patterns. So, because the brain works as a whole, the entire organ would have been focused from stem to stern, both in rehearsal and in the heat of battle, on vocalizing, interpreting, and comparing verbal formulations. In this way, the precursors of the human vocal apparatus, and of the vocalizing aspects of the human mind/brain relationship, emerged as unintended consequences of hominid selective breeding practices. Music, poetry, and rhetoric would later grow from this fertile soil.

Our Creation Story

Out of the larger breeding community of rapping hominids, a few became isolated, and bred the human genome. The most likely scenario is that a small group, perhaps no more than fifty, wandered in search of food such a distance from the greater community that they lost contact. This group then became an isolated breeding community.

Animal breeders learned long ago that selective breeding can raise particular traits to the level of dominance in a breeding group. This has been done, for example, to enrich cow's milk. Cows producing watery milk are removed from the herd, and cows which produce creamy milk are added to it. In this way, the genetic formula for rich milk production becomes a dominant element of the herd's gene pool, and the calves born to the herd grow-up to be producers of creamy milk. Mating members of the same family of rich milk producers can accelerate the process. Then, what might take several generations of removing some cows from a herd and adding others, could be accomplished in one or two generations.

However, such intensive inbreeding also increases the risk of accelerating the development of undesirable characteristics. The selective breeding of cows for rich milk has produced herds that have lost their former ability to resist certain bovine viruses. Large herds under natural conditions maintain this immunity. But the specially bred herds must be kept on antibiotics, or risk losing the whole herd to disease. Dogs inbred for fighting ferocity sometimes develop an undesirable tendency to see children as status rivals, and to maul them.

The Hapsburgs were a royal family that ruled in central Europe for several centuries. Their family members reigned over numerous kingdoms, before and after Europeans formed nations. Hapsburgs often married within their extended family, both to strengthen political ties, and to "breed royalty." But rather than breed a superior form of human, they produced a series of "mad kings" and murderous princesses. They also sprouted a prominent chin that sometimes stretched out and curled up towards their nose, like that of a cartoon witch. One old story tells of a Hapsburg duke who could not chew his food, because his jutting jaw could not close. This hapless Hapsburg had to sip his soup from a silver spoon, at the side of his mouth, because his chin curled up and blocked a direct approach!

Happily, the Hapsburg experiment shows that genetics favors democratic breeding practices over selecting for "royalty." It also shows that royalty cannot be bred, and that humans are not immune to the hazards of intensive inbreeding. Unfortunately, that defective gene has not gone away. There are still Hapsburg descendants who must take their "mandibular prognathism" to a plastic surgeon for correction.

The principles of applied genetics, which we have been illustrating here, help to explain what likely happened to that isolated group of gracile hominids. Because the supply of sex partners, which was once available from the larger community, became sharply limited, while the demand for sex likely remained constant, inbreeding increased. Hominids may have had an instinctive resistance to mother-son incest, because that rewards timidity, while the courage to go out in the jungle was necessary for group survival. However, the incidents of father-daughter and brother-sister relations would have gone way up in these conditions. As a result, the genetic brain growth tendency, which had acted slowly over the preceding several million years, rose to a higher position in the gene pool. The momentum for growing the speech and reasoning parts of the brain, which had been carried on by the culture of rap, accelerated. This led to the creative reconfiguration that became the human brain. Within a short time, perhaps no more than a few generations, sperm carrying the 23 chromosomes needed to form one half of the human genome, began to fertilize eggs carrying the 23 chromosomes needed for the other half. In that generation, there was born not only an Eve, but an Adam, and at the other side of the camp, a Peter, there a Paul, and here a Mary. If not the angels in Heaven, then surely these hominids on Earth sang joyfully in celebration of their fertility! Such an extraordinary set of circumstances could not have come together at any other place or time. This moment was truly unique.

The great human genome, now with *seven billion* replications, creator of science, art, philosophy, and literature, builder of grand cities, international commerce, public education, and miracle-making hospitals had its humble beginnings as a tiny zygote in the fallopian tube of an incestuous hominid.

After examining the results of DNA analysis by experts who sought to calculate when humans came into existence, Richard Leakey has concluded that it was likely around "150,000 years ago."[xxxiv] While this is surely a rough approximation, we see no reason to reject it. For now, this is the best that science has to offer. We know for certain, however, that the first generation of humans begot a second generation, which produced a third, etc., and that our hominid ancestors passed into extinction. In the next chapter we will consider how the two species separated. We will hypothesize based on empathy as to what life was like for that first generation of humans, and for the next one hundred thousand years of human life. In chapters following that, we will bring our story up to date. In the remainder of this chapter, however, we would like to bring into closer focus the causes of our under performing Schucman Corridor, our high intelligence, and the natural order of values.

The Locus of Man's Misery

The proportion of gray matter in the brain, rather than the size of the organ, seems to be the source of the human superior ability for abstract reasoning and imagination. However, that neocortex also appears to be associated with the human burden of having to *find* one's happiness, instead of having it naturally. From these observations, we have concluded that the swelling of the cerebral cortex in the human brain caused a reconfiguration of the prior hominid mind/brain relation. Recall that in Chapter One we distinguished between the need-based self-reflective consciousness of the animal mind/brain relationship, and the human meaning-based mind/brain relationship. Meaning awareness, of course, entails a far more complex process of mind/brain communication than does need awareness. In the passage from hominid to human, the animal's direct awareness of needs has been transformed into an awareness of "my needs;" i.e., an awareness of needs mediated by the self-created self.

In this metamorphosis, the instinctive, or naturally regulated, production of contentment causing chemicals was lost in the human mind/brain relationship. This is humanity's "Hapsburg Jaw," or genetic defect. The genetic formula for natural contentment in the hominid animal genome has been either garbled, or left incomplete in the transition to the human genome. As a result, each person is left with the responsibility to repair his or her own personal version of the human birth defect.

The reason why humans must self-adjust their production of contentment causing chemicals may be due to a hyper-attenuated link in the Schucman Corridor, caused, in part, by the swelling of the cerebral hemispheres. Neuro-scientists may have found the physical evidence of this defect. The authors of *The Human Brain*, a widely used textbook, describe a string of tissue in the limbic system, which is technically composed of the "hippocampal-dentate complex" and the "supracallosal gyrus."[xxxv] While intended for medical students, their discussion is well worth considering. They write:

> Although this constitutes a complete arc surrounding the corpus callosum *in most mammals*, it is *reduced in human beings* for the most part to a lobulated form (hippocampal-dentate) hidden deep to the medial border of the temporal lobe. The superior remnant of this arc of cortex is a vestigial, thin plate of tissue (supracallosal gyrus) lying on the superior surface of the corpus callosum beneath the overlying cingulate gyrus (emphasis added).

In other words, the human brain has only a "remnant" of what is "a complete arc … in most mammals." Here, then, may be a comparative anatomy of the Schucman Corridor in man and animals. That loss of crucial tissue in the hyper-attenuated section of our Schucman Corridor may constitute the organic basis of the human birth defect.

Incidentally, *The Human Brain* may also have described the link in the brain over which *the right intention* passes to initiate the operation of the Schucman Corridor. According to the textbook,

> Recently, direct neocortical input to the hypothalamus, in the form of fine corticohypothalamic fibers, has been reported. These fibers have been shown to originate from

the posterior part of the orbital gyrus of the frontal lobe. *The functional significance of these fibers is not yet clear* (emphasis added).

The hypothalamus is the "switch board" that links the frontal lobes with the brain stem, which is a rich source of contentment-causing chemicals. Those who are engaged in the quest for the locus of the Schucman Corridor may now be able to clarify the "functional significance of these [recently discovered] fibers." They could play a major role in achieving and maintaining human happiness! A definitive statement about our hypothesis as to this connection of function and location can only be made by neuro-scientists. Our task here is but to illustrate the kind of progress that can be made when empathic science and natural science work together.

Introspection shows, as we will explain at length in later chapters, that the culture which modern humanity has created is an extension of our defective mind/brain relationship. As a result, the burden of self-correction for the individual has been rendered far heavier than need be. Those chapters will trace the development of human, or world, culture from its beginning to the present. We will show how, and why, man has laid this needless cultural burden over his natural burden in Chapter Five. We will offer a complete program for self-correction, inspired by Dr. Schucman's writings, in Chapter Six. To conclude this chapter, we will complete our discussion of how the natural order of values came into being.

How the Natural Order of Values Emerged

In *The People of the Lake*,[xxxvi] Richard Leakey proposes a theory as to how the means by which hominids lived contributed to both the growth of the hominid brain, and the increase of their intelligence. One of the purposes of his discussion is to refute the popular and dramatic "killer ape" hypothesis. That notion explains modern man's aggression, attraction to war, and other murderous behavior as the result of our inheriting the genes of a killer ape who violently conquered all his rivals long ago. However, Leakey argues that a close examination of the paleo-anthropological facts shows that the killer ape hypothesis is more science fiction than science fact. While modern humans certainly do many dastardly deeds, the cause of this behavior is cultural, not genetic.

Empathic science finds Leakey's proposition persuasive, not just for his reading of the objective facts, but because introspection confirms it. As we stated in Chapter Two, introspection, empathic observation, and intersubjective agreement show that the natural order of values is an inherited structure in the complex neuropathways of the brain. The healed, and therefore normal, human mind/brain relationship feels as a matter of fact that one is a member of the family of man, and that each person is too precious to use. This order of values is locked into the A's, T's, C's, and G's of the human genome. The connection between brain stem, limbic system, and the neocortex, when not inhibited by fear and false beliefs, naturally produce these feelings as an element of everyday perception and understanding.[xxxvii]

Leakey's argument against the killer ape hypothesis serves an additional function. It provides an evolutionary explanation for how hominid selective breeding gradually set the stage for mixing the genetic formula that produces the natural order of values in the human genome.

We begin our novel application of Leakey's argument with his observation that from all the evidence available, anthropologists tend to select those facts which will confirm their preexisting opinions of man. Even in little matters, the presumption that man is naturally aggressive colors the way the facts are presented. For example, the way hominids lived for millions of years, and the way humans lived for the first centuries of their existence, is widely characterized as a "hunter-gatherer" way of life. That view is deeply etched into contemporary humanity's self-image.

The facts are, however, that *gathering* was massively more important than hunting to hominid existence over the last six million years, as well as to the early life of humans. Meat was a treat, and never a staple. Gathering nuts, berries, and other fruits, digging up roots and tubers, snatching insects, and pulling up grasses was always the hominid mainstay. If hominids had tried to live exclusively on meat, as do lions for example, they would have soon perished. Hunting by male hominids was a game far more so than it was a means of living. Indeed, more meat was obtained by scavenging carrion than by hunting.

Leakey attempts to correct this widespread misperception by reversing the term, and calling the hominid way of life that of a "gatherer-hunter." But in our view, even this seems to be too much of a concession to convention. To be sure, hominids killed for meat when they could. On occasion they likely killed and ate large prey, and even other hominids. However, the number of bones found in cave trash heaps suggest not only that meat was a minor part of their diet, but that small animals were far more likely to be eaten than large ones, and then only as a side dish. The dramatic and unusual moments of life do not define a way of life. As we will show in Chapter Five, man became "a hunter" somewhere between 35,000 and 30,000 years ago. Before then, both the hominid and the human way of life was, in our terms, that of a *communal gatherer*; that is, both our hominid ancestors and our human forbearers gathered the great bulk of their food, and shared it with their community.

According to Leakey, the key element in this hominid way of life was "food sharing. … Sharing, not hunting or gathering as such, is what made us human."[xxxviii] He compares this with the observed behavior of modern primates. Chimps, gorillas, and orangutans, for example, are foragers. They move through the jungle in groups, and each individual picks and eats his or her food as they go. Leakey notes emphatically that "no primate gathers food – ever!"[xxxix] Also, except for mother and child, primates rarely share food. Nor do they have "meal times."[xl] Like four-legged grazing animals, primates eat on and off throughout the entire day without planning for a common meal.

Leakey argues that hominid behavior provides a sharp contrast to that of primates. Early in their evolutionary history hominids began to practice a division of labor and an ordering of their daily life, which was far more extensive than that seen in any contemporary primate group. In general, everyone gathered; although males may have spent some time engaged in the game of hunting, or of competing with buzzards and other scavengers over the remains left by true hunters, like lions. Probably at a regular time, they came together for a common meal. Of course, this practice began as a tendency, perhaps in the time of Lucy, which, over millions of years, gradually grew into an established way of life.

These practices had some very significant effects on the growth of the brain, on the increase of intelligence, and on the breeding of a natural value predisposition. For example, the hominid way of life required a more focused intellectual involvement with the environment than that of foragers. Gatherers, like foragers, had to know which plants provided needed nutrition, and which were inedible, or toxic. But hominids, unlike apes, learned that buried under the ground, out of plain view, laid luscious roots and tubers. However, some items were only tasty when ripe. So, the hominids had to know not only where, but also when to gather them. To ease their labor, they invented tools. One example is the digging stick. Males likely specialized in the tasks of chipping sharp stone blades, and of using those to carve a point on the digging sticks. Hominids likely devised bags of animal intestines to fill with nuts, berries, and other foods. Females may have used these natural shopping bags to carry water, or their babies. They had "baskets" made from sections of bark stripped from trees. Primate intelligence was incapable of such inventiveness.

In the game of hunting, as well as when scavenging, males had to focus their minds on the study of animal behavior. Even to capture small animals, hominids had to know enough to be able to predict how the creatures would respond to the approach of the hunter. From predators they would learn both the techniques of stalking and attacking prey, and they would learn how to avoid or scare-off predators that were stalking them. To obtain those "shopping bags" we mentioned involved a considerable amount of observation, learning, and invention. After seeing the intestines, and examining them closely inside and out, they would have had to put two and two together. That is, someone who understood the inefficiency of carrying handfuls of berries would have had to suddenly realize the usefulness of stuffing them into an animal's stomach so that the "groceries" could be transported back to the camp in greater quantity for the common meal.

The invention of the bag may not have been possible until the hominid brain had grown sufficiently for them to knap stones sharp enough to butcher large animals with tough hides. This way of life also involved some planning ahead, having some consideration for others, and the regular practice of teaching youths. Children had to be taught how to make and use tools, how and where to find the right plants, how to transport them, and also not to eat them until they "got home." Young males would likely have learned stone chipping, point carving, hunting, trapping, and butchery. Young females would likely have learned childcare, and the fine points of finding, gathering, and preparing plants for both eating and perhaps for medicinal purposes. Hominids had developed the use of fire for warmth, and perhaps for cooking, about one million years ago. This continuous teaching of the young would also convey to them that they were *worth* the time, effort, and attention of their adult mentors.

Foraging apes do not exercise their intellects in the same way as did the hominids. Their minds are less challenged because they tend to repeat a very limited range of techniques for obtaining food. Indeed, under the principles of evolution established by Hardy-Weinberg and Gould-Eldridge, we may surmise that the genomes for chimps, gorillas, and other primates may have undergone very little change over the past several millennia. Lacking the hominid brain growth tendency, and being so well adapted to their stable environment, there has been little to cause any significant change in the primate genome.

In contrast, hominid behavior was breeding a new kind of brain. For example, the anti-social male hominid who only fed *himself* during the day was less likely to have the same reproductive appeal as those who "brought home the bacon." The female who refused to work, and wanted only to "stay home" and be supported by others may have ended-up feeding the clan in a way she had not intended.

Primate society is structured so that "free loading" is never a problem. Since each ape feeds himself, the ones who refuse to forage die. But hominid society would have had to formulate rules as to who should work, what each one should do, and as to how much work would be expected of each group member. Without such rules, the moochers would soon over-load the workers. Here, then, is when the seeds of "justice" were planted. Other values, along with a nascent sense of fair play, were also being cultivated by the gathering way of life. As hominid mating favored those who shared and cooperated over loaners or selfish group members, they gradually bred a genetically transmitted predisposition towards brotherhood.

This process worked in the same way as dairymen breeding cows for creamy milk, or dog fight fans breeding killer canines. The trend towards growing the brain, and cultivating an altruistic predisposition within it, gradually picked-up momentum during the two to three million years after Lucy's breed of hominid had faded from the scene of evolution. The pace of this momentum may have increased somewhat in the million years that rapping hominids lived before the human genome was forged. While hominid society outshined primate society as to both inventiveness and altruism, neither group, as we have said, ever rose above animal culture. Nevertheless, a genetic momentum was firmly established by some of those hominids, and eventually it gave rise to the natural order of values in man.

Hominid culture also put a higher premium on learning skills than does primate society. The division of labor would have added more complexity to hominid society than that of primate society. Thus, as we have seen, in addition to jockeying for Alpha positions and mating privileges, hominids had more work roles to fulfill, and more rules to enforce. For the youth to be physically and mentally prepared to meet the challenges of the communal gatherer required a longer childhood than does the life of the forager. Individuals who could more easily manage the demands on their cognitive abilities would likely have tended to receive reproductive rewards, intelligent males being attracted to intelligent females, and vice versa. Thus they created a rising tide in their gene pool, which lifted all boats.

Also of inestimable import, as Leakey noted, the hominid division of labor created significantly more *interdependency* among individuals than is found in primate society. As the males and females of a hominid group dispersed to carryout the day's labors, they depended upon and trusted one another to return. They also cultivated a devotion to one another not seen in ape society. While primates have calls to warn their fellows of danger, and engage in grooming and other social contacts, adult individuals are mostly on their own. Only in hominid society did mature members of a group depend upon one another for the food they would need to live. The *social emotions* of trust and devotion also elevated the value of other hominids in the minds of each individual. Trust and devotion necessarily raise the worth of the other, just as suspicion and rejection devalue the other. Bringing food to others for sharing assumes a substantial value in them. Receiving food from others grows gratitude and a sense of oneness.

Leakey understood that permanent, genetically transmitted neuro-connections were being set in the tissue of the hominid brain by the behavior and selective breeding practices associated with their mode of production, or method of collectively sustaining their lives. He argued that hominid altruism was not an act of calculated, or rational, self-interest, but an act of inbred behavior. This behavior came naturally to the hominids because "over countless generations natural selection favored the emergence of emotions that made reciprocal altruism work, emotions such as sympathy, gratitude, guilt, and moral indignation."[xli]

Hominids lacked the gray matter needed to calculate the long-term self-interest in conforming to an altruistic society. They lived by social emotions based on instinct. If hominid instinct had not impelled the individual towards social service, their social order would have collapsed. This biological commitment to service had to override selfish impulses automatically in the hominid mind/brain relationship for its animal society to survive as long as it did. The mere learning of altruism could not have sustained a widely dispersed food sharing society for all those millennia. Only by instinct could such an animal society stay the course between the destructive impulses of freeloading and self-aggrandizing acquisitiveness. Thus, as Leakey writes, "these elements [of altruistic behavior] provided the principal stimulus to the organization and growth of our fore-bearer's brains."[xlii]

The beginning of a clear distinction between valuing other people intrinsically and instrumentally, which was being woven in hominid cortical tissue, can be inferred from the evidence of hominid behavior. Leakey infers that unlike apes, male hominids, for example, would have willingly shared meat with females, the young, perhaps the sick, and other males who did not directly participate in a successful hunt, "for no better reason than that they are members of the same band."[xliii] In other words, they naturally valued their own kind intrinsically, and not just for their use value. We suggest that when the human brain emerged, this natural sense of caring extended universally to include the whole species.

Let us not loose sight, however, of the rough realities of hominid life. They cooperated with each other, but they also killed one another. Anthropologists often mention evidence of cannibalism. Hominid "fellow feelings" were not driving passions, but rather slight inclinations. These feelings tilted the shape of their behavior just enough to clearly distinguish them from the primates. Mating choices were likely made more by the chance confluence of lust and opportunity than by a principled determination to pick the most altruistic member of the band. This process of breeding for values was a loosely adhered to policy, and so took millions of years to show significant progress. The hominids did not act with the calculating mind of a dairyman. But the momentum established by the hominids leapt to its culmination when the inbreeding of some of them intensified to the point of producing man.

In summary, then, we reiterate our view that the discovery of the human genome, and that there is a human genome to be discovered, has huge consequences for humanity's self-understanding, which reach backwards to the point of man's beginnings, and forwards far into the unknown future. While the human genome divides into lesser-included formulas of gene pools all over the world, the human essence is contained in each. That essence has a physical and a mental dimension. The physical part centers on our swollen cerebral hemisphere. Although average height and weight, body shape, facial characteristics, and skin color change on the physical periphery, the key physical essence of humanity is the proportion of neocortex in our brains, along with the defective line of tissue described above. These characteristics remain uniform and universal within the species.

The *mental* essence of humanity entails its unlimited capacity for abstract reasoning, problem solving, and imagining, as well as the individual's burden of self-recalibrating the Schucman Corridor. These aspects of the human mind/brain relationship, too, are as uniform and universal as are the heart, lungs, stomach, kidneys, and other elements of the human body. Because each person shares in the human essence, the discovery of the human genome is a confirmation by science of the *feeling* of human oneness.[xliv]

Because the human genome defines what it is to be human, a clear bright line can be drawn between "human" and "animal." The hominids of the past were as much animals as are the primates of today. Also, because the very first humans possessed the human essence, their mind/brain relationship was as much like those of modern man as were their skulls, bladders, and bowels. Each experienced himself or herself through the self-created self. Those first people lacked the language and learning of contemporary humans, but their mental capacities, and their existential burdens, were every bit the equal of ours. This is why we can understand them. Let us then move on to the next chapter, where we will present empathic science's understanding of how it *felt* to be one of the first human beings on Earth.

Chapter Four

Primitive Communism –

150,000 to 40,000 years ago

The First Philosophy of Life

We have discussed the theory of punctuated equilibrium. It holds that organisms will evolve in a manner that replicates their genome until some intervening cause results in a sudden change of evolutionary direction. While no one can know for sure, we suggest that the first humans were produced by an isolated group of inbreeding gracile hominids. The inbreeding caused previously latent characteristics to rise to dominance in some of the babies born to this community. As a consequence, the first generation of offspring with the human mind/brain relationship were nurtured and raised by animal parents.

All tots learn their orientation to life at the knees of their parental figures. The first human tots acquired their orientation from the hominids that bore them. As those hominids were, of course, animals, their brains lacked that extra thick layer of cortical tissue around each hemisphere, which is necessary for thinking at high levels of abstraction. Also, those hominids, like animals generally, were naturally contented. These two differences have several implications.

As we have seen, animal contentment is regulated automatically by their brains. Hence, their decision-making for action is guided far more than ours by direct need awareness, without our longing for happiness. Their perceptions, too, are organized by instinct, rather than meaning. Hence, like other animals, our ancestor hominids relied on learning not to answer abstract questions or to give meaning to life, but only insofar as learning was necessary to fine-tune their adaptation to their environment.

When baby's mind takes its first halting steps towards trying to make sense of birth, he or she lacks language and the analytical tools necessary to think like an educated adult. Long before left side language and analytical capacities have any experience to work with, baby's right hemisphere is engaged in nonverbal, preconceptual, holistic meaning making. As we stated earlier, the experience of birth compels baby's mind to first of all understand itself as a center of sense data. This bombardment of experience is sorted-out, in part, by the formation of a body image. Where "I" ends, and the rest of the world begins, is gradually defined in the mind/brain relationship by learning through experience. Implicit in this process is the formation of the body identity; that is, the self-reflective baby mistakenly commingles his or her body image with his or her sense of self. This erroneous notion becomes established before the tot can talk. These meanings then become the major premises, which direct all other conclusions about oneself, and about life itself, throughout childhood and adulthood. We will see that, as tots learning about life in the caves and camps of their hominid parents, the first humans simply extended, as their understanding of their condition, the premises about life that they had formed as babies in response to the birth trauma.

Then, as now, baby's self-understanding provides an interpretative framework for processing new experience. As the first human babes observed and interacted with their animal parents, there was a kind of harmony between the instinct-driven behavior of the parents and the rapidly forming self-made meanings of the human children. The notion that "I am a body" parallels the intentional thrust of animal instinct. That is probably what animals would think, if animals could think. Thus, as the first babies grew into children the materialistic trajectory of their thinking was reinforced by the behavior of their animal parents, to whom the tots looked for guidance. Baby's experience of bumps, scratches, discomfort due to cold, heat, hunger, etc., went into his or her self-created understanding of self as vulnerable in a hazardous situation. Baby's mind generalized these original materialistic assumptions as baby grew and observed the behavior of his or her animal parents. Guided by instinct, these parents were fully aware of their vulnerability in the predatory world in which they lived. The children needed no lectures to understand the lessons to be learned from the behavior of their role models.

That we humans survived shows both that our animal ancestors were well prepared to teach us survival skills, and that we learned our lessons well. Had the first human babies been abandoned, they would not have known how to get by, and we would not be here to contemplate their life experience. Leakey noted that the behavior of our hominid ancestors was shaped by millions of years of evolution. Natural selection produced a breed of creature that knew how to survive in the jungles and grasslands of Africa. Our animal parents were well equipped to teach the first generation of humans.

Animal knowledge is far more iconic than verbal. That is, animals sort through and classify the objects in their world by the image of the thing and its emotional significance, rather than by its abstract name. Like today's primates, hominids lacked the neocortex required for any substantial verbal knowledge. But through example and nonverbal communication, each hominid generation would have passed on its survival knowledge to the next. This would have been how the first humans were taught to live. Besides techniques and implements needed for survival, the first humans learned the orientation to life conveyed by hominid instinctual behavior through animal forms of communication and thought processes. The first human mind was filled with animal content.

Precisely because our neocortex has replaced instinct with our brain's meaning making function, humans must learn what it means to be human so that they can act in the world. Our self-understanding is our reference point for decision making and action. This learned and shared understanding, or culture, becomes the functional substitute for animal instinct in decision-making. As we have said, the learning of culture is an extension of baby's process of forming a body image and sense of the world around him or her. Baby's body image is, of course, a form of meaning – the meaning of who one is to oneself. It is based exclusively on baby's self-reflective integration of sense experience with this meaning making process of self-understanding. The learning of culture is also meaning making, but based more on baby's interaction with his or her caretakers. In this interaction the human child learns, mostly from parental figures, what is important in life, how the world works inside and outside the clan or family, and what it means to be a member of that social unit.

Without too great a risk of being wrong, we may assume that the first children learned by observing, internalizing lessons, and absorbing the most subtle attitudes and emotions of their parental figures. Since the hominids had strong social instincts, the children would have learned to identify themselves as social creatures. Of course, they would not have seen themselves as "humans in a hominid society." They would have simply assumed, at first, that they were members of the group, just like everybody else. Human children would have played with hominid young in complete innocence of the knowledge that each was of a different species. The young humans, then, learned to engage in social bonding. They were socialized into a society of communal gatherers. They learned to share food, and to carry their fair share of work responsibilities. They learned to form alliances for hunting, gathering, and mutual protection. They learned about the political hierarchy in their group, and about gender roles in the division of labor. Males learned that winning "word wars" would gain them social status, leadership positions, and sexual advantages with the females who had learned attraction to men with power and status.

Because the hominids passed on their slender builds to their human offspring, the first humans surely did not learn to think of themselves as the "kings of the jungle." Hominids were easy prey to a variety of more powerful carnivores. Lions, leopards, hyenas, and other creatures would have been regular predators on the weaker, slower hominids who ventured from the safety of the campfire or their allies. The first children would have learned from the fear of their parents that "its a jungle out there," and a "dog eat dog" situation, in which we are "meat on our feet" for any large predator who can catch one of us alone and unprotected.

We call the meanings made by the first humans, as they were being socialized into hominid society, the "first philosophy of life." While no one was taught a specific doctrine, and there were no schools or catechism classes, individual children would have formed similar meanings from their similar experiences. The first philosophy of life is a configuration of nonverbal, preconceptual meanings made from a variety of fact and value presuppositions. An analytical separation of these presuppositions will help to clarify what they are, how they came to be, and how they fit together as a whole.

The way one defines the world factually goes a long way towards determining how oneself, others, and the world around one will be valued. To define the world as a "jungle" was a rather reasonable characterization of the conditions in east central Africa 150,000 years ago. Because this world was full of predators, and hominids were frequent prey, humans could reasonably emphasize their prey status in their self-understanding.

Value priorities are often established by moments of intensity. Parental alertness during the day would have contributed to junior's understanding of the world as a dangerous place, but witnessing a large carnivore attack, maul, and perhaps devour that parent, or some other member of the group, would have seared into his mind the imperative to stay vigilant. As a factual assumption, the understanding of being vulnerable in the jungle ties-in with the body-identity and baby's feeling of being in a hazardous situation. This tie-in reinforces the factual assumptions of the first philosophy of life, and helps to raise self-preservation to a top spot in its value hierarchy.

The first philosophy of life is the transformation of animal instinctive behavior into human meaning. It is the product of young humans turning observations of animal behavior into an understanding of their own life situation. Hominid instinctual behavior was an automatic process built into their animal mind/brains by eons of evolution, and only supplemented slightly by learning. Although animals have no philosophy, instinct guides their behavior with the kind of consistency that a believed philosophy would guide the behavior of a human. If instinct were to be translated into a philosophy, one could say that it is based on a primarily pragmatic value system, or a system which is largely on the plane of what Hartman calls "extrinsic" value. Extrinsic value entails use-value. It is the valuation of a thing, another person, and even oneself for its usefulness in need satisfaction. Thus, extrinsic valuing would likely have been a part of how each of the first humans learned to value himself or herself, one another, and the world around them.

Such pragmatic instrumentalism would have included the idea that in the eyes of predators man is meat. This understanding would have reinforced the notion that the body is a thing, which could be used for food if not protected. Indeed, the very preconceptual understanding of the roles of "prey" and "predator" imply a use-value to both – the one as the object of use, the other as the user. The bodies of prey and predators are also instruments to themselves; that is, instruments to be used for the "four Fs" – fighting, fleeing, feeding, and reproducing. As they experience needs, animals become satisfaction-seeking opportunists. Whether their purpose is fight, flight, quelling hunger, or the pleasure of mating, animal behavior is highly pragmatic, body-centered, outward (rather than inward) looking, and action oriented. These predispositions, which are natural to animals, became the principles of orientation in the imitative worldview of the first humans.

The first philosophy of life was modeled by parents whose contentment was guaranteed by nature. To their minds, self-preservation and the satisfaction of physical needs were their only problems. Because the first humans were apprentices to animals, they could only learn what animals had to teach. But humans must learn to acquire contentment; unfortunately, the animal parents of the first humans had nothing to teach about how to do that. Thus, as the first humans replicated the "animal worldview" in their own minds, they failed to prepare themselves to understand and to satisfy their unique emergent need to adjust their Schucman Corridor. This gap between what the first children had learned, and what they needed to know, is also a part of the first philosophy of life. We will discuss how the early humans learned to live with the problems of the first philosophy of life later in this chapter, but before that, let us further clarify what that philosophy is by comparing it as a theory of value to the natural order of values.

The natural order of values, as we noted in Chapter Two, has two dimensions. In the pre-consciousness of consciousness state, the achievement of one's full potential for contentment is life's prime want. Awareness of that want may be dim and easily distracted, but after contentment is attained one sees retrospectively how urgently one had desired this happiness. Only in the post-consciousness of consciousness condition can one fully experience the natural order of values.

The natural order of values is not, to borrow a phrase from Oliver Wendell Holmes, jr., a "brooding omnipresence in the sky," ready to condemn every thought or action of humanity. It exists only as an inclination in the mind/brain relationship of individuals. It is neither a "bad conscience," nor an abstract product of the intellect, like the prattle found in much of philosophy and religion. Nor is it in the mind by choice or commitment. Flowing from a complex system of neuro-connections in the tripartite brain, it is not a theory, but the natural attitude of a person whose consciousness has connected with its own source of being. Because it is an attitude, or understanding, it is neither an ethical doctrine casting judgments on "sinners," nor a political philosophy around which to rally the masses.

The natural order of values is the clear feeling of joy and satisfaction at the felt oneness with humanity, and with the world of which one is a part. It consists of what Hartman calls "intrinsic" value. Rather than the usefulness of self, others, and the world around one, its focus is on their uniqueness. On the plane of intrinsic value, one sees that use diminishes uniqueness. On this plane, oneself and others become too precious to use.

Animals never worried about the seeming contradiction between valuing others intrinsically and instrumentally, because these are abstractions outside their ability to comprehend. Only humans worry about logical contradictions. Hence, hominids cooperated with one another out of instinct rather than a considered theory of values. Each was an instrument used for the survival of the others, and happy with the situation because their brains kept them in contentment. We humans have inherited the neuro-structures that are the bases of hominid contentment, but that feeling does not come to us automatically as it did to our ancestors. The first philosophy of life is man-made meaning over-laying and obstructing the realization of our natural value tendency. In other words, the first philosophy of life is not what humans need to know, but misinformation, and a distraction from what we need to know.

The first philosophy of life, then, is the oldest human artifact on Earth. However, it is not some sort of relic from a far removed past, like the thousands of stone flakes the first humans and their hominid family members left behind. Empathic science has found that the first philosophy of life is *still* the operative philosophy of humanity. It is as much a fundamental decision-making criteria and interpretative framework today, on all four corners of the globe, as it once was at a small camp site in east central Africa, some 150,000 years ago. In our view, the first philosophy of life has been, and continues to be, handed down nonverbally from generation to generation as the meaning of life for man, from the !Kung! in Africa to the richest socialites in New York. We are all cohorts in contemporary world culture. We will show, in this chapter, how this core of world culture has been modified, added to, covered over, and communicated without ever transforming its essential elements.

The first philosophy of life is the result of humans learning from animals what it means to be human. Obviously, in this experience, the early humans did not learn what it means to be human as such, but only what it means to be an animal in a hominid society. What it means to be human, in a human culture, is still a riddle. As a practical matter, this contradiction of humans learning from animals what it means to be human was unavoidable. However, its continuation is certainly not a necessity. Once the problem is seen clearly, it can be resolved.

A healthy skepticism may lead one to doubt the existence of the first philosophy of life and/or the natural order of values within oneself. But doubt has two sides. On the one side is the doubt that they are there, on the other side is the wonder whether they could be. Only superficial introspection is required to find both the first philosophy of life and the natural order of values within oneself. Merely a small measure of value sensitivity is needed to feel the contrast between the two. With just a jot of courage, one can recognize the influence of the first philosophy of life on one's own thought processes. Who can honestly say that he or she has not thought "it's a jungle out there," or that "people use each other as instruments," and that "one must protect oneself from being preyed upon by others"? Seen within the interpretive context of the first philosophy of life, these comments seem to express immutable aspects of human nature.

However, who can make these statements without at least a hint of regret that they seem so true? The natural order of values within a person leads him or her to wonder whether people can do better than to value one another solely as instruments. Also, anyone with even a slight intuitive awareness of the natural order of values will suspect that he or she could be more contented with life than he or she is now. Or, one may suspect that there is another, perhaps higher, happiness than that derived from material pursuits. Also, one may have a vague sense that somehow one could feel more unity with others and with the world than one presently does. Each of these "suspicions" is based on one's self-reflective sensitivity, and is not a matter of arbitrary opinion, or of some learned doctrine.

Who among us can deny the intuitive pull of the axiom that people are too precious to use? Who could deny without at least some misgivings that he or she sometimes uses others, and that use diminishes others? And, who would not admit, with some pique, to sometimes feeling used by others?

One need not have achieved the consciousness of consciousness to appreciate the difference between the natural order of values and the first philosophy of life. Many people have experienced leakage of the natural order of values, through intuition, into consciousness. This will be enough to convince them that the values which flow naturally from the brain are more a part of their being than are the values which have been acquired from their culture. One can learn to recognize that, as a product of the brain, the natural order of values has a quality of immediacy and organic connection in consciousness, which is lacking in the first philosophy of life. The latter configuration of meaning is entirely fabricated, and for some folks might have a foreign quality to it. Although it defines the nature of the world, and how one should relate to the world and to other people, to one who is aware of the natural order of values, that philosophy feels alien and unnatural. Despite attempts to give that philosophy a scientific gloss with slick titles, like "Social Darwinism," few self-sensitive people would agree that it adequately defines who they are, or how they feel. Indeed, the focus of the first philosophy of life on the use-value of oneself and others can cause a sensation of sickening emptiness in one who has come in touch with his or her organically based natural order of values.

Animals can live on the plane of use-value, unlike humans, without feeling degraded, alienated, or empty because instinct keeps them in contentment. Thus, our animal progenitors could not teach their human children *the principle* that all people are of the same species, as both fact and value, nor that each person is too precious to use. While they taught survival skills well, they could not teach their children about the possibility of finding contentment within. For this reason, humanity has survived in discontent from that first generation to the current one.

In sum, the natural order of values and the first philosophy of life can be seen as two conflicting theories of value. Each one posits its own hierarchy of import. Each one exists on a different plane of value. One value theory is entirely on the plane of extrinsic, or utilitarian, value. The other is on the plane of intrinsic value. One value theory holds that the self and others are things to be used and allied with for mutual protection. The other holds that the self and others are unique self-reflective consciousnesses, each longing for the consciousness of consciousness, and each being an instance of potential joy and love, too precious to be used. While one values the world for its utility, the other values the world for its awesome beauty and uniqueness.

The first philosophy of life desensitizes people to the natural order of values, but awareness of the latter heightens a person's sensitivity to the former. Post-consciousness of consciousness, one sees retrospectively how one had suffered in the pre-consciousness of consciousness state, and how other people are still blindly and needlessly suffering in their pre-consciousness of consciousness condition. One also understands with greater clarity than before how dangerous people can be to one another because of their belief in the first philosophy of life, and their lack of awareness of the natural order of values. In the consciousness of consciousness one acquires a new point of view. But it is not a point of view with blinders, as is the first philosophy of life, it is a viewpoint which illuminates all of life. Once the natural order of values is fully felt, one sees how great the need is to reconfigure one's philosophy of life so as to bring it into closer alignment with the natural order of values. The monumental task of remaking world culture is all the more difficult because so few people see the need for it.

Leaving the Nest

The absence of teaching about contentment in the first philosophy of life has had repercussions extending to our times from that first generation. Our first parents gave their children no instruction as to how to recognize the early signals from the Schucman Corridor that its operation was constrained. As the Schucman Corridor began signaling its readiness to work in the minds of human adolescents, the first philosophy of life, including baby's error, would distort those benign signals which can lead one to love, into terrifying threats of the death of self. These children were not taught that any higher form of happiness was a possibility for them. Nor was the willingness to surrender control of the self-created self ever modeled for them by a parenting figure. When their Schucman Corridor was ready, and their first feelings of something missing in life emerged in their self-awareness, there was no preparation for these feelings. There was no way to talk about it, because there was no language for such discussions. Even if the hominids had had a sophisticated language (which they did not), they would have had no comprehension of the discontent their human children felt, because the parents felt content, and always had.

In addition, by the time the Schucman Corridor reached maturity, the first generation of young humans would already be engaged in reproductive behavior. They would have been loaded with their share of adult responsibilities for childcare, food gathering, tool making, etc. They would have had no models for introspective contemplation, and no time for it. These adolescents would not have known what to do about this onslaught of strong negative feelings, because the first philosophy of life had a gapping Black Hole where knowledge was needed. Thus, before the first generation of humans had a language to speak, they had feelings of emptiness with which they had no idea about how to deal. The experience was something which they simply had to endure. They were teenagers with no education about themselves, no parental guidance, no language, no one to talk to, and feeling deeply troubled.

In the theater of the mind the fight or flight mechanism uncritically responds to semblances. The examination of how realistic such responses are is a separate process involving the translating of semblances into a symbolic form which can then be analyzed and criticized by the intellect. An uncriticized semblance will continue to evoke the physiological response appropriate to it, as if it were true. If the meaning is "I am in a dangerous situation," then the appropriate level of anxiety and alertness will be generated until the meaning changes to "all clear." However, if *life itself* is defined as a dangerous situation, then the production of anxiety will not be cut off. Thus, to keep oneself from being immobilized by fear, one must find ways to desensitize oneself to the feeling. Instinct enables animals to move from appropriate anxiety back into contentment; but humans, lacking instinct, lack this return mechanism. Hence, in the absence of critical examination, humans are condemned to live in the anxiety caused by their own understanding of themselves as potential prey living under the threat of imminent predation.

In their innocence, early humans would have unguardedly experienced fear as every Schucman Corridor signal was interpreted wrongly as a death threat to the body-identity. Lacking modern man's efficient techniques for the denial of pain and feeling, early humans would have naively *felt* every bit of fear they had. All told, this would have included their unresolved responses to the birth trauma, the anxiety of baby's understanding of the immediate world as a hazardous place, and the higher anxiety required to stay alert for predators caused by the fist philosophy of life. Then comes the fear of the death of the self-created self, brought on by their misinterpretation of the Schucman Corridor signals.

These four sources of anxiety would have converged in consciousness to be experienced as worry and pain; indeed, as a tormenting terror. Such was the mood in which the first humans lived, if one can call that "living." Actually, that was the rawest form of survival – suffering, yet clinging to life. The first humans learned well how to survive but not how to live. Learning to live remains one of humanity's greatest challenges.

The emerging need for contentment in the growing human youth was likely a cause of friction between them and their hominid elders. Young humans would have appealed to their parenting figures for help in easing their angst. But the animal parents would have been baffled and soon annoyed by the pleading and whining of the children with big heads. The more the humans grew, the more intense their misery would become. Every mammal has an instinctive sense of when their off spring are old enough to be independent. Even birds have an instinctive notion of when its time to send their chicks from the nest. But human pleas for help would have become more and more urgent as they matured – as if each had a fire on his head!

It would not have been long before the unhappy ones learned to identify one another. Each person would have been pushed away by his or her exasperated parenting figure, and attracted to the other by the recognition of their common life crisis. A sense of compassion in each for the suffering of the others would have kept them together. Thus, on the principle that misery loves company, the first human group was formed. At first, there were likely no more than a dozen teens. Having learned well how to survive, they would have gathered and shared food. They would have assumed the gender responsibilities they had been taught by the hominids. As women bore children the human group would have knitted together all the more tightly. The children would only have known human parenting figures, and therefore formed an identity of being a member of this group as distinct from any hominid group. Because the human and hominid experiences of life were so different, the groups would not have maintained contacts with one another for long. Thus began the human race.

World Culture

Humanity's original challenge, then, was, after assuring their survival, to intersubjectively and cooperatively find a way to ease their common pain. Early humanity met its challenges as best it could. There were no books then, discussing alternative solutions to the human dilemma. Nor was there even a language by which clear thinking minds could express their insights, or give guidance to their brothers and sisters. The human genome gave the first humans self-reflective minds like ours, with the same burden of finding happiness, but without any of the learning or language that humanity has acquired since then. Insofar as our brains and conscious experience replicates theirs, they had persistent feelings of fear, anguish, and emptiness like ours. They also longed to be free of these feelings, as we do. But they lacked our clever means of suppressing and denying the awareness of these painful emotions, or of deadening ourselves to them through such devises as drugs, drink, "entertainment," and so forth.

Lacking instinct's regulation of contentment, and having the first philosophy of life, and the other sources of fear that we have mentioned, gave these early humans a chronic case of the jitters. Each day was like that moment in a horror movie when the screen darkens and the eerie music starts to play. The first humans constantly felt that they were in a death threatening situation, as if stalking predators were all around them. Unlike the moviegoer, however, early man could not run out of the theater if he got too scared. They had to find a way to ease their terror and pain.

These teenagers wove together the tiny threads of understanding that would become the common basis for the longest unbroken period world culture has had. The first of those threads would have entailed the understanding of each that the others were also in pain. This compassion is what pulled the first humans together. Seeing this compassion and understanding in others would have brought some comfort of itself to each individual. At least each knew that he and she were not alone in their pain. Here was something to build on. To their credit, the solution that the first generations of humans fashioned was satisfactory enough to endure for over 100,000 years. In resolving that problem together, however partially, world culture was born.

The Cultivation and Nonverbal Communication of Love

Empathic science research has found that early humans learned to comfort one another through the practice of "cultivated love." They discovered, perhaps within the first generation, that by giving love to one another, they could ease one another's jitters, and fill, at least a little, one another's emptiness. Let us consider for a moment what the biological bases of cultivated love are, how this love is made, and how it is sent and received. We will suggest how humans likely perfected the cultivation of love, and how we can know these things. In Chapter Five we will show how and why this art was lost.

Cultivated love consists of the self-created feeling of love within oneself, for the purpose of conveying that love to another so as to comfort him or her. Natural compassion makes this strategy an apt choice. To meet the challenge to ease their common pain, early humans drew from the only knowledge base they had. Their hominid parents had impressed upon them the value of social service, and of forming alliances for mutual aid and safety. Their fondest memories would likely have been of those tranquil moments when hominids and humans sat together resting around the campfire, perhaps grooming one another, after everyone had eaten. Since they had no instructions about how to find their own inner source of contentment, they used what they did know to fashion a way to compensate for their self-ignorance.

Early man did not turn to speech to sooth his pain, for speech can distance people more than it brings them together. To use words requires shifting attention from right hemispheric processes to left ones. Speech, thus, draws attention away from feeling and on to conceptions. But early man lived in, and for, feeling to an extent that is incomprehensible for most moderns. Actual, wordless feeling was broadcast and received person-to-person, in completely unguarded, trusting openness. Modern man's fumbling efforts to learn to "express feelings" is a measure of his alienation from his own right hemisphere. Feeling is a direct experience, and is unrelated to words. That we are in the absurd position of trying to use speech to bring feelings into consciousness is one of the legacies of the Great Shift in world culture, to be discussed further in the next chapter. We will also see there how and why the development of spoken language has destroyed and replaced the art of nonverbal communication, which once gave humans their only reason to live.

What, then, is nonverbal communication? This subject is worth examining because the dominant cowardly sciences are so skeptical that nonverbal communication exists in any substantial degree, if at all. In the course of our examination we will reconstruct the typical day in the average life of an early human, to illustrate the role played by the cultivation and communication of love. After that, we will take a more encompassing view of how early man lived prior to the Great Shift in world culture.

Animals have oral communication, but they appear to rely far more on nonverbal communication. Much of their communication is governed by instinct. For example, birds and other animals engage in courtship rituals. Highly social mammals in the wild, from horses, to wolves, to lions have forms of body language related to greeting, mating, and recognizing who's the boss in the group. Primates have a variety of facial expressions and hand gestures that express subjective states like joy, anger, and fear. They learn from one another far more by observation and demonstration than by oral instruction. Flocks of birds, schools of fish, and herds of grazing animals can turn on a dime in unison. How is that possible? Perhaps it is due to an ability to communicate without sound that we humans do not fully, or at least consciously, understand.

Animals that live by cooperative hunting appear to have the ability to communicate strategies and tactics nonverbally. Wolves and lions, for example, often seem to be following an agreed upon plan to cut an intended victim out of a herd, and close in for the kill. One crew of naturalists filmed a matriarch lioness smack a younger lioness in the head, apparently for bungling a hunt by charging a herd of wildebeests before the other lionesses were in place. This appeared to be a punitive slap for failing to follow a nonverbally communicated strategy. Hunting animals appear to learn a "play book" from their elders as they grow up within a group. The leader of the hunt then signals the plays to be followed.

Neurologists have found that nonverbal communication is largely a function of the right hemisphere of the brain. For example, the recognition of emotion communicated by the facial expressions or posture of another is a right hemispheric function. The areas for composing and interpreting speech are generally located in the left hemisphere. Humans have inherited their capacity for nonverbal communication from hominids. The first humans also learned how to develop and use this capacity from their animal elders. As we have said, the first children were socialized into hominid society through animal forms of communication and thought processes. This learning set the pattern for the first uses of the human mind. The knowledge of how to survive in the wild was conveyed and learned primarily through right hemispheric processes. Raw, blunt, animal emotions, attitudes, and intentions were the core curricula in the education of the first humans. While instinct guided the formation and projection of animal feelings, humans made right hemispheric meanings from those models.

Early humans had a very long way to go before developing any sort of speech, as we now know it. To develop the rules of word usage, grammar, and syntax requires an intense, sustained effort over a period of several generations. Such an effort would only be undertaken in circumstances in which its need was clearly perceived by the leading members of the group. In our opinion, the human community felt no such need for thousands and thousands of years. Having learned to live from animals, the early humans expected no more from the material world than to live as animals do. Since the animal forms of communication were well suited to fulfilling animal expectations of life, and those were the expectations of humans, humans felt no need to improve upon animal speech as a tool for survival. In the next chapter we will offer an illustration of the kind of conditions that likely produced sophisticated speech.

Politics for the early humans would have been conducted as it was for their hominid forefathers. Not speech, but stylized vocalizations were likely used to determine Alpha status. These encounters would not have been meaningful debates, or even name calling, but only ritualized shouting matches. Thus, for them, political conflicts were not settled in moments of great oratory, such as some of the fine speeches given in modern campaigns for public office. This primitive form of politics, and the secondary role of speech in human life generally, would not have changed significantly until the time of the Great Shift.

Early humans surely engaged in forms of oral communication outside the areas of politics and economics. Jokes or phoneme puns are possible without any complex system of grammar or syntax. Specially designed sounds may have been developed for courtship, or in quibbling over possessions, or wounded pride. Forms of singing may have been used. Their vocabulary for the names of things was likely expanded. But until a group had an established grammar and syntax, story telling would have relied on gestures and body language far more than upon words. This may have led to dance as a form for expressing meaning. Because chimpanzees and other primates in the wild display many of these forms of communicative behaviors, we may reasonably infer that our hominid ancestors engaged in similar sorts of activities.

Animal nonverbal communication has limitations that do not apply to humans. Instinct and their lesser amount of cortical tissue restrict the range of meaning that the animal brain can fashion. But human nonverbal communication is only limited by the range of preconceptual meanings that their brains can make.

Unlike animals, humans have a particular need for nonverbal communication that comes out of the self-reflective nature of consciousness. Solipsism, the theory that only the self and its experiences can be known, necessarily haunts the human self-reflective consciousness. Nonverbal communication enables the individual to offset the terror of epistemological isolation by the reassuring experience of intimate communication with others of his own kind. But because animals are naturally contented, they do not experience what for man is one of the deleterious effects of having a self-reflective consciousness.

Empathic science concurs with Schucman's oft-repeated observation that the body is an instrument of communication. This function goes way beyond the constant stream of verbiage that occupies modern social interactions. As we will explain here, in all likelihood, nonverbal communication held the prominent position in human consciousness and behavior for roughly three-quarters of man's existence on Earth. Humanity became obsessed with verbal communication only after the Great Shift, commencing about 35,000 years ago.

We will argue that, despite the modern obsession, right hemispheric communication continues as naturally as the heart pumps blood and the lungs breathe air. Indeed, in our view, right hemispheric communication is the dominant communicative function of the human brain. While speech is intermittent, nonverbal communication is a constant, at least during waking hours. Only our attention has shifted away from the nonverbal to gloat over the mendacious bedazzlement of words. Why and how this shift of attention occurred will be explained thoroughly in the next chapter. Here, let us consider the nature of human nonverbal communication, how it works, and what it can convey.

Some of the evidence for the existence of nonverbal communication is fairly obvious. Sometimes people speak of feeling the excitement in a crowd, or the tension in a room, or the love of an intimate and supportive group or family. Lovers witness these processes when they feel the love of their beloved. Confidence men, salesmen, politicians, and Don Juan's exercise right hemispheric abilities when they "get the feel" for who would be an easy mark, sell, supporter, or conquest. Sensitive therapists can sometimes detect the exact fears and confusions of a client who is out of touch with their feelings, and full of denial about them.

An American TV commentator once told a story about a visit he had taken to Moscow in the late 1990's. As he walked the streets admiring the architecture and generally people watching, he began to notice that they were staring at him. After a couple of days of that, he shared his observation with his Russian host. The latter replied, "its because you're not afraid."

In other words, some people found him to be a curious sight because they did not see in him the same fear they personally felt, and saw in one another. This is empathic, nonverbal communication. People broadcast feelings. People are also highly receptive to the messages emanating from others. Of course, people can be deceptive. Sly people can sometimes hide their feelings from others. Talented actors can project the appearance of feelings, which are not truly their own. But in the normal course of events, the body is a system for broadcasting and receiving feelings. This is true of both man and animals. Like animals in the wild, early man showed his feelings quite openly. Modern humans have complicated the process by selectively suppressing awareness of both their personal feelings and their receptivity to the feelings of others.

The normal Muscovite, it seems, still harbored the fears of living under a Stalinist regime loaded with KGB-type secret police. They also had severe economic insecurities. Seeing these fears in each other everyday reinforces them and keeps them active. When they see a government-trusting, economically secure American strolling the streets without those fears, its surprising. It's also a reminder that life without such fears is possible.

The human genome meets out right hemispheric communication abilities, in varying proportions, to all humans. The range of potential for the ability to broadcast, and the sensitivity to receive, nonverbal communication is the same today as it was for early man, because it is an element of the formula for humanity. However, modern humans have largely abandoned the cultivation of the art of nonverbal communication. Also, the skepticism of behavioral science has turned us into the fish who doubt the existence of water.

If people are in constant nonverbal communication, one may ask what it is we are communicating to one another. To answer that question we must engage in an act of translation of distinct feelings into fairly representative verbal meanings. That requires creating a bridge of attention across the corpus callosum so as to connect right and left brain processes. Once this has been done, one can clearly say what one can clearly feel. Speech, of course, can never be more than a mere symbolic portrayal of feeling. Hence, our discussion of cultivated love, and the meaning conveyed in nonverbal communication, is best understood as only suggestive, and not the thing in itself.

The Genetic Basis of World Culture

Because we are each a product of the formula for humanity contained in our genome, the basic content of our nonverbal communication is constant. The needs this communication serves are genetically given, from the very first humans to we of the present. Like modern people, the first humans, then, having a self-reflective consciousness looked to one another for reassurance that each was not alone in his or her suffering. "Do you feel it, too?" "Are you with me?" each asked the other. But people need to know more than that. Each seeks confirmation of his or her fundamental beliefs about the realities of life. "Are you as afraid as I am?" "Do you feel that predators are all around us, too?" "Do you feel the same emptiness and pain that I feel?" "Is there some way to relieve my pain?" "Can you help me?"

These were some of the messages broadcast by the first humans to one another throughout the day, everyday, probably commencing in adolescence with the readiness of the Schucman Corridor to go to work. If these nonverbal transmissions could have been recorded, it would have sounded like agonized pleading, perhaps punctuated with screams of despair. Early man's attention was focused, at first, on his own pain. But he soon learned that expressions of compassion and love for one another could distract attention from his pain. The causes of the pain were not removed, but attention withdrawn from that feeling, and put onto the balm of another's love is at least a second best remedy.

The feelings of helplessness and powerlessness over one's angst and ennui were never denied, but were acknowledged nonverbally and frankly to all. In the developing human culture, each person learned from his or her youth that redemption from emptiness and isolation can only come from one's relationships with others. Their experience was that by isolating or withdrawing oneself from others, one would only condemn oneself to merciless pain. Through socialization into human society, each person learned to define himself or herself as one who needs to be nourished by others as much as he or she needs the nourishment of food.

Every jilted lover has awoken to the feeling expressed in the song best sung by Billy Holiday, "Good Morning Heartache." In this pain, each person knows that only the love of another can heal the wound. And so it was for early humans that when each awoke in the morning, the message would go out from one to the others,

> Is there anyone out there who cares about me? Please don't let me feel my pain! Mary, Joe, I'm with you. I'll always be here for you. Do you feel the same for me? And John, I'm with you too brother. I don't want you to live in pain. I feel so much love for all of you. And, yes, now I'm beginning to feel your love for me! I feel so grateful to you. I want to express my gratitude by serving you throughout the day.

The day, then, was passed in service. Those who were able went out for firewood. Others collected roots, fruits, and vegetables. When not needed for gathering, some of the men left together to hunt, trap, or to scavenge meat. Some of the women stayed at the campsite to tend to the children, and prepare food for the common meal. As Karl Marx understood, this "primitive communism" was the first human mode of production. Those folks lived by the principle later articulated by Marx: from each according to his ability, to each according to his need.

Throughout the day, the nonverbal communication that people needed to ease their pain continued. Verbal communications were limited, and subordinated to the nonverbal. Nouns may have been used as names of things, and some verbs may have been used to speak of actions, but these were used sparingly. Verbal communication was used only when needed to supplement nonverbal communications, as animals in the wild do today. Thus humanity lived from generation to generation, in relative tranquility, for approximately 3500 generations. Both physical and introspective evidence shows that humans lived in animal culture, like the hominids, from their beginning until the Great Shift, starting about 35,000 years ago. But before we get to the evidence, let us complete our explanation of how cultivated love was communicated and received.

Nonverbal communication was likely as prominent a feature of early humanity's daily life as verbal communication is to modern man's daily life. When people communicate nonverbally, they project meaningful feelings. Two-way communication consists of such feelings being extended, received, and replied to. Participants who consciously engaged in the process experienced a sharing of feeling that was as sensual as a naked embrace. Not only the physical presence, but also the feelings of another can be felt. Each early human lived in this emotional embrace with his or her brothers and sisters. Community for early man was not simply individual bodies living in close proximity, and interacting for common purposes. Community was the experience of each person feeling the distinct emotions of others, as well as he or she felt his or her own feelings.

The feelings that modern people associate with private romances between two people were once the feelings that whole communities shared together. Let us imagine Mary, for example, cleaning the dirt from roots for the evening meal. As she works, she feels the warm embrace of the love she knows as John's. She accepts this feeling and dwells happily within it. Meanwhile, Sue sends Mary a call for help. Sue's pain is creeping up on her, and she feels too weak just now to fight it off by herself. Mary feels the plea, and replies by sending Sue love, and the nonverbal reassurance that "it will be alright." Sue accepts the support, feels the love, and her spirit is lifted.

The empirical properties of such nonverbal communication are not now known, due to the lack of solid research on the process. Behavioralist and cognitivist physicalism keeps us all ignorant. However, empathic science hypothesizes that such properties do exist, and can be known. Our hunch is that messages are sent as waves through the air, from sender to receiver. Prior to the projection of such messages, a sender forms an intention to send a specific message. Thus, when John sends his love to Mary, he feels that love in the moment he sends it. When Sue sends her cries for help, she is feeling her pain and despair. Making an analogy to radio waves is tempting, although the two may not be exactly the same. One may choose to narrowcast on one channel to a specific person, or to broadcast to any and all open receivers. The message would not be John's or Sue's actual feelings flying through the air; rather, it would be a set of electric-like coded instructions sent from one person's body, and impacting the senses of the receiver. Those instructions would be carried from the receiver's nerves to his or her brain. There they would be deciphered and put into a form that could be passed into his or her consciousness.

These instructions would direct the brain of the receiver to combine particular chemicals, in specific measure, so as to produce the feeling, in the consciousness of the receiver, intended by the sender. Every feeling is the product of brain chemistry. Each person's feelings, from the chemistry point of view, carry his or her unique signature. John's love differs from Mary's love in that his has a pinch more of one element than hers does, and a dab less of another. Thus, John's brain sends the recipe for his love to Mary's brain, which mixes her brain chemicals together, as instructed, to produce the feeling of his love in her consciousness.

All love is self-made. Dr. Michael Liebowitz shows, in his path-breaking work, *The Chemistry of Love*, that when one person loves another, the emotion he or she feels is the result of complex chemical combinations being mixed in his or her brain. We add that just as one's meanings and feelings can cause chemical reactions in one's own mind/brain, so chemical mixtures in one person can be nonverbally communicated to cause meanings and feelings in the mind/brain of another person. The love John feels for Mary is something he has made. His experience of being loved by her, in return, is also his own brain-made cocktail. Thus, in his brain there are two compounds, one he mixes for his love of her, and the other he mixes according to her recipe, for her love of him. She is doing the same in her brain. Hence, their lives were rich in love.

The science of brain chemistry is still in a crude beginning stage. Terms such as "endorphin," "serotonin," and "dopamine" create the illusion of three distinct brain chemicals, but as more scientists start taking a closer look, they are finding that what once appeared as one chemical is actually a compound of several. Consequently, the number of subtle chemical mixtures that each brain is capable of producing is infinite.

Without any left brain knowledge of chemistry, early man intensely focused every waking hour of his life on the brain-to-brain communication of complex chemical formulas. This was not done as an intellectual exercise, with words or concepts, but with intentions and feelings. The process was cognitive, but not conceptual or literal. Each person had a clear idea of what he or she wanted to do when each sent feelings of love, or cries for help. This was the use of right hemispheric knowledge, not left. Right hemispheric knowledge can use the distinction-making power of the left to its own ends, and remain in the form of nonverbal, preconceptual meaning. Hence, while awareness resided more in the right hemisphere than in the left for early man, he was every bit as capable of making clear and subtle meanings with his mental materials as is a modern philosopher, or artist, with his materials of words or paints.

The cultivation of love is a human art form. It is an activity for which all individuals are given the potential by the human genome. This potential can be perfected by practice. As with running, or painting, or chess, some people are born with a gift for the practice. Most people fit somewhere in the continuum from mediocre to masterful. The modern notion that love can "strike like lightening," and is therefore an involuntary process, is entirely due to a widespread lack of self-awareness. Minds choose to whom the brain will send love, and minds chose to receive, to return, or to reject the message. Our self-ignorance is perpetuated by the myths we spin about ourselves.

Those Yogis who can intentionally control their respiratory and circulatory systems also belie the claim of the cowardly sciences that these processes are completely "automatic," or "involuntary." Positivistic science reifies its blind spots to defend the validity of its false premises and to conceal its fear of the subjective. Its self-serving propaganda has become the "common sense" of world culture. But real life pioneers like those Yogis show that intentionality can go far beyond the "limits" arbitrarily set by special interest groups with a vested interest in keeping people ignorant. Behavioralists use modern man's experience of himself as evidence that love is an involuntary process, and modern man believes it, because that is his experience of himself. But what is true of our time is not necessarily true of all time. Simply because we do not know how to use our genome-given potential, is not proof that such potential does not exist. Empathic science takes the position that just as intentionality can learn to control other bodily functions, so it can learn to control the chemistry of love in the brain. Mind directs the mixture of love's chemicals, and can do so at will.

Empathic science research leads to the conclusion that cultivating the art of sending and receiving such basic emotions as fear and love was the central aim of world culture for over 100,000 years. As children were born and socialized into the human community, they learned the first philosophy of life. As we saw, this philosophy had no way to understand or ease the pain of being human. But in addition to that philosophy, the youth also learned the techniques for ameliorating the pain that came with maturity.

Juanita and little Eddy, for example, learned to make and send, and to ask for and receive, the cultivated love of others. Simply by being present at the practice of the art, they absorbed the knowledge of how to do it from their elders.

Parental figures discouraged activities which would distract the minds of the young from the practice. Children will play, of course, and fight as well, especially the boys. But elders would intervene when children went into excess, and remind them of what life is all about. If Joselito and Billy became too involved in "word wars," while imitating the Alpha males, an adult would step between them and send his love to each of the combatants. In most cases, the children would respond by ceasing their testosterone bravado, accepting that love, and sending love to one another. In this way, the community was their school. As they grew, their own pain was their strictest disciplinarian. Those adults who slacked-off in the communication of love were soon reminded by their own misery as to why they must keep up the practice.

Adults would also recognize talent in children. Those children who learned to send and receive love quickly, and with little instruction, would have been given an extra reward of notice and admiration. This early training developed a mental framework, which defined what it means to be human. To be human was to live in fear in a predatory world, but also to have the gift of love to give and receive for comfort. With that understanding, world culture was given the most enduring structure it has ever had.

We know from experience that the human genome distributes intelligence and ability on a curve. In any human endeavor there are klutzes and there are the incredibly gifted, with the majority in the middle. The potential for sending and receiving love would have been progressively developed as those of a higher aptitude set new standards for the masses. Each generation produces fast runners, for example, but almost every season Olympic records are broken because of improved techniques of training. The same principle applied in the early development of world culture.

The human genome seems by chance to produce an individual of maximum brilliance on a periodic basis. Suppose, for example, that such persons were produced every 5000 years. If so, then in the long period from man's beginning, about 150,000 years ago, up to his big entry into Europe, about 40,000 years ago, early man would have seen 22 of these marvels. Such outstanding talents would have served as models for those around them. Their genetic gifts could be returned to the community as education. For example, in the early generations of world culture individuals may have felt the love of one or two others, as their initial limit, and may have been reticent about sending all the love they could muster. They likely had no idea of how much love they could make, send, and receive.

Gifted people would be natural teachers to the others. We moderns, like the very first humans, have no idea what natural limits the human genome sets on an individual's capacity for nonverbal communication. But in the long stretch of 100,000 years, humanity surely reached these limits, and then exceeded them by focused training. The key question here is "how much love can one person send and receive?"

Suppose John's brain mixes the chemicals for his love. How many people can he send this message to at one time? Two? Four? Six? Sixteen? Conversely, what is the limit on the number of persons whose love John could consciously experience at the same time without becoming confused? Three? Five? Seven? Nine? Nineteen? When it comes to answering these queries, modern behavioral science is impotent.

Just as in the making of music, left brain and right brain abilities would be working together in this process. The left brain plays an important role in discerning differences. This ability would be employed by John as he learned to distinguish Mary's love from Juanita's, Mohammed's, and Jose's. From the pharmacological point of view, John's brain would be mixing his own love potion, as well as the potion according to the recipe sent by each of the others. A future brain chemist could do research to discover if the number of love potions a brain can make at once is limited to nine, or if it can make less, or even more.

The knowledge of another's love may be had without words. That love can be recognized simply by the experience of it. Color sensitive people can see shades of red, green, or yellow without words for each subtle change. They can also educate their less sensitive fellows to appreciate what stands there before them, but which at first was not seen. A brilliant wine taster can discern, without words, far more elements of a wine's bouquet than can those with a more ordinary pallet.

In the same way, early humans became connoisseurs of love. Each learned to filter fear from love so that it could reach degrees of purity which the first humans likely never dreamed possible. In the progress of human culture, the ability to both broadcast and to narrowcast love would have reached the natural maximum for strengths of signal, and then gone beyond that with the coaching of gifted people.

The conductor of an orchestra, as well as musicians and educated listeners, can discern the quality of sound for individual instruments in an ensemble of fifty instruments, or more in the gifted. The ability to discern gradations of quality was no less sensitive in early man's mind than it is in modern man's mind. They simply applied their mental discipline to different abilities. Thus, just as an orchestra learns a symphony by practice, the early human community devoted itself, with all the energy, intelligence, and concentration it could muster, to the perfection of feeling and projecting love.

Suppose the best of times could have been recorded, say by placing special microphones throughout a campsite. The device would have recorded a man or woman, with an extraordinary power to lead in loving, encouraging others to give freely of all the love they each had inside them. A booming, harmonic melody of joy would have rung through the air. Each person would be experiencing his or her maximum ability to send his or her purest love, and to receive the highest number possible of signals of pure love from others. This would not be for a moment of a day, but a daily routine – even the theme of a generation led by a genius. If ever there were a time in human history in which one can wish to have lived, it surely would be when all enjoyed a generation-long love-in, with each person basking in the "good vibrations" of his or her brothers or sisters.

While a matter for further research, as we have suggested, there may have been 22 epochs of maximum love in our prehistory. Perhaps more, or perhaps less. Of course, goodness in life has its ups and downs. Also, the human population would have been increasing, and communities separating, during this long period of time. The fortunes of each community would have varied, some blessed, some cursed. There were likely some groups, as with modernity, which had lost that loving feeling. Great teachers may have led whole groups to enlightenment. Some groups may have risen to the level of a gift economy, in which each gave to the others all he or she could as a sheer expression of honor, love, and appreciation. While the availability of food and water would have played a large part in forcing groups to split apart and move away, the average ability of people to experience love may have had something to do with the size of a typical human group. These were wandering populations, rather than settled. People along the fringes may have felt that they could have a more satisfying experience of communal love if they parted from the core group and formed their own love-cultivating community. Groups of less than fifty would be small enough for each person to be familiar with all the others, yet large enough to keep all but the most daring carnivores at bay.

Indeed, carnivores would have been a constant threat. They would have kept the human population small, along with disease. Life spans may not have exceeded thirty years on average. These people lived like animals. There is no evidence that they built shelters, or wore clothes, until after the Great Shift. In the rain, they got soaked. In the heat, they had only the shade of trees for shelter. Bone evidence suggests that vitamin, mineral, and protein deficiencies were rampant. Arthritis would strike people in their twenties. Rates of infant mortality, and of death in childbirth, were very high. Their over taxed and under-nourished immune systems would not have been able to carry them into what we moderns think of as old age.

But there can be no doubt that their lives were richer than ours. While they were material minimalists, they were communal maximalists. In other words, although they lacked things, they had each other. Contrast their condition with the middle class American who is loaded down with cell phones, PCs, TVs, CDs, DVDs, SUVs, taking anti-depressants, sleeping pills, diet pills, who is miserable at work, and unable to give or receive much love. Which is better, a long and empty life, or a short love-filled life? Fortunately, there now is another option. In our view, a long love-filled life is also an alternative. But this is a matter for future generations to decide upon.

Also, early humanity had none of modern man's alienation from nature. They felt as at home in nature as does any animal born and bred in the wild. Despite his abject poverty, early man had a strong sense of efficacy. The sense of efficacy is directly related to one's expectations of oneself as a "bread winner" in life. Early humans expected to live like animals, and they were well trained by their hominid parents to live as animals do. Hence, they easily fulfilled their self-expectations. Unless there were droughts, floods, pestilence, or other disasters, early humans were well satisfied with their material conditions, because they had all they expected to have. Their biggest problem was easing the pain and fears they felt. Humanity was consumed in this long period of world culture with reconciling the contradictions between their emptiness and misery, and their inherent need to feel happy and whole. Of course, in this respect, we moderns are no different.

The Evidence

Let us now consider the evidence for our accounting of early man's way of life. We will present two types of evidence. These are the intentional and the extensional. The latter is physical and objective, the other is based on introspective methods, therefore, it is more subjective, and intersubjective. Our concern here is to answer the question as to how the feelings, meanings, and the modes of communication of men long dead can be known by us.

Empathic science can understand early man's mind, at least in part, because our minds are structurally the same as theirs, just as are our brains. Our common mind/brain relationship enables all people to understand each other through self-critical empathy. That process entails the problem, as Hartman noted, of distinguishing one's own self from that of others. The limits of natural solipsism have never been fully tested. But through the methods of empathic science the potential for growth in human self-knowledge today is like the potential for growth in the natural sciences at the time of Galileo and Copernicus 500 years ago. Our self-reflective consciousness need not be a barrier to understanding one another.

Let us first consider the intentional evidence. We have already invited the reader to engage in some introspection. We have noted that many people have an intuitive feel for the natural order of values within themselves. This intuition is a form of introspection, or self-awareness. This line of introspection follows the links between the neocortex, the limbic system, and the ancient brain. The natural order of values exists primarily in the mind/brain relationship involving these links.

There are other lines of introspection that may be followed. Empathic science also conducts introspective research into other functions of the brain's right hemisphere. As we have seen, one objective of this research is to access right hemispheric communication processes. The empathic scientist seeks to dwell within those processes, to grasp the meanings conveyed, and to recover the lost art of sending and receiving those meanings. Another introspective research project aims at accessing the right hemispheric memory. That memory stores feelings, as well as nonverbally communicated meanings.

The memory that people practiced cultivated love for most of their time on Earth is accessible to people. Indeed, many have done so, albeit not with the clarity of science. The archetypal literature on the theme of lost love is voluminous. In *The Book of Genesis*, God's beneficent love turned to anger over Adam's disobedience. Milton's epic poem, *Paradise Lost*, tells of how some angels fell from grace. Lost love is a major theme in the songs, writings, and films of popular culture. This theme resonates because people self-reflectively feel that it touches upon some deep, personal truth. Empathic science turns the intuitions that lead to these feelings into a method for interpreting them. This chapter constitutes a preliminary report on the introspective findings thus far yielded by these several lines of research. The recall of such meanings and feelings, when combined with paleo-anthropological facts, is the basis for our understanding of the existence and the role of cultivated love so long ago.

Our right hemispheric memory contains a text that tells a story. The great pioneers of empathic science have taught us how to read that text within. Hartman has provided an exposition of its logic. The psychologists and philosophers of intention have given us direction. Schucman has provided a poetic portrayal of its content. We merely report now what they have enabled us to see.

Perhaps it was Nietzsche who coined the term "the archaeology of meaning." The giants who he inspired to pursue this thesis, and who wrote under such rubrics as "phenomenology" and "hermeneutics," set the stage for our distinction here between extensional and intentional evidence. Our task is to show how the two can be used together to explain our ancient past. From the point of view of intentionality, that early man lived by the principle of cultivated love can be *felt* to be true. Just as the color-sensitive person can show us how to see different shades of color, so these meaning-sensitive pioneers have shown us how to see different shades of meaning.

Humanity shares an ancestral memory. This memory is not conveyed genetically, as Carl Jung once thought, for genes do not contain meanings. Meanings are always self-made by each person. Nonverbal, right hemispheric communication is the vehicle of man's ancestral memory. Signals sent brain-to-brain cause a weaving together of those neuro-pathways that store the meaning of what it is to be human. That preconceptual, yet cognitive, meaning includes the first philosophy of life. It also entails the understanding that cultivated love can ease one's pain.

Prior to the Great Shift, these were the two major themes of the human ancestral memory. Everywhere people went, they took the story of what it means to be human with them. Around campfires, whether in caves or under the stars, people told this story to one another nonverbally, repeatedly, and without ever tiring of it. During the Great Shift, humanity withdrew attention from right hemispheric processes, and refocused their attention onto those of the left hemisphere. But the shift of attention did not change the workings of the right hemisphere. It continued its function of telling the story about the human condition. After the Great Shift, the theme of cultivating love became something that humans used to do. As we will show in the next chapter, a new theme emerged in the meaning of being human. Now, to be human means that one eases one's pain not by cultivating love, but by pursuing the more electrifying pleasures of exercising power. Thus, the Great Shift also entailed a huge change in human behavior. This change of behavior lends credence to one of the fundamental axioms of empathic science. That is, that human beings generally act so as to fulfill their self-made self-understandings.

We find support for many of our claims about nonverbal communication in the writings of anthropologists Edward T. Hall and Mildred Reed Hall. These experts on the subject have written that nonverbal communication is the "only language used throughout most of the history of humanity."[xlv] Indeed, according to the Halls, "it is the first form of communication you learn." We have observed that since the Great Shift, humanity's focus of attention on left hemispheric processes has not stopped the continuation of those on the right. The Halls have made a similar observation; viz., "All people communicate on several different levels at the same time but are usually aware of only the verbal dialog."

For this situation to exist, everyone must agree to make it happen. Hence, one of modernity's great illusions is that mind can conceal truly felt meanings, and control the meanings one wants to communicate. Here, like the Wizard of Oz, is a comic self-deception! Experienced empathic observers like the Halls know better, because, "Nonverbal communication systems are much less subject to the conscious deception that often occurs in verbal systems." The empathic scientist learns to detect incongruence between spoken language and its nonverbal accompaniment. And, as Schucman knew so well, the body is an instrument, not for the mind to use as its communication device, but as a device which communicates the mind. The body naturally emanates the mind. Modern world culture rests upon a conspiracy to create the illusion that one can control what one communicates. The chief pay-off, as we will explain further in Chapter Five, is that the illusion stimulates a small amount of pleasure from thinking one has such power. People believe they are exercising a secret power when they put on their "best behavior," or their personal persona, or whatever act they wish. They think that their "hidden" feelings are unknowable to others. This is but one of the many illusions of our self-alienated modern times.

To make this self-deception work, everyone must pretend not to receive the communication of one another's concealed feelings. In reality, however, the body is a transmitter of feeling, which is in operation during all of one's waking hours. One has the power to narrowcast one's messages, or to turn-off one's receiver, but no one has the power to stop broadcasting, any more than they can stop breathing. For these reasons, cultivating one's awareness of right hemispheric processes is a deeply subversive activity. Modern society cannot survive as it is presently structured, if any appreciable number of people become aware of the inner reality, which behavioralism fanatically insists does not exist. This is why "the taboo against knowing who you are," to borrow from Alan Watts, is an extreme necessity in the modern world.[xlvi]

Ultimately, then, our intentional evidence depends for its validation upon the courage of the critic to engage in two acts. One is to look within, and to see if what we say is there. To fully develop one's self-sensitivity requires that one have the courage to dwell within the same dread, confusion, and pain that the first humans knew as their daily experience. While not necessary to achieve the consciousness of consciousness, this process is necessary to acquire a thorough knowledge of oneself and one's culture. The second act needed to verify our claims is to turn on one's right hemispheric receiving units, and listen to the testimony to torment that, we claim, other people are always sending out. But if our critics refuse to look through our new conceptual instruments, as the Church Fathers refused to look through Galileo's new-fangled telescope, they will never understand the merits of our case.

Let us now consider the extrinsic evidence. If the first human group emerged on Earth 150,000 years ago, by the end of the first 50,000 years it had grown, divided, migrated, grown some more, divided, and migrated again and again, something like the cell differentiation in a pregnancy. In that time, small bands of humans had spread all over Africa from their point of origin in the east central section of that continent. As they migrated, of course, they carried the seeds of the human genome, and the foundations of world culture, with them.

The method of nonverbal communication remained constant, because it is inherited. The content, or meaning, of the communication also stayed the same, because then, as now, it was uncritically accepted. Thus, as groups separated, they continued telling the story of man, independently of one another. They continued, for the most part, to focus all their creative energy on the nonverbal communication of cultivated love. As we have seen, such feeling-to-feeling communication was so enriching to their lives that, by and large, even the most brilliant people ever born never gave a thought to trying to improve the material conditions of life. Generally, people were satisfied with their hominid knowledge of how to survive. Sticks and stones were their main tools. Gathering and sharing food was their mode of production. Most people relied on this technology, without improvement, to obtain "the necessities of life." Even man's notion of what was "necessary" to life was taken from this animal culture. Like their hominid forebears, they followed the communist principle of distribution, which is, as we have said, from each according to his or her ability, and to each according to his or her need.

As to the tools of production, however, anthropologists have found in Africa physical artifacts which clearly demonstrate that the human potential for technological innovation existed in full from man's earliest days.[xlvii] Cave deposits in southern Africa reveal physical evidence that humans cut animal bones into harpoons for fishing, and skillfully carved decorations along the sides of these implements. They also had tools made of colored stones that were carried to the caves from several miles away to be crafted. Experts on the finds estimate that this work was done between 100,000 and 70,000 years ago. Two thousand miles north, in the area of Katanga, Zaire, of west central Africa, miners have unearthed spears made in a style similar to the harpoons found in southern Africa. These findings are also estimated to be from as far back as 100,000 years ago. Here, then, long before modern people entered into Europe are the first known instances of both technological innovation and of chattel art. The craftsmanship of these items suggests that their makers were likely trained in techniques that may have taken several generations to develop.

Hence, contrary to contemporary Euro-centric prejudice, humans in Africa were the first to exercise their skills in technological innovation and artistic decoration. These findings have other important implications. They suggest, for example, that the human genome turned out humans then who had as much innovative genius as humans now have. The great difference is that early man lacked the will to use his creativity extensionally, but kept it focused on the intentional application.

For us, these artifacts are the exceptions that prove the rule. In a couple of discrete pockets of Africa, and for a limited time only, some humans sought to improve upon animal culture. Such acts were a major deviation from the norm for that time. How can this deviant behavior be explained? Were such endeavors as technological innovation somehow inconsistent with the cultivation of love? We suggest that at that time, the two acts were, indeed, inconsistent. One can convey and receive love, and create a fine bone harpoon, too, but probably not at the same time. Such craftsmanship requires concentration. To focus on that task requires drawing attention away from the task of nonverbal communication, which was to send and receive specific prescriptions for love. For a person who is not focused on easing the pain of the constricted

Schucman Corridor, attending to craftsmanship could allow that pain to creep back into consciousness unmollified.

We suggest that the experience of turning away from the cultivation of love, so as to pursue material improvements, was something like the experience of touching hot coals. A few groups tried it, and burned their fingers. Other groups simply learned from observation, or used what for them was "common sense." The majority of humanity continued the cultivation of love, and the life of animal culture, and regarded material innovation as folly.

Indeed, even the innovating groups soon learned that the game was not worth the candle. All signs of innovative culture suddenly ceased. No lasting cultures were based on these technological advancements. They occurred in no more than a few spots, between 100,000 and 70,000 years ago, and then disappeared. Within the context of world culture as it was at that time, man's first experiments at material improvement only showed the wisdom of staying the course of cultivated love. Only with the Great Shift did humanity veer completely off that course. Then creativity became an expression of power. As material innovation came to be seen in a new light, the road to modernity was opened.

In sum, the absence of material innovation evinces not ignorance or lack of skill, but a choice for an alternative. That alternative was the cultivation of love. Although people had the ability to improve their material conditions, they chose not to. To their minds, at the time, they were making the better choice. Because such innovative activities distracted people from cultivating love, and permitted pain to slither back into consciousness, like a poisonous snake, the whole idea was abandoned as ill conceived.

But that is not our only empirical evidence. There is something else. Anthropologists have found a group of contemporary low-tech people who may have once lived just as early man did. The Tasaday were discovered in 1971. They lived in a mountain jungle on the island of Mindanao, in the Philippines. Observers described them as communal gatherers, with a stone age technology, who lived in a cave. There were only 26 individuals at that time.

In a volume entitled *The First Men*, by the editors of Time-Life Books, the Tasaday were reported by one observer to be among "the gentlest people on the face of the earth."[xlviii] According to all reports, when first found these people were a model of material minimalism and communal maximalism. They are depicted as living in tune with their environment, and so cooperative that they "have no headman, and no serious rivalries." They had few needs, and these were easily satisfied. They spend most of their time together, and "often sit in silent, closely knit groups."

Unfortunately, the first anthropologists to observe the Tasaday had been trained to fear the subjective. Given their intellectual framework, these intruders from industrial society neither knew what to look for in those long periods of silence, nor how to see what was before them. Instead, like physicists, they objectively described the actions of bodies "sitting in silence;" of course, stones do the same thing. Lacking empathic training, they did not have a clue as to what was transpiring between these ancient people. Were they too ignorant to think of anything to say to fill the silence? Were they bored? Or, were they communicating cultivated love? Having learned to dismiss the "subjective" as either irrelevant, or unreal, the scholars who studied the Tasaday neither asked nor answered these questions. While one academic anthropologist has challenged some aspects of the early reports about Tasaday life, there is widespread agreement that these quiet and gentle people once lived in a world untouched by Western "civilization."[xlix]

After that initial contact was made, however, the roar of helicopters shattered the sounds of silence. These noisy whirlybirds brought in linguists with notepads and tape recorders. The machines also carried in wealthy celebrities, and other anthro-tourists, who sought a glimpse of these primitive people before they became corrupted by modernity. Of course, as Heisenberg knew, the observer inevitably changes that which is being observed. The Tasaday soon learned that powerful high-tech people put great value on the spoken word, and now completely disregard nonverbal communication. Thus, they have remained silent about their silence. They have become regular talkers now. They use metal tools, live in houses, wear pants and dresses, keep busy, engage in trade with industrial people, and intermarry with outsiders. What transpired in those periods of silence is still an unknown. Perhaps the language they speak has no way of conceptualizing that practice, so that it cannot be talked about. Now, the old ways are no longer followed, and little is known about what they had meant to the Tasaday. Still, the very existence of these people lends some support to our hypotheses about the ways of early man. The Tasaday may have been the last practitioners on Earth of the original culture of cultivated love.

The Critique of Cultivated Love

We have, here, presented cultivated love as humanity's first, and to date, most successful collective way of easing man's natural pain. Cultivating love enabled people to cope for over 100,000 years. However, in our view, the practice of cultivated love is not above criticism. In the first place, the full-time cultivation of love could only be carried on in the primitive communist mode of production. We do *not* recommend a return to that way of life! Our hope is that a synthesis of material production and institutionalized efforts to heal the human birth defect can be realized in the future. We will discuss how to begin that process in Chapter Six. We will close this chapter with a list of some of the major defects that we see in the practice of cultivated love, and which make it an undesirable goal for modern world culture to return to.

The first defect we see in the practice of cultivated love is that it fails to remove the cause of the problem, and merely distracts attention away from the pain the problem causes. In the long era of cultivated love, society was organized to sooth human pain by providing distractions and teaching the suppression of its awareness. Of course, this practice replicates mother's soothing of baby's pain by helping baby to "forget" the trauma of birth. But, as Rank has shown us, the stimulus of the pain is not rendered inoperative by disregarding its affect. Unconscious processes continue unabated. Just as the motorist who drives with one foot on the brake and the other on the accelerator unnecessarily wears down his car, so the nervous system of man was worn down sooner than need be by cultivating love rather than by opening the way within for it to flow freely.

To best understand the culture of cultivated love, let us contrast it with post-consciousness of consciousness objectless love. As we indicated in Chapter Two, objectless love flows freely with the opening of the Schucman Corridor. It is grounded in the experience of one's oneness with humanity, with the world around one, and with other sentient creatures. Objectless love is simply the conscious experience of all systems working well within the human organism. Once the effort to form the right intention has succeeded in starting up the Schucman Corridor, objectless love flows as effortlessly as the heart beats and the lungs breathe.

Cultivated love must be cultivated. That is, an intense and hard to sustain effort is required to produce and communicate it. Early humans would have had "bad days" when they could not make the effort. These would have been painful times. There may have been whole generations, or epochs, when the will to generate love failed. The most miserable periods of history were those in which some human groups had forgotten how to suppress the awareness of their pain. Perhaps these were the conditions in which those first material innovations were undertaken.

Because cultivating love requires effort, it distracts attention from the beckoning whispers of the Schucman Corridor. Thus, cultivating love is a false happiness conditional. That is, it promises the contentment that one longs for, but it is unable to deliver fully on that promise. As Schucman noted, one cannot find the truth by pursuing an illusion. Forming the right intention is so difficult, in part, because it must be free of illusions and hidden agendas.

Cultivating love does not change the first philosophy of life, but perpetuates it. Cultivating love assumes that life is as the first philosophy of life defines it, a dangerous situation for bodies. Then cultivating love becomes the key strategy for living in accord with that definition of the situation. But one's real problem is to let go of one's self-created understandings, along with the self that is woven into them. Such understandings, including the cultivation of love, are merely the contents of consciousness; however, it is the consciousness of consciousness which one needs to achieve.

Objectless love is communicated to others without any expectation of something in return. Cultivated love was given, in effect, as part of man's first "social contract." The terms of that social contract were "I'll sooth your soul, if you'll sooth mine." This created a set of expectations of love-in-return. These expectations would have been instilled in children, and enforced against adults by social conventions. But, objectless love is given without obligation. Indeed, as Schucman and others have often said, the more one gives it away, the more one has of it.

Cultivating love creates a society of co-dependent relationships. One must depend upon others both to validate one's love by receiving it, and to supply one with their love. The risks inherent in this situation would have generated their own brand of nervousness. For example, if one sends love, which no one wants, then one may feel abandoned to suffer alone and helplessly. If others take one's love, but offer none in return, then one will feel unfairly treated, and one's bulwark against agony will be weakened. Co-dependent relationships are susceptible to all sorts of abuses. If cultivated love could be given or withheld as an act of power, some people could victimize others.

Early man was addicted to his medication. This, of course, raises its own insecurities about supply, and the possibilities for abuse. We will see in the next chapter that during the Great Shift humanity quit its addiction to cultivated love, but substituted for it a less satisfying and far more self-destructive addiction. This addiction plagues us today.

Love becomes a commodity in the culture of cultivated love. Some people may have felt deprived of their "fair share" of love. Some may have felt resentful or envious that others seemed to receive more love than did they. In bad times, social conflicts may have erupted over perceptions of an unequal distribution of love in a group. The human genome provided for pettiness then, just as it does now. Because objectless love is freely given, it avoids all conflicts peculiar to an exchange of commodities. This is love on the intrinsic plane of value, not traded, but given for its own sake. In the natural order of values there is no quid pro quo.

Cultivated love objectifies humanity as a condition for its operation. To feel one's own love for them, one must use them as objects to which one's love is sent. To feel the love of others, one must be their object.

All of the adverse possibilities implied by the principle of cultivated love are made possible because they are elements of use-value. Cultivating love assumes that the value of others is their usefulness as a remedy for the pain of life. Each seeks to use the other as a balm to ease his or her agony. Obviously, if each would take responsibility for easing his or her own pain, no one would need to use the others as a balm. But, tragically, early humans, on the whole, were no more sensible in this matter than are we moderns. Thus, both the first philosophy of life and early man's response to it kept world culture on the plane of extrinsic, or use, value. In the first philosophy of life, one values oneself and others in the utilitarian roles of potential prey, predator, or ally. Cultivating love continues along the plane of extrinsic value by using others as a salve. While this use is surely positive and well intended, it is still a use.

The practice of giving love to others in exchange for their love is inconsistent with the natural order of values. The highest priority in the natural order of values is that one achieve one's own personal happiness. The cultivation of love evades this responsibility by using others as a source of love. In the natural order of values, oneself and others are too precious to use. But the cultivation of love is based entirely upon using. In an alliance for the cultivation of love, use-value overrides intrinsic valuations. Intrinsically another person is valued only as a unique instance of self-reflective consciousness, like oneself. Allies, however, are valued for their usefulness. Some are worth more than others, depending on how well they sooth one's pain.

Validated by the cultivation of love, the first philosophy of life sustains pain. Believing in that philosophy also turns one's attention outward to search for relief. Animals are instinctively outward looking, because they are naturally contented inwardly. In humans this animal thinking is an extension of baby's materialism, and acts as a powerful force that misguides reason when the Schucman Corridor signals its readiness to go to work. Early man's mind was thus oriented to look outwardly for happiness. Allies, both in the struggle for survival and as a balm, are always outside oneself. This outward orientation is perpetuated, and exploited, by the cowardly sciences. Because of their propagandizing in the schools, the tendency to look outwardly for happiness remains today unbalanced by *any* knowledge about either the need to attend inwardly, or about how to do so.

The practice of cultivated love may be criticized as discouraging authenticity. If one does not feel like making the effort to send love, or does not feel like receiving it from others, then why should one do it? Perhaps there were early humans who took that position against the conventions of their time. If such independent thinking enabled them to get in touch with the homing signals of their Schucman Corridor, then they certainly made the right choice. Otherwise, that position would have been very difficult to maintain. Without the balm of cultivated love, one's pain would have been tormenting. Also, social pressures would have been intense. Nonconformists who made a nuisance of themselves may have been punished, ostracized, expelled, or even executed.

Even spiritual heroes, such as Zen Masters, may have suffered an undeserved fate. The primitive mind is very traditional and conservative, with little tolerance for variation from accepted practices. In modern times, too, the message of change is often resisted.

Modern people cling to the romantic dream of individual love, although it often proves to have been an illusion. The illusion is that "he" or "she" will "fill my void." This dream replicates, to a large extent, the illusion that moved early humans. The culture they created led each to depend upon the love of others to "fill my void." Amazingly, the illusion of salvation in the love of another worked well enough that they clung to it for over 100,000 years.

The memory of cultivated love strikes a nostalgic cord in modernity. We call it the "return to love" theme. We discussed earlier how Otto Rank dealt with this theme insofar as it was connected to the longing to return to fetal bliss. The frustration of an underperforming Schucman Corridor creates another source of discontent. In ignorance as to the exact meaning of one's longings, the right hemispheric memory of cultivated love seems to float a promise of contentment. Christianity's command to "love thy neighbor" evokes the memory in many people that cultivating love once brought some salvation from pain.

However, we hope that we have shown that the allure of returning to both prenatal contentment and the practice of cultivated love are false happiness conditionals. Why long for the past, when the future holds much richer possibilities? Humanity can move forward, and create a culture that contains all the best of past and present, when our practices have been brought in-line with the natural order of values.

Cultivated love is like the collector's love of a beautiful vase, for example, one from the Ming Dynasty of ancient China. He would never use this precious item, for instance, to serve lemonade on the tennis court. But he is deceiving himself if he thinks he really values his vase as too precious to use. This is a "love" that is wholly involved with using. At bottom, his Ming vase is a commodity to him, worth more, to be sure, than an ordinary plastic pitcher, but nevertheless a useful investment for both profit and prestige. Any love that is involved in using is not an objectless love.

Unlike cultivated love, objectless love is blind to use. However, use-value and objectless love need not be mutually exclusive. One can feel objectless love, and still engage in the use-valuing of others. When practicing kickboxing, for example, a healed person may value a worthy sparring partner over a weakling or a coward. Few people would choose a spouse who habitually cheated, and therefore put his or her partner at risk for STDs. When playing golf, even a healed person would not want a partner who threw his clubs in anger, or a business partner who consistently lost money for the firm. Every sort of employment can be, but rarely is, an instance of use-value added on to objectless love. Use-value need not diminish the intrinsic worth of another, if the other has knowingly consented to be used.

These two planes of value can be like parallel lines that go on and on without ever intersecting. They need not be confused, as they are in our times. Once the basic distinction between intrinsic value and extrinsic value is both understood and experienced as a part of one's being, then use-value no longer diminishes another because it is a secondary activity, and incidental to the love which is freely given. Social contracts, or relationships based on exchange, are not inherently inconsistent with the natural order of values. Use-value diminishes others when it is given as the only value. When use-value is given subsequently to intrinsic value, it is consistent with the natural order of values. In *The Structure of Value*, Hartman offers a formal axiology that enables the experts to measure the elements of intrinsic and extrinsic value in any given idea, situation, or social practice with mathematical precision. Over time, these parallel lines can be untangled, and set straight.

Conclusion

World culture has never fully grasped the distinction between these two separate realms of value. Indeed, as we have said, the essence of animal thinking is to value others only for their use. This habit of mind is deeply ingrained in world culture. It was the choice of the earliest humans, and it is the choice of humanity today. They could have done otherwise. Their Schucman Corridor was signaling to them that the way to freedom from fear and emptiness lay within. They could have found ways to support one another in their individual efforts to realign their mind-brain relationship by forming the right intention. Then they could have cooperated with one another to achieve material goals in the spirit of objectless love.

Indeed, there might have been generations that did this, but no way to sustain a healed mind across generations has ever been found. Instead, early humans did the best they could with the knowledge they had at the time.   Unfortunately, what they did not know did hurt them, and us. We are now mired deep within the patterns of thought learned from the hominids that bore us. Our task is to find a way to clear away the muck of use-value as humanity's primary mode of valuing, and to devise institutions and practices that will retrofit world culture with a foundation of intrinsic value. But before we discuss how to begin that culture repair project, we must see how the culture of cultivated love was brought to a sudden end, to be replaced by the unhappy practices of modernity.

Chapter Five

The Genocide of Neanderthal, and the Genesis of Modern Culture

Was Neanderthal a Man?

More than any other event since the formation of the human genome, man's encounter with Neanderthal has made him who he is today. In this chapter, and the next, we will continue to draw from both extensional and intentional evidence to reconstruct the past in a way that will explain the present. Only with a clear understanding of where we are and how we got here, will we humans be well positioned to chart a course for our future.

Because we say that Neanderthal made us who we are now, we believe that it is extremely important to understand the nature of that creature. Indeed, understanding Neanderthal will enable us to better understand ourselves. Who, then, was Neanderthal? How did he live? Was he animal or human? How intelligent was he? Could he speak? What kind of mind/brain relationship did he have? After addressing these, and other, questions we will discuss man's encounter with Neanderthal and its consequences for both him and us. Throughout this discussion we will interpret the facts, which have been accepted by the experts, from the theoretical perspective that we have presented in the preceding chapters.

Paleontology has the position, resources, and professional responsibility to inform the public about humanity's nature and evolution. Unfortunately, it has shown sever misfeasance in the execution of this fiduciary duty. That profession has allowed itself to be overrun by careerism, fraud, incompetent fieldwork, hucksters, and, with a few exceptions, empathic ineptitude. These are the forces that have shaped the popular image of Neanderthal. Only since the 1990's have efforts been undertaken to clear away the trash which has accumulated since the first Neanderthal bones were found in the mid eighteen hundreds. Thus, we must begin with a review of the most recent efforts at debunking the misinformation. To start the Twenty-first Century with a clean slate, responsible paleontologists have had to rake through about 150 years of accumulated muck.

Tales, which are sad but true, abound. In 1912 one ambitious and unscrupulous paleontologist fastened an orangutan mandible to a human skull which he had apparently robbed from a grave. Claiming that he had discovered it in an excavation in Piltdown, England, he proclaimed it to be the "missing link." He promptly received the highest praise and honors his profession had to offer. His con went undetected for nearly fifty years, long after he had died.[1]

Otto Hauser was the first "fossil hunter" to cash-in on promoting the myth of Neanderthal burials. The old Darwinian notion that man had evolved from apes had reached its peak of popularity in Europe. The sale of "antiquities," such as chipped stones and old bones, had become lucrative. Then, as now, there was money to be made in tourism. One example was that pilgrims to the

Lourdes site in France were spending lots of money on hotels, food, and souvenirs.

In 1908, the shrewd Hauser announced his discovery in Le Moustier, France, of a Neanderthal buried on its side with its hands lovingly folded under its head.[li] The town swelled with tourists. Then Hauser made a second find in Combe Capelle of a buried Neanderthal whose body was prepared for the after-life with stone tools and shell ornaments. He was among the first entrepreneurs to promote his business with picture postcards.[lii] Excursions to his cave sites soared.

Over in Monte Circeo, Italy, a hotel owner had some amazing "luck." In 1939, a paleontologist discovered a cave with a Neanderthal skull carefully placed in a "circle of stones."[liii] By happy coincidence, this firm evidence of a religious ritual was found right on the hotel property! The hotel guests surely appreciated the convenience. A competing hotel business in the same town had no stones and bones for the tourists to see. So, the owner did the next best thing. He renamed his establishment "The Hotel Neanderthal," and they came.[liv]

In the Middle East, more Neanderthal burials were found. At a time when the flower-wearing Hippies were still in the spotlight of the press, TV, and movies, a discovery was announced that the Neanderthals were "the first flower people."[lv] In the Shanidar cave of Iraq, some Neanderthal burials were unearthed. A couple of the skeletons had been interred in a "flexed" position; that is, arms and legs folded in. Samples of flower pollen and red ocher were sifted from the dirt. This immediately became proof positive that Neanderthals were a near-human species with mystical feelings, a metaphysical philosophy, belief in an after-life, and perhaps supernatural connections. Given these giant inferences, the debated hypothesis that humans evolved from advanced Neanderthals became a verified Truth for those paleontologists who had already taken that position.

However, since some other members of the profession have started getting more serious about doing science, one myth after another claiming ritualistic and reverent burials of Neanderthals have been debunked. That cave on the hotel property with the "circle of stones," really was not a Neanderthal sanctuary. It is now known to be an old hyena den. The stones were strewn about in random order, and had not originally formed a circle. If the skull had not been planted there by a paid agent, it was probably dragged into the cave as part of a hyena meal.[lvi] The skeleton, which had been buried with shell ornaments, was later found to be a human's, not a Neanderthal's.[lvii]

That Neanderthal which Hauser had promoted as lovingly laid to rest on its side was, years later, determined to have been killed in its sleep by a cave-in.[lviii] Indeed, falling roofs may have buried more Neanderthals than were ever interred by kin. Several million Neanderthals lived and died during their approximately 200,000 year sojourn on Earth. If burials had actually been a regular religious ritual, thousands of graves, and perhaps dozens of graveyards, should have been uncovered. But the number of actual graves found suggests to Ian Tattersall that "burial appears to have been a rather uncommon practice among Neanderthals."[lix]

While experts agree that some deliberate Neanderthal burials occurred, the mystical explanations for them are no longer accepted. The pollen found at Shanidar was part of the sediment on the cave floor. It had been blown in over the years, and was swept into the grave when the body was covered over. Incidentally, many of the "tools" found in Neanderthal graves are now regarded not as supplies for the after-life, but as debris pushed "into the grave by accident."[lx] The bodies were likely buried in a flexed position so that a larger hole did not have to be dug in the hard cave floor.

The burials themselves had nothing to do with religion, belief in an after-life, or respect for the dead. Throughout the Neanderthal record, there is "no suggestion of a coherent symbolic system."[lxi] Neanderthal behavior was highly pragmatic. Buried bodies would not attract bothersome rats, or larger carnivores, into the cave.[lxii] Also, burying dead bodies hides the stench of their decay. Finally, Neanderthals were cannibals. They may have buried bodies for storage, like a dog buries a bone.[lxiii] Ocher may have been sprinkled on the body as a form of seasoning, or as a preservative. The few deliberate burials that have been found are probably forgotten food, or the storers met their own fates before they could exhume their meat for consumption.[lxiv]

Another false implication of the myth of ritualistic burials by Neanderthals is that a human-like brain guided their behavior. While no Neanderthal brains have yet been found, because the soft tissue quickly dries into dust after death, our view is that the Neanderthal brain was an animal brain, not human. Anthropologist Marcellin Boule, and renowned neurologist/brain surgeon Paul Broca, agreed over 100 years ago that the Neanderthal cranium, or brain case, could not have housed a human brain.[lxv] Their brain was similar to ours in size, but not in shape.[lxvi] The Neanderthal skull has a low forehead which slopes back from protruding brow ridges. Our brows are comparatively smooth because our light jaws do not require ridges to support thick facial muscles. Human skulls have a dome shape with a high, roomy forehead, to accommodate our bulging frontal lobes. Their brain case is typically low slung and elongated.

Neanderthals probably had a three-layer, or triune, brain; but, the major differences lay in how the parts related to one another within each brain. As we will discuss further below, Neanderthal bodies were much thicker and more muscular than human bodies. As a general rule among hominids and humans, bulkier bodies have bigger brains than smaller bodies. Because of their bulk and larger internal organs, the Neanderthal brain stem would likely have been proportionately larger than that of humans. For the same reason, Neanderthals may have had a comparatively bigger cerebellum to manage the operations of their massive musculature. The larger eye sockets in their skulls suggest larger eyes. If so, and given their body mass, they might have had larger occipital lobes, at the rear of the brain, than do humans. Their prominent nose may have been connected to correspondingly large olfactory lobes in their brain, which may have given them a superior sense of smell compared to humans. Being hominids, and therefore highly social, these stocky creatures would have had a large size limbic system atop the big brain stem.

Humans are also unique in the relationship of their forebrain to their hindbrain. Richard Leakey points-out that in "apes, the occipital lobes [which manage vision] are larger than the frontal lobes; in humans, the pattern is reversed."[lxvii] The Neanderthal brain case has less room in the frontal portion than the human brain case, strongly suggesting they had smaller frontal lobes. Thus, since Neanderthals had smaller frontal lobes and larger occipital lobes than humans do, their forebrain/hindbrain relationship was, like that of the apes, well within the animal range, and a far cry from being human.

Finally, the cortical tissue wrapping around the two hemispheres of the Neanderthal brain would be the key to classifying their brains as either human or those of animals. In the chimpanzee, for example, the cortical layer is thinner and less convoluted than that of humans. As we mentioned in the previous chapter, the chimp cortex constitutes about 65% of their brain volume, but a whopping 85% of ours. Because Neanderthals probably had larger reptilian and mammalian sections, in a brain case with just about a human volume, their cortical wrapping must have been thinner than ours. Also, because the known behavior of the Neanderthal demonstrates very little abstract thought, we surmise that their percentage of cortical tissue was in the animal range.

The dimensions of the Neanderthal brain, of itself, belie all the speculation about their capacity for rites, rituals, or abstract thought. Nor could they have developed speech without the frontal lobes needed to think abstractly. Indeed, careful studies of Neanderthal skull interiors and computer modeling of their vocal apparatus show that the Neanderthal capacity for speech was likely on a par with contemporary apes. In other words, they lacked the speech anatomy necessary to make the complex combinations of phonemes that are required for speech. Like chimpanzees, they could grunt and call, but that is all. [lxviii]

The absence of a "symbolic sense" also negates the claim of Neanderthal "cave bear cults." Cave bears lived and died in caves. That is where their skeletons collected. Sometimes they were killed and eaten by invading packs of four-legged predators. When Neanderthals moved-in, they tossed the bones into piles to get them out of the way. Later, ambitious, or naïve, paleontologists came along and wrote attention getting papers about cults, rituals, and Neanderthal worship of higher powers. Experts now agree that "none of these instances stands up to close scrutiny." [lxix]

While human intelligence and innovation has lead our kind to create vast, highly complex, ever-changing societies with a multitude of products and services, animal societies are comparatively simple and routine. During their long stay on Earth, Neanderthals showed very little capacity for innovation. Their ways of tool making changed very little compared to the style used by other hominids for a million years before them. They continued to use the Homo erectus "tear drop" hand held axe without ever thinking to haft it for more leverage and force.[lxx] Nor did they fasten stone tips to their wooden spears. Clearly, Neanderthal behavior, like its brain, was animal in nature.

However, they did gradually develop a variety of stone implements. They had stones that could be used as cutters for butchering meat, and scrappers for scrapping the fat off hides. Indeed, although Neanderthals never knew how to sew, they probably wore animal skin cloaks slung around their shoulders. They may also have used this material for bedding, like gorillas use leaves and branches to make beds. Holes dug in cave floors suggest that Neanderthals may have stuck posts in there and draped bearskins across the poles as lean-tos. But there is no evidence of them having invented footwear. No one knows if they tied animal skins around their feet, or walked barefoot, even in winter.

Barefoot or not, however, Neanderthals were amazingly well adapted to the frigid, ice age conditions in which they lived. Anthropologists are at a loss to explain how those creatures, with hominid bodies much like ours, could have endured such cold. What is more, they were not the first hominids to thrive in those conditions. Neanderthals probably evolved in Europe out of a breed of Homo erectus hominids, which may have migrated to Europe from Africa a half million years ago. Shreeve supposes that the huskier, larger brained Neanderthals emerged about 130,000 years ago, but Tattersall cautions that it may have been considerably more.[lxxi] Apparently, Neanderthals learned the survival techniques of their Homo erectus ancestors. Those ancestors had fire, and probably animal skin cloaks. But these were hardly enough to forestall hypothermia in nearly naked hominid bodies. So, what was their secret?

Remember those Tibetan monks who can dry their sheets by raising their body temperature through meditation? The Homo erectus in Europe may have had enough imagination and ingenuity to discover that they could beat the cold simply by "thinking warm." That is, perhaps by maintaining a right hemispheric deliberate dream, or semblance of being next to a warm fire, those ancient creatures could run barefoot and half-naked through freezing cold forests, and survive for over a quarter of a million years. They may have taught the technique to their young through a combination of example, and verbal and nonverbal instruction. The tradition that those Tibetan monks preserve may have been learned from Neanderthals who, long before, had been driven into the Himalayan Mountains by European man.

Neanderthal tool making innovations show that their mental powers rank above those of any other animal; but by how much is still a debated issue. Neanderthals were not the only animals to use stone tools. Chimps and otters, for example, use two stones like a hammer and anvil to crush shells to get at the food inside. Chimps crack open nuts, and otters, mollusks. A chimp knows how to break a branch off a bush, strip it, and stick it down a termite mound to fish for the tasty insects. Chimps have also learned to squash up a leaf and use it as a sponge to hold more water to drink than it could get by hand.

Clearly, the animal mind is capable of some rudimentary element of design. Neanderthal innovations go a step or two further than the chimp's stick, sponge, or the gorilla's bed. But the Neanderthals probably stretched the animal capacity for design to its limit. Indeed, even the term "tool making" implies a more focused purpose than the Neanderthals may have actually had. Neanderthals had strong hands with dexterous fingers. Evidence in the caves suggests that the males enjoyed sitting together and knapping stones. Chipped stones are strewn around cave floors, and piled in numbers far in excess of what they needed for their limited purposes. Knocking rocks together appears to have been more of a way to occupy their free moments than as an "industry." Neanderthals took to chipping stones like good old Fido relishes retrieving a stick thrown by his master. Because the dog is fulfilling main parts of its nature, its delight always outlasts its owner's interest in the game. Neanderthal eye, hand, and brain coordination made rock knocking a favorite hobby to while away his spare time.

As this pastime was learned by children, new shapes were hit upon as much by chance as by design. Delight in the activity moved the Neanderthals to maintain a small repertoire of patterns to follow. Thus, styles of stone knapping show no more regional variation than would be expected from chance. Individuals simply learned, and passed on, those styles, which had evolved incidentally in their region. When the time came to butcher meat, or scrape hides, or carve a spear tip, a Neanderthal would rummage through the rubble on the cave floor and pick up a piece of chipped stone which suited the task at hand. Many experts now agree that the idea of deliberately assembled "tool kits" is a projection of human practices onto animal behavior.[lxxii]

Unlike Neanderthals, humans chose particular kinds of stone for special uses. They also used wood and bone to achieve finer edges than those of the Neanderthal tools. Human stone work reflects far more training and intellectual involvement than the Neanderthals were capable of. Neanderthals had no art, no jewelry, and no decorations on their tools. A Neanderthal knife blade could be knocked out with a few dozen strokes, taken from only two or three different angles. By contrast, a man-made knife blade, of the same period, required over 250 strokes, taken from several different angles. The human knife was thinner, sharper, and a piece of thoughtful craftsmanship. The Neanderthal blade could saw through tough hides, but the human blade was capable of fine slicing.[lxxiii] (Scratches on Neanderthal front teeth suggest that they held raw meat in their teeth and hastily cut off mouthfuls with their knife blades.)

The proximity of Neanderthal ingenuity with that of other animals suggests proximity of intelligence. Like other animals, they used their ingenuity to fine-tune their adaptation to their environment. However, the Neanderthal's adaptive capacity excelled within the animal kingdom by solving a much wider variety of problems than has any other non-human creature. They were the brightest by animal standards, but not human. They were incapable of forming more than a rudimentary conception of how an implement, or a situation, could be improved. The capacity to envision abstract ideals is man's alone. We will soon see when and why man became committed to using that power to its fullest.

Neanderthals lacked the "planning depth," as well as the communication skills needed to organize the mass hunts that have been wrongly attributed to them for popular consumption.[lxxiv] Evidence does exist that over the past couple hundred thousand years there have been a few instances of mass deaths of herd animals, such as horses and reindeer. During this time, huge herds of animals grazed in the rich grasslands where these deaths occurred. In each case, the likely cause was lightening, brush fire, or the charge of four legged predators. The herds panicked. Those on the edge were driven by their own kind off cliffs, or into quicksand pits. Nearby Neanderthals then came along and scavenged meat from the carcasses. According to Tattersall, "few archaeologists are prepared to conclude today that [Neanderthals or other non-human hominids] ever systematically hunted the bigger animals."[lxxv] Neanderthals were much less of the "noble hunter" than they are often made out to be.

As judged by the number of animal bones found in caves, meat was a treat and not a staple for Neanderthals, just as it was for other hominids.[lxxvi] They inherited the altruistic gathering way of life common to the hominid species. Being highly social, they had strong bonds within their small bands. The bones found in Neanderthal trash heaps, mostly of small animals, show that when prey was caught, or carrion captured, the males brought the meat back to the camp for the common meal. There is evidence that males occupied areas of the caves which were separated from the quarters shared by women and children. But the concentration of bones and meat cutting stones around hearths suggests that everyone ate together before retiring to their separate sections. We will see why they parted shortly.

From the above facts, we conclude that Neanderthal consciousness was need-based. Their decision-making was guided by their species instinct. Like primates and other animals, they had no self-created self.[lxxvii] Of course, each Neanderthal had a unique personality. The neuroconnections in each Neanderthal brain, which determine the individual's temperament and predispositions formed a unique configuration in every instant. But Neanderthal behavior, like that of mice, cats, or elephants followed patterns which were typical of the species. One of the main elements of instinct is regularized behavior. In contrast, human decision-making is guided more by meaning. Since meaning, unlike instinct, can be creatively reconfigured into endless numbers of patterns, it is not restricted to easily predictable stereotypes. That is why there is such variety in human cultures.

Unfortunately, as we have seen, our creativity comes at a price. Humans lost the natural contentment of animals when the swelling of our neocortex caused a reconfiguration in the tissue and functions of our brain. The inner connections needed for natural happiness have been so attenuated that they have become too tenuous to work naturally. We must mend this flaw in our mind/brain relation by an intentional act. But Neanderthals, having an animal mind/brain relationship, were spared the human birth defect.

As we have seen, the Neanderthal brain volume was within the human range, not because they possessed an expanded neocortex, which they did not, but because the reptilian and mammalian sectors of their brain were larger than those of humans, due to the great bulk of the Neanderthal body.[lxxviii] Neanderthals have a bell shaped rib cage, suggesting rounded rather than V-shaped torsos. A typical 25 year old Neanderthal male stood around 5' 6." Yet, he could easily have weighed 225 pounds. Much of his weight was concentrated in his husky chest and shoulders.[lxxix] Neanderthal's bones tell of his "heavy build."[lxxx] According to Tattersall, Neanderthal's "load-bearing joints … are large, and the shafts of the long bones are much thicker than is typical of Homo sapiens."[lxxxi]

For decades Neanderthal was depicted as a lumbering ape-like creature, half way between a gorilla and Quasimodo. Then anatomists discovered that the leg bones upon which this image was based had been improperly assembled. Modern experts on Neanderthal anatomy agree that Neanderthals walked upright, with a well-balanced, even athletic gate.[lxxxii] There is also widespread agreement that Neanderthals were extraordinarily powerful. Shreeve remarked that a Neanderthal could easily pick up and throw an NFL linebacker.[lxxxiii] Trinkaus expressed amazement at "how massive and robust Neanderthal legs and feet were."[lxxxiv] Not only was he more muscular than any human, according to Trinkaus, Neanderthal's muscles were attached to their bones at angles which enhanced their might and agility.[lxxxv] Trinkaus and Dr. Pat Shipman observe that "No Olympic athlete of today has a comparable overall robustness."[lxxxvi]

Although a foot shorter, a Neanderthal could easily flip and pin a heavy-weight wrestler, like the 6' 6" Jessie Ventura, or break Jessie's neck with a head lock. A heavyweight boxer, like Mike Tyson, could shatter the bones in his fist by socking a Neanderthal on his enormous jaw. Then a lightening fast Neanderthal right hook to Tyson's temple would crush his skull.

Perhaps the most noteworthy aspect of this powerful creature is that his "hands were especially strongly built."[lxxxvii] The hands were broad enough to palm a basketball, with knuckles the size of walnuts, and as hard as ball bearings. Numerous lesions and fractures on skulls, ribs, leg and arm bones show repeated exposure to blunt force trauma, as well as stab wounds. A Neanderthal skull is rarely found with all its teeth. Incidentally, the experts have found that much of this trauma occurs on the left side bones. "This is the side that would tend to be most easily injured if there were combat between right-handed opponents."[lxxxviii] These and other features of their bones speak volumes about their politics and how they lived.

As we suggested in Chapter Three, man evolved from a gracile line of hominids whose politics (or means of sorting out Alpha status) centered on ritualized verbal confrontations. Neanderthal's ancestors were of the robust sort whose heavy jaws and lack of speech anatomy precluded them from participating in the more parliamentarian style of politics. Since Neanderthals inherited these linguistic limitations, we may assume that their politics were not the same as those of the gracile types. Indeed, just as rams butt heads, to see "who's boss," we may infer that Neanderthal males relied on their "dukes" to determine Alpha status. The injuries on their bones show that they often used their "fists of iron" on one another, as well as using rocks, stone knives, and wooden spears. Trinkaus has recently commented that, "I've yet to see an adult Neanderthal skeleton that doesn't have at least one fracture, and in adults in their 30's, its common to see multiple healed fractures."[lxxxix]

Every athlete knows the joy of pushing his or her body to do what it seems designed to do best. Whether dancer, swimmer, or master of the martial arts, exercise pain is a welcome sign that one is developing one's full potential. The compensatory joy follows from the successful realization of the full potential in one's physical attributes. The evidence shows that Neanderthals were natural-born brawlers. Fisticuffs were their form of self-fulfillment. When the day's food gathering was done, and the common meal eaten, the men would sit together chipping stones until someone's grunt triggered a melee. The females and their young prudently occupied separate quarters for their own safety. After a fulfilling fight, the males who had proven their Alpha status would likely saunter over to the female area for a reward of horizontal refreshment before retiring for the evening. Because Neanderthals were guided by the hominid instinct for altruism, it seems unlikely that they would deliberately kill one of their own band members for a meal. More likely, being born to brawl, Neanderthals fought each other for Alpha status, and coincidentally ate the casualties.

The facts show that Neanderthals were the greatest hand-to-hand combatants that the species Hominidae has ever produced. All the human heavyweight boxers, wrestlers, and cage fighters who have ever shamelessly claimed "world status" are mere pretenders in the safety of Neanderthal's absence. No man, not Sampson, Goliath, Spartacus, John L. Sullivan, Gorgeous George, nor Muhammad Ali could have gone one round with this agile, athletic, iron-fisted brute.

Here, then, is the creature that caused humanity to change. The change was not physical or genetic, but rather the *culture* humans followed for over 100,000 years prior to their encounter with Neanderthal was transformed into its opposite by that experience. Let us now consider how meeting-up with that beast made us who we are today. Our aim will be to explain what happened to the culture of cultivated love. In our view, that culture did not undergo any lasting change until it was transformed in Europe by man's encounter with Neanderthal.

Man Meets Beast

The weather probably played a significant role in determining when the people living in the northern regions of Africa and the Middle East entered Europe. Ice age conditions began thawing around 40,000 years ago. Prior to that time people likely settled on the warmer side of the European borders. The migrations out of tropical Africa, east from Ethiopia through and beyond Yemen, may have begun long before entry into Europe was desirable or feasible.

Settlements ranging from Morocco, in the northwest of Africa, east along the Mediterranean Sea through the Levant, Lebanon, Syria, and into southern Turkey may have existed for thousands of years before warming weather tempted the wanderlust of man to enter Europe. These areas did not have the arid desert-like conditions of today. There were vast grasslands on which grazing animals lived, and forests full of nutritious plant life. The sea provided fish. Numerous small gathering communities could have lived well along this strip of land between Africa and Europe. Indeed, this region may be seen as humanity's staging area prior to meeting its European destiny. Unfortunately, for paleo-anthropology, much of this staging area became flooded as the ice age glaciers melted and the Mediterranean Sea grew to its current size.

Humanity's population growth curve is impossible to draw, because so little is known about the number of people who lived between 150,000 years ago and the time of the large scale entry into Europe by humans about 40,000 years ago. We can infer that man was doing well at this time. There were surely thousands of little communities throughout Africa. Human bones and artifacts found in southern Africa show that man was living there at least 100,000 years ago.[xc] As we will see, findings in the Levant suggest that humans may have been in the staging area outside of Europe also as much as 100,000 years ago. With such a widespread population, there could easily have been ten to twenty thousand people in that broad staging area. In addition, whatever direction any of these migrants went in, they carried the human birth defect with them. We may assume that they also took along the practice of cultivating love that we described in

Chapter Four. Indeed, humanity's reproductive and survival success may have begun to undermine the strength of that culture long before the encounter with Neanderthal finished it off.

The cultivation of love requires conditions that permit a sustained focus on right hemispheric processes. This is possible in a small, stable, and homogeneous community that feels secure in its routine methods for satisfying the necessities of life. But once such a group begins to move into unfamiliar territory, more attention to left hemispheric processes is required. Moving requires at least a minimal degree of evaluating the pro's and con's of the change, some planning, discussion, and the use of logic to make probability estimations (e.g., will there be sufficient water a day's walk ahead?).

Decision-makers must draw from practical knowledge and experience, and employ and develop their vocabulary. All of this draws attention from right hemispheric processes. When done in small increments, such distractions from cultivating love likely caused very little discomfort to most people. However, the more that people moved along, the more they experienced such distractions. Gradually, those who could tolerate less cultivated love likely migrated further than those who could not. Hence, by way of "cultural selection," as populations radiated out from the point of human origin, they developed greater propensities to engage in left hemispheric processes. These were the people who occupied the staging areas outside Europe.

Within that staging area, some travel, trade, and interbreeding surely occurred between communities. Items of trade likely included colored stone for tool making, sea shells for ornaments, sharp tipped stone spear heads, and other stone, bone, and wood implements, animal skins for toting and wearing, pitch from the pine forests to be used for keeping torches burning and as a topical ointment, as well as a variety of herbs and food products. These may have been carried on man-drawn stick sleds. Traders may also have developed the first form of counting at this time. Thus, trade and travel tended to further the development of left hemispheric abilities.

Richard Leakey recognized that early trade practices likely influenced the development of language.[xci] Travelers and traders needed to talk much more so than did stay-at-home folks, who stuck with nonverbal communication. Travelers have stories to tell, and their presence moves curious people to ask questions that the traveler is likely eager to answer. Trade, of course, entails bargaining, which is entirely a left hemispheric activity. Haggling would not have been conducted in complete sentences, for a sophisticated grammar had not yet been invented. Instead, animal forms of communication, such as gestures, grunts, and groans would have been mixed with words that had a commonly understood meaning. With these words, travelers and traders knitted the first tiny threads of a common language throughout the staging areas around Europe.

Even with all the activity, however, the over-all influence of trade and travel on that staging area culture would have been relatively small. The majority of people probably did not engage in travel, and the influence of trade was likely quite limited. As Marx observed in the 1850's, and Eric Fromm in the 1950's, bargaining can erode love. Perhaps man's fate would have been different if there had been a clear understanding of the consequences for feeling from trade. That desperate need to compensate for the awful effects of the defect in the human mind/brain relationship kept the attention of most people on right hemispheric processes. Those few individuals who engaged in trade likely felt less discomfort than the typical person does from the reduction in love that is a necessary element of business. But, as everyone knows, giant oaks grow from small seeds.

The Levant has been called the "gateway of prehistoric migration into Europe."[xcii] Caves in the Levant were untouched by the rising waters of the Mediterranean Sea during the warming period that began forty thousand years ago. While no one knows exactly when the first people came up into the Levant from central Africa, Shreeve cites authorities who estimate that it was about 100,000 years ago.[xciii] Trinkaus and Shipman suggest that humans occupied the Qafzeh cave in the Levant about 90,000 years ago, and the Skhul cave about 80,000 years ago.[xciv] Tattersall puts man in Qafzeh 92,000 years ago.[xcv] Shreeve points-out that the uncertainty is due to imprecise dating techniques which can only yield ballpark figures for this time frame.[xcvi]

Humans first encountered Neanderthals in the Levant. Here again, the exact times and places are not now known. Richard Leakey estimates that people were in the Levant before Neanderthals "by as much as 40,000 years."[xcvii] Other experts agree.[xcviii] Thus, it appears that some Neanderthals wandered into the Levant from the north about sixty thousand years ago. These creatures were somewhat less robust than the ones man would encounter in Europe.[xcix] Perhaps they were less aggressive as well. Richard Leakey suggests that over a period of several thousand years, small bands of Neanderthals migrated south when the weather got too cold in Europe, and either died-out in the Middle East, or moved back up north when the weather in the Levant became too warm.[c]

Human occupation of the Levant was not continuous. Humans seem to have dispersed during the periods of Neanderthal occupation. The experts agree that "Neanderthal and early modern fossils never occur in the same cave deposits."[ci] Little is known about the relationship between the two species. Louis Leakey, Richard's father, has speculated that if there was any interbreeding, the results were likely infertile hybrids, like when a horse and a donkey produce a mule.[cii] Bones that look semi-human have been found in the area, and may be such "mules." Analysis of Mitochondrial DNA show no signs of human-Neanderthal off-spring. We will discuss sexual relations with Neanderthals in Europe shortly.[ciii]

Apparently, contacts between the two species in the Levant were very limited. Man probably learned quickly to avoid Neanderthals. Although the two groups both lived by animal culture, and used stone technology, the evidence suggests that they rarely, if ever, mingled; hence, they "remained anatomically and genetically separate."[civ] While they appear to have lived in very similar cultures, they did so for very different reasons. Neanderthals were living by their species instinct, and lived in an animal culture by nature. Humans lived in an animal culture because they still defined themselves as hominids, and their culture was an expression of their self-definition. But that culture would soon change.

The Neanderthals were not the first hominids in Europe. As we have said, they probably evolved there from migrating Homo erectus hominids that may also have once occupied the Levant.[cv] Thus, the Neanderthals had many thousands of years to adapt, and to grow their population in Europe. More than a half dozen Neanderthal sites have been found in Spain, and another half dozen in Italy. A few have been found in Wales and England. Over fifty sites have been found from the west of France to as far east as Uzbekistan, largely concentrated in south central Europe.[cvi] Of course, there is no way to be sure how many individuals existed at any one time, but it is not unreasonable to speculate that around 40,000 years ago there could have been as many as 1,000,000 Neanderthals in Europe.

Human migration into Europe did not begin all at once, as with a starter firing his pistol. In Richard Leakey's opinion, some humans may have begun to enter into Europe around 50,000 years ago.[cvii] Shreeve suggests that a few people may have migrated across the border as much as 60,000 years ago.[cviii] At that time, as we said, northern glaciers had sucked up so much ocean water that land bridges connecting Europe and Africa existed in Spain, Italy, and Turkey.[cix] The fate of the early pioneers who crossed those bridges is unknown. They may have never seen a Neanderthal, because the wide area that Neanderthals occupied was sparsely populated. On the other hand, many of them might also have been Neanderthal dinner guests. Those first humans in Europe made no lasting settlements.

The first enduring influx of humans into Europe began as we have said, with the warming of the climate around 40,000 years ago. Many points of entry were used, but the route from the Levant, and points East through Turkey, was likely the heaviest traveled. People did not go into Europe by the busload; rather, small bands trickled-in, taking several generations to walk from the Levant into the Balkans, or into Spain and western France. Sites in both Bulgaria and Spain show human occupation "about 40,000 years ago."[cx] Leakey suggests that a substantial human presence was well entrenched in Europe by 35,000 years ago.[cxi] All the authorities agree that by 30,000 years ago, the Neanderthal species had become extinct.

Exactly how long man and Neanderthal knew of each other's presence in Europe is unknown. Both groups lived in small bands of 25 to 50 individuals. Much of the vast area of Europe at that time consisted of forests and tundra, which could sustain life without the need to roam far from home. So, the two species may have had little or no contact on any sizable scale for hundreds or even thousands of years. Richard Leakey suggests that man and Neanderthal may have knowingly coexisted in Europe only "for a millennium or two at most."[cxii] So, whether it was for a ten, five, or two thousand year period, we do know that a large-scale interface took place, and that something very intense happened. An entire species of gladiators disappeared, and also the culture of cultivated love was effectively erased from Earth.

A man-carried virus almost certainly did not exterminate the Neanderthals. They were far too hardy to have been lost to ill health. Also, had a virus afflicted them there surely would have been more survivors. Sickness rarely destroys an entire population. The majority of people survived the plague in Europe, and some people in Africa are even immune to HIV. There is no genetic over-lap of European Neanderthals and the descendents of the first humans in Europe. So, we did not absorb them through mating. More likely, Neanderthals succumbed to another cause. In our view, man wiped-out the Neanderthals in an organized massacre. This, of course, is not a new idea. Shreeve credits Marcellin Boule with having first proposed this notion in the late 1800's.[cxiii] What we add is the idea that the pogrom took place in three stages. Our hypothesis is that in the first stage, humans were the victims of Neanderthal crimes and abuses. In the second stage, rage drove the victims to organize both to stop the abuse and for revenge. In the third stage, man became the victimizer. In this process, modern culture was born. Let us consider the likely details.

As we have seen, humans managed their relationships with Neanderthals in the Levant by avoiding them. But this experience was surely forgotten by the people who entered deep into Europe several generations later. No sophisticated language yet existed to sustain a detailed memory of their recent history. So, those who were born in Europe felt that this was their home and had no idea that their ancestors had come from Africa. In addition, those who survived the treacherous trek through the forests and winters of Europe were among the most rugged humans our species had yet produced. Natural selection saw to that. Hence, these people may have been a little more inclined to fight over flight, than were their more cautious brothers in the Levant.

When humans and Neanderthals first met in Europe, they probably saw each other as being of the same kind. Both had hominid bodies. They likely saw, heard, and smelled one another at a distance long before meeting face to face. Some encounters may have been friendly. According to Tattersall, some Neanderthal sites contain stonework that was made by Neanderthals but in the human style.[cxiv] But in other meetings, people were not so lucky, and eventually, even the friendly encounters likely went sour. The two groups simply could not understand each other. In the human culture, one person would send signals of love to the other. But Neanderthals were contented by nature. They did not need human love. Gradually the repeated experience of unrequited love would surely have alerted people that Neanderthals were not of their kind. As a result, humans would have begun forming the conceptions of "them" and "us." To refer to such distinctions, man would have had to add new words to his vocabulary.

While humans soon learned to see Neanderthals as different, the reverse is not likely. Neanderthals, unlike people, lacked self-conceptions. They related to one another by social bonding, instinct, and perceptions of physical appearance. Just as other animals in the wild, Neanderthal individuals would have bonded with their band, but that would not stop them from having sexual relations with members of other bands. Indeed, such inter-band relations are essential to keep the breed's gene pool stable. Preserving the Neanderthal type depended upon them breeding outside their bands.

Thus, that sexual relations occurred between Neanderthals and humans is a near certainty. There were, no doubt, men who wooed Neanderthal females, and Neanderthal males who had sex with women, or girls (since twelve and thirteen year olds were ready for conception). Some of the human-like bones found in Europe may have been those of "mules." There were probably more Neanderthal males getting it on with human females, than there were men doing it with Neanderthal females. A quick consideration of the power relations between the couples would support this inference.

A 5'2" 130 pound Neanderthal female was just as strong as was the typical man of 5'10" and 160 pounds. He would have to woo her, because he risked his life if he tried to rape her. Even an amorous "love tap" might leave him with a broken jaw. So, Neanderthal females were more dangerous for a man to approach, than human females were for Neanderthal males to take. The fact that she was an animal, and he a human, may not of itself have been a deterrent for sexual adventurers. Man has a long history of bestiality, especially in the shepherd's fields.

The Neanderthal male, however, could have just about any girl he fancied. Suppose a Neanderthal male entered a small human encampment. Those who first saw him might send him their love. His lack of response would confuse, and perhaps frighten, them. Following his natural instincts, he might sidle up to a little "cutie," and throw his arms about her. Unless she was pleased with the beast, she would likely scream for help. If the Alpha male was close by, he would surely be determined to put a stop to this by shouting down the offender. This intruder had not properly established his political status; so, the angry man would bravely march right up to that Neanderthal. But the last sound the brave man would ever hear would be that of crunching noises in his jaw, skull, and neck. A fast right hook would have felled him before he got out his second "boogally!" The Neanderthal could wrap his left arm around the girl's waist, and carry her away, perhaps breaking the jaws of a couple of other would-be rescuers along the way. Once he had ravished her in the bushes, he would likely have let her run back to her people, blood and semen dripping down her legs.

Trinkaus and other experts on Neanderthal anatomy have expressed surprise at how broad the pelvis of that creature is. Commenting on the size of the female Neanderthal's birth canal, Trinkaus has remarked that it could have accommodated a twelve-month gestation period.[cxv] In other words, at the time of birth, a nine-month-old Neanderthal fetus was likely the size of a three-month-old human infant. Thus, if a Neanderthal female delivered a man's baby it would have been an easy birth. But for a woman, or a girl, to be impregnated by a Neanderthal would have been the "kiss of death." At six months, a Neanderthal fetus could have been the size of a full term human fetus. For a mother who did not miscarry well before her third trimester, disaster lay ahead. In some instances, her skin might begin to stretch beyond its ability to hold together. If it did not split and bleed in places, it would surely have been extremely sore. By the end of the seventh month, the fetus might already be too big to pass through her birth canal. A girl, who did not die of infections, or other complications, would have suffered a slow, horrible, agonizing death as her birth contractions erupted into hemorrhaging, and her heart stopped, or she bled to death, the Neanderthal fetus kicking in her womb.

The culture of cultivated love had no way to deal with this experience. Against Neanderthal, it was as useless as a limp penis on a Saturday night. Humans had had a long experience with predators. Lions or hyenas occasionally took someone who strayed too far from the campfire, or who got caught alone while gathering food. Their death was painful, but mercifully quick. Everyone mourned the loss, and gave each other love. But campfires were no deterrent to Neanderthals. They had fire, too. What's worse, Neanderthal incursions surely increased every year, thus increasing the needs of the bereaved for comforting love. This can be inferred from their nature.

As we have seen, Neanderthal politics were based on slugfests. The guys duked it out, and those left standing won the Alpha status. Of course, there were many more losers than winners in this system. Loser Neanderthals were probably the ones whose behavior ruined the culture of cultivated love. At first, the losers would have learned by chance that they could be "top dog" in any human encampment. To them, a human was a hominid. And, to be an Alpha hominid was the thrill of a lifetime for every loser. A loser Neanderthal could enter a human group, prove his superiority in a fulfilling fight with a half dozen men, and grab any girl at hand to help him celebrate his new honors. He had no malicious intent, he did not want to be a demon, he was just following his bliss. After finishing with the woman, the loser would wander back to his band. His brothers would notice his elation, and soon learn the reason why, as they followed him on his next venture in search of a human group.

Forest rangers know that bears around national parks can become addicted to human food. The officers will give an intruder one or two chances to redeem himself by carting the offender off to the other side of the mountain. But bears that have the taste in mind of a ham sandwich, dripping with mustard and mayonnaise, have an uncanny ability to find their way back. Such recidivists must, reluctantly, be shot. Similar patterns of animal behavior occurred in Europe early in the interface period with which we are concerned. Loser Neanderthals became addicted to the sweetness of dominating human communities.

The Birth of Speech

Humans did not rise above the level of animal forms of communication, prior to their encounter with Neanderthal, for many reasons. One is that man's animal parents had no sophisticated speech to teach him. As we have seen, the first generation of humans learned to live by animal culture, and that includes animal forms of communication. Oral communication had been used by hominids, and is used by other animals, for a myriad of reasons, such as to instruct the young, to convey information, to entertain, express emotions, and so forth. Even Fido has a bark to express joy, or the desire for attention, and a whimper to express submission, and a growl that warns not to come any closer. The hominid form of oral communication was as well adapted to its needs as Fido's "speech" is to his. Thus, the human descendants of hominids did not see, or did not agree upon, the need to make the effort to fashion a sophisticated language, so long as their expectations of life were being fulfilled by the ways of animal culture. Those expectations had matched perfectly with the realities of animal life in the jungles and forests of Africa, so humans felt, as we saw in earlier chapters, satisfied with their material lot. Hardships were accepted, and love was given as the best balm for any pain. But this mind set was unable to adapt to conditions that contained Neanderthals.

We find support for our hypothesis that sophisticated language first emerged in the course of the genocide of Neanderthal in the writings of Aristotle, the great philosopher of Ancient Greece. In our view, the elements of public speech that he analyzed have an intentional trajectory that runs back to their point of origin in the genocide. Aristotle writes, in the *Rhetoric,*[cxvi] that there are "three kinds of speeches." These are 1) deliberative, 2) forensic, and 3) epideictic. The first concerns exhortation or dissuasion. The second, accusation or defense. The third, praise or blame. Let us consider how these kinds of speech relate back to the time when sophisticated speech emerged out of the confines of animal culture and into the beginnings of human culture.

Hominids, no doubt, had words for each of the types of predators that might prowl about their campsites. For example, "leopard in tree," or "lion in grass." The hominid form of oral communication was a part of the package of animal culture, which people had originally learned from their parents. But as they encountered Neanderthal, they had to add new words to their vocabulary, and invent new rules of usage. Neanderthal's appearance and behavior were so different from that of other predators that they required additional discussion. Humans, for example, who had seen a Neanderthal could not convey a detailed description of the creature nonverbally to those who had not seen one. Nonverbally, one can understand that another person is in shock, or has been horrified, or deeply hurt, but the reasons and causes of such feelings can only be conveyed verbally.

Within the frontline communities, speech and social relations were changing together. The initial human response to Neanderthal's rapacity was to comfort the survivors with love. Unfortunately, however, the supply of such love rapidly diminished as demand for it increased with the rising number of Neanderthals that followed their bliss to human communities. Hence, the common fear of Neanderthal, and the growing rage at his abuses, was the fertile soil in which human speech grew. At first, terrified women would have turned to their men with nonverbal pleas for protection. But as more girls were raped, and nine months later died slow, painful deaths before their helpless brothers and sisters, women found words to cajole and exhort men to take action. Because they lack the strength of men, women had no choice but to rely on the power of language to save their lives and the lives of their children. One cultural remnant of these events is that, following ancient social pressures, modern girls progress earlier in the learning of language than do boys.

Many generations of such hard experience were required before one man could say to a group of others, "we must do something about this menace!" The best minds of the time strained to formulate plans of action in words. Fear and prudence forced a thorough deliberation over alternative proposals and their likely consequences. Humans have longer legs than hominids, including Neanderthals. The human ability for distance running also helped establish man's first sophisticated language. Runners carried words great distances, and helped to preserve their uniformity. Thus these discussions could include wise persons, with similar problems, yet who lived far apart.

At the same time, travelers and traders made reports to groups of people who had never seen a Neanderthal. The speaker's passion compelled the interested listeners to learn his language. His emotions carried the message that their own lives were at stake. So, the need for survival justified the intellectual discipline and sustained effort required to comprehend the threats that the words conveyed. Threats to life can create a feeling that learning is a matter of great urgency. Spanish only became the national language of Mexico, for example, because the conquistadors threatened to kill those who spoke their native tongue, and the padres warned them that their souls would be condemned to eternal damnation. Fear for their lives on Earth, and for the happiness of their spirits in the after live, plus a prudent desire for peaceful relations with the invaders, persuaded a people of at least one hundred different languages, and many more dialects, to acquire new skills. Within two centuries they learned to speak Spanish as well as any Spaniard. Having the same intelligence and linguistic ability as the native Mexicans, European man likely formed the first sophisticated language in a similar span of time.

Forensic speech was central to this emerging language. This is the speech of accusation and condemnation. Names were needed for the crimes of Neanderthal. Principles of right and wrong became a focus of discussion. A vocabulary of criminal justice was fashioned as the notions of rights, violations, and of retaliation, revenge, and retribution took shape for the first time on Earth. Such notions were new to people who had practiced acceptance and love for over 100,000 years. Whereas people had once accepted predation as a fact of life, they now began to think of Neanderthal's actions as unnecessary, intolerable, and unacceptable. Once acceptance gave way to such judgments, the path was opened to the uniquely human presumptuous Knowledge of Right and Wrong. Because love makes no such judgments, but simply extends itself, humanity had never before engaged in declaring on the rights and wrongs of deeds.   Such pronouncements are entirely a left hemispheric endeavor.   Humans shied away from postulating moral principles because it drew them out of love. But now, the feelings of fear, frustration, and rage, plus the failure of cultivated love to ease their mounting sufferings, drove attention to these more cognitive processes. Along with the new nouns and verbs needed to convey moral condemnation, came a syntax for ordering them. Discipline was required to enforce adherence to the rules of usage. Children had to be taught the difference between the statements "Neanderthal is bad for raping Mary," and "Mary is bad for raping Neanderthal," or "Neanderthal is a beast for eating John," and "John is a beast for eating Neanderthal."

The discovery of the power and the vocabulary to morally condemn Neanderthal brought with it the capacity for an associated kind of speech. Men who fought and slayed Neanderthals received public praise, while those who ran were excoriated for their cowardice. Those with a warrior's courage leapt to the forefront of social status, as those who once were honored for sending love lost their usefulness. The image of the most praise-worthy man as "hero," or "dragon slayer" emerged to take a place in world culture that it has never given up. Alpha status, social privilege, and sexual favors became the rewards for killing Neanderthals.

In Chapter Three we noted that, according to Richard Leakey, a sense of "fair play" and a need for rules evolved in hominid genes, out of the gathering way of life, and shaped the hominid instinct for some minimal degree of altruism and cooperation. This was the precursor of the human sense of *distributive* justice; that is, the way goods and services are shared. De Waal has observed a similar sense of justice in some primates.

But only humans have a sense of *retributive* justice. For example, a televised film taken by a crew of naturalists showed a scene in the wild in which a female chimp was apparently jealous of another's new born infant. Suddenly the jealous chimp, which may have been superior in status, grabbed the infant from the mother's arms and smashed it to the ground, killing the baby. The horrified mother screamed in protest, but did not attack the killer. The mother picked up the tiny corpse and mourned her loss. But within a few days, murderer and mother were filmed grooming one another in a tender way, as if nothing had ever come between them. Also, the observation has often been made that a male lion will take over a pride after defeating the old male in a fight, or where the pride is found without a male. Over the protests of the mother, he may kill her cubs. But not long thereafter, she submits to his desire to mate with her.

In human culture a woman would be considered insane for restoring her friendship with a person who had murdered her infant only a few days before. The same judgment would almost universally be applied to a woman who made love with the man who had shortly before murdered her children. A woman in those circumstances would be expected to feel outage and the desire for retribution against such a man. Yet, natural selection requires that animals have no desire for revenge. That is one reason why there are no animals that organize against their common enemy. If wildebeests had a sense of justice, they would organize a war of genocide against lions. These prey often outnumber their predators by as much as 2000 to one. If ants had a sense of justice, we humans would be in serious trouble. They outnumber us by more than a million to one.

The human sense of retributive justice was not bred slowly into the structure of our brains, but stems from the *idea* of intolerable behavior and the desire for revenge. Revenge, as a uniquely human expression of anger, frustration, and the desire to teach a wrong-doer a lesson, emerged as the practice of cultivated love failed to perform well in humanity's changing conditions. Unlike distributive justice, which has roots deep in nature as an expression of the desire to share, the sense of retributive justice is purely a human artifice, and is an expression of murderous rage. Man first developed his idea of justice as "getting even" in the course of his experience with Neanderthal.

Terror and rage, then, forced the simultaneous development of language and the idea of vengeful justice as the key elements of an emerging human culture. But for our encounter with Neanderthal, this may not have happened. Aristotle's *Rhetoric* shows that the most salient function of speech is to stimulate a sense of retributive justice, and to stir-up a response to injustice. Sophisticated language developed in the service of that function some thirty-five thousand years ago. The notion of retribution-as-justice has been refined and reshaped by various cultures since then, but here is where it was conceived.

Animals that hunt use oral communication as an instrument in their trade. To be sure, the amount of such "speech" is minimal. Lions, wolves, hyenas, and other cooperative hunters use growls, hisses, calls, and barks both to teach their young their hunting play book, and to adjust plans in the heat of the chase. Because up to the time of the genocide humans were not, in fact, the great hunters that popularizers have made them out to be, they had no idea that speech could be used as a weapon. The development of sophisticated speech was a slow go before its application to stopping Neanderthal abuses was discovered.

On those increasing occasions when a loser Neanderthal appeared in a human encampment, his mere presence would cause shock waves of terror. We can imagine what happened. The screams of women, the shouts of men. Brave men who approached the beast with their fiercest yells and hollers only stimulated the joy it felt at the prospect of a good old-fashioned fight. Unlike humans, Neanderthal gladiators could easily overcome their natural fear of death, because fighting was their means of fulfilling life.

Obviously, the natural contentment of predators, whether lions or Neanderthals, does not compel them towards peaceful, non-violent behavior. All predators have contentment, or inner peace, but they must also be themselves; that is, they must prey upon the innocent creatures they eat. They must also fight to protect their territories, and to protect their young. The violent urges that disturb contentment, and drive predatory behavior, come from different brain modules than does contentment. But once these urges are acted upon, and satisfied, they recede, and contentment is restored.

Eventually, as human speaking skills increased, they would have seen that Neanderthals lacked the power of speech. Thereafter, a new pattern emerged in the man-Neanderthal relationship. Rather than screams as an expression of panic, a woman would scream an alarm, "its here!" Rather than holler at the beast, an Alpha male would begin to yell commands: "Joe, when I give the signal you dive for his right leg. Pete, you dive for his left leg. I'll run into him and knock him down. Juan, you pick-up that big rock behind the beast and smash its head with it. You women bring the spears from inside the cave!"

The Neanderthal would not have understood any of this. He would have seen the fear he struck in the humans.

This may have led him to smile confidently, showing that half his teeth were missing. The communication here would be like trying to explain to the family dog where you plan to go on your next vacation. Just as Fido would stand there wagging his tail, so Neanderthal stood grinning.

Then the leader gave the command – "ready, go!" Suddenly three brave men were upon the creature and brought it down, while a fourth man pounded on its head with a heavy stone. Women rushed up with spears, and more men came with knives. There may have been eight to ten people punching, kicking, choking, pounding, and stabbing the struggling creature. In the first two or three seconds, the beast fatally wounded the leader by breaking his back with a bear hug. But in the next few seconds, the animal was made to bleed profusely from several spots. It was blinded from the blood, sweat, and the dirt that women were throwing in its eyes. Its consciousness was fading fast from the blows to the head, and the loss of blood. The humans kept at the fight with a furious pace. In three or four intense minutes, which seemed to the fighters like hours, the monster was dead.

My God! What emotions they felt! Every bit of energy they had was spent. Their nervous systems caused them to quiver with the overload of adrenaline. Triumph exploded into consciousness. First there was disbelief, then jubilation. They had defeated the dreaded beast! No one said it at the time, but they all knew that speech was their secret weapon. Nonverbal communication could not express their feelings, they had to jump and shout with joy!

Now runners, traders, and travelers had something new to talk about. More words would be needed to tell the story of that winning strategy, which centered on speech as its decisive weapon. Storytellers rose in status, as they enabled listeners to participate vicariously in the thrill of victory. Language enabled men to agree upon a common strategy for dealing with their common Neanderthal "menace." With language, they could organize war parties consisting of fighters from far away bands. Fast running messengers could convey plans for strikes at specific times and places. Sprinters enabled men to scout ahead, and to quickly adjust tactics in changing circumstances.

While men would, on occasion, have had to directly confront and fight these great gladiators, that would not likely have been their first choice of tactics. Their preferred method of attack would more likely have been to slaughter females and their young as they were caught out gathering, and away from the more dangerous males. Unless men held something like an eight to one advantage, heroic confrontations with male Neanderthals most likely occurred as individual animals intruded in campsites, rather than out in the open. Where there were no women and children who needed protection from Neanderthal males, men were more likely to run from the beasts than to engage them in battle. Man's surest and safest long-term strategy was to attack the reproduction capacity of Neanderthals. That was their Achilles' Heel.

Once humanity began fighting back, rather than simply comforting victims, they soon learned that killing Neanderthals did not trigger retaliation. Men quickly learned that Neanderthals had more in common with wildebeests than with themselves. That is, while humans shared a desire for revenge, Neanderthals, being animals, had no sense of retributive justice. From the Neanderthal point of view, it was "nature's way" if a band of human warriors descended upon a group of gatherers, and slaughtered them. In the early stages, the males were more likely to gorge themselves on the meat of the dead than to organize for revenge.

The musk ox, which forms a circle for defense, never organizes to either seek revenge, or to eliminate the wolf menace "once for all." Likewise, North American bison once out numbered white target shooters by 10,000 to one. If the animals had had the capacity for abstract thinking necessary to perceive a common threat, and to organize for their defense against it, the settlers would have built their railroads in other places. But natural selection cannot allow such thinking, or else the natural world would self-destruct. The natural Buddha-nature of animals is the key to maintaining the balance between prey and predator. Just as it restores calm to prey after a herd has been struck, so once the predator has killed, its contentment keeps it from killing more than it needs. Humans, however, lack natural contentment. Once they experienced the intense pleasure of killing for revenge, there is no natural mechanism to curb their quest for the thrill.

The Rise of Power-Pleasure

At first, it may seem that man began killing Neanderthals to satisfy the noble aims of "justice." Aristotle has written that justice is "the equality of proportions." If so, then at some point in the process humans would have killed as many of them as they had killed of us; and, at that point, justice should have been satisfied, and the killing stopped. But that is not what happened. Retributive justice was then, as it is now, a thin veil used to cover the real motives of self-alienated men. Love was failing to adequately temper the torment of living with a constricted Schucman Corridor. A new type of fix was needed, and fast. Man found his fix in murder. People probably used "justice talk" to help them in the transition from giving love to taking revenge, but by the time any "equality of proportions" had been reached in the numbers of victims, humanity did not need any such shibboleths as "an eye for an eye" to excuse killing.

Social rituals are generally meant to be a means of evoking and expressing specific feelings. For example, funeral rituals are generally intended to evoke and express grief and mourning. Church services are generally used to evoke and express religious sentiments such as reverence. The use of ritual to evoke and express martial feelings began in the time of the genocide. Preparations for war invite everyone to participate in the thrill of the kill. Ritual also extends the pleasure by enabling people to savor anticipation. In martial rituals, society spotlights the young heroes who will go off to fight. Good feelings, which are ultimately animated by blood lust, are to be had by all. Old ladies and old men, the infirm or ill, those who are too young to fight, and the highly fertile females (about whom the men at war will often dream), can give themselves a strong shot of their power-pleasure brain chemicals as Johnny marches off to war. And so it was, in the course of the genocide, that martial rituals were created for everyone's enjoyment. These highly intense feelings drove out the practice of cultivating love.

Once humans had learned the appropriate techniques for killing Neanderthals, a systematic approach to the slaughter could be organized. Perhaps forays were synchronized with lunar cycles. Harvard anthropologist, Alexander Marshack, has identified what may be evidence of man's method for carrying-out the pogrom. After studying a 35,000-year-old piece of carved antler, with 69 marks cut in it, he has determined that it is a type of calendar depicting the stages of the moon.[cxvii] This palm sized tablet, and others like it, may have been carried by runners from camp to camp to organize regular strikes on Neanderthals.

We may reasonably surmise that a new custom gradually developed throughout Europe to manage the progress of the genocide, and to maximize man's pleasure in it. Perhaps on a quarterly bases, bands and tribes all over the land would have festivals and feasts culminating in a grand Neanderthal hunt. If there were once a million of these magnificent combatants, and the ritual resulted in the slaughter of a couple thousand each year, the whole lot of them would have been finished within about 500 years. Of course, some years may have been more productive than others. The stresses of surprise attacks and of suffering frequent losses of fellow band members likely drove Neanderthals into distant places and remote mountain hideaways. There, where food is much harder to find than in the forests, few would have survived.

But the disappearance of Neanderthals was no deterrence to the killing rituals. Indeed, all the evidence suggests that these rituals flourished over the next 20,000 years. Europe was also the home to a variety of other huge, powerful mammals. The famous cave bear was larger than a modern grizzly. Neanderthals competed with these bears for cave space, but rarely killed and ate them.[cxviii] Ritualized killing of these creatures was, however, carried on by man. "One Austrian cave held the remains of 30,000 bears."[cxix] "Probably the biggest cat that ever lived – at least 25 percent larger than today's African lion – [was] the cave lion."[cxx] It, too, was once common in Europe. The giant European hyena was once "one of the most numerous mammals of the ice age."[cxxi] The wooly rhinoceros, with a three-foot long front horn, once grazed contentedly all across Europe. "The hefty 12-foot long aurochs was the ancestor of all domestic cattle."[cxxii] Although men intensively hunted it too, the species survived long enough to be selectively bred and domesticated by humans who practiced agriculture. The great European bison once grazed in huge herds, but that species, like most of the others in this bloody list, had "disappeared from Europe [by] 10,000 years ago."[cxxiii] The enormous wooly mammoth once roamed freely over Europe, Siberia, Asia, and North America. Descendants of the Clovis People killed the last one about 10,000 years ago. The great Irish elk, with 14-foot wide antlers, also found its match in man, as did the giant ground sloth, and other extinct species.

The killing rituals might have gone on until there were only ants left to step on, but the growth of the human population, and the development of agriculture and then of urban living, a little less than 10,000 years ago, forced man to modify his power-pleasure mind set. The deep fulfillment that man found in acting out his murderous rage had to be achieved through other means, so that a settled civilization could be cultivated. While early European art depicted symbols of power and fertility, the invention of "higher powers" was not necessary until Ruling Elites needed to control human behavior outside of their visual field. Religion was used to subdue and re-channel the blood lust of men with the threat of attack from invisible, blood-lusting gods. Animal, and sometimes human, sacrifices to their gods allowed settled people to continue to participate in the pleasure of blood-letting, albeit vicariously. The need to regulate wars against each other also helped people to keep their murderous rage under control during peaceful interludes. Spectator sports are a spin-off of the old killing rituals.

Religion devised another clever means to assist the growth of mass society. It taught people to stimulate the power-pleasure centers of their brains by using their imaginations. The invention of "sin," and the idea of "evil," empowers people to mentally cast "killer judgments" at one another. In this way, we can each experience, to a small degree, the same thrill of the kill that European man discovered so long ago. We will discuss this process further in the next chapter; but, first, let us summarize briefly what we see as the key messages of this chapter.

Using introspection, the spoor of the right hemispheric memory can be read, like lines in the desert sand can show which way the wind last blew. These tracks record a sudden increase in the movement of attention from right hemispheric processes to those of the left. Those songs and stories about the loss of love, as we have said, have their poignancy precisely because they are reminiscent of the nonverbally transmitted ancestral memory held in the mind/brain relationship of every human. Each person has at least a faint whisper of awareness of these acquired memory connections in his or her neocortex that tell this tale. Empathic science has learned from those who are the most sensitive to the subtleties of right hemispheric memory to carefully connect the facts of paleo- anthropology to these feelings. Through intersubjective agreement, humanity can now know, *as a matter of science*, that the human mind/brain relationship underwent a revolutionary shift during the period of the genocide of Neanderthal and the other great creatures mentioned.

Conclusion: The Legacies of Genocide

Man first greeted Neanderthals with nonverbal messages of love. But they did not need our love. Early on, the ones that man saw the most of were the loser Neanderthals. Each of them only needed humans to fulfill its natural desire to reign as an Alpha male over a hominid band. Those hardy humans who had known no other home than Europe chose to stand their ground and fight. They could have done otherwise. Humans in the Levant, for example, gave up their space, and kept their inner peace, as Neanderthals came along. In this way, the two species shared the Middle East for thousands upon thousands of years, until the transformed Europeans came south to hunt down the last Neanderthals.

Humans in Europe underwent a mass conversion experience during the time of the genocide. The numerous legacies of that experience, which even now shape world culture and politics, are further evidence of the genocide's occurrence. These legacies include organized warfare, and the development of sophisticated speech. Also, a Great Shift took place from cultivating and communicating love with the natural capacities of the right brain, to using the more cognitive processes of the left. Each side of the brain has the capacity to produce a balm for the suffering that humans are subjected to by their species birth defect. In the absence of taking the necessary intentional act to attain the consciousness of consciousness, people must have some sort of balm for their pain and confusion, or life would be intolerable.

This shift of attention from right to left entailed a new practice of looking outwardly rather than inwardly for relief. Whereas humans living in primitive communism attended inwardly to the comforting feelings of cultivated love, the more intense thrill of the kill compelled them to look outwardly for more victims to sacrifice. In the course of the genocide, man discovered that by stimulating the power-pleasure centers in his brain, he could distract attention from his emptiness and despair with jolts of joy generated by fulfilling what Nietzsche rightly called "the will to power" (itself a legacy of the genocide). Many millennia later, this outward looking for the power-pleasure of conquest would spur the Age of Exploration, imperialism, and, on a more civilized level, even natural science. Indeed, behavioralism's outward looking quest for objectivity, and fear of the subjective, are themselves a legacy of the genocide.

Nietzsche understood as clearly as anyone ever has that language is among man's primary sources of power-pleasure. The power to name things, he writes, is the power to assert dominion over the whole world. Language, of course, was man's secret weapon over Neanderthal and the other mute giants. Man, then, learned in the genocide to define himself by this source of power. The genocide ushered in the Age of the Articulate. Thereafter, humans have defined themselves as special in nature because they can speak. To be "of those who speak" became a badge of honor. As speaking people moved out over the world, those who still cultivated love never stood a chance.

Everyone who participates in world culture today does so as "a speaker." But the arrogance of the articulate has at least one comic failing, which exposes the weak foundation of its edifice. Unlike the ancient mind, which once dwelt in the quiet feelings of cultivated love, the modern mind streams chatter. This chatter serves as a reminder to oneself that "I am one of the powerful ones." Through chatter, one uses left hemispheric processes to constantly stimulate the power-pleasure centers of one's brain. Chatter usually lacks focus and sense, but that is not important because its function is to sooth anxiety, like thumb sucking. Chatter is the ultimate proof that humanity is helplessly addicted to substitutes for oneness. For now, it is our burden of Bad Karma. But, let us not encroach further on Chapter Six.

Chapter Six

The Errant Legacy of the Genocide, and Its Correction

Introduction

In Chapter Three and Four we saw that humanity had lived for over 100,000 years in a right brain culture. All the intelligence and ingenuity of which human genius is capable poured into the cultivation of right hemispheric potentials. Life then was richer in loving feelings than any living person now could possibly imagine.

In the culture of cultivated love, humanity had reached the highest degree of community feeling that man has ever known. But this achievement came at a high material cost. The level of material "luxury" then, for humans living in the plains of Africa, was equal to that of primates in the jungle today. In the rain, humans got soaked. In the cold, they froze. In the heat, they sweltered. Living in caves was not much of an improvement. Hungry predators prowled outside of cave entrances, and along the borders of human encampments. Girls likely began bearing children at thirteen, whether they wanted to or not. Poor nutrition weakened their immune systems. "Old age" came at thirty.

Times have changed since the genocide. Now women can control the time for reproduction, and many choose to bear children after age thirty. "Old age" has been pushed up to the mid-seventies, and climbing. The list of material conveniences is endless, and too tedious to mention. But in the midst of this wealth, health, and longevity, people ache for some feeling of community. Modern man pines for love. Human creativity has been applied to the invention of distractions, entertainment, and self-deadening practices, all to divert attention from any deep feeling.

Through all these changes, the first philosophy of life, which was formed in the African savannas, has continued to define the human condition. The first philosophy of life is an instance of human culture defining itself as animal culture. Since people tend to act so as to fulfill their self-definitions, they have lived as animals do for as long as they have believed in that philosophy, or understanding. Of course, this includes our times. As we have seen, humanity accepted the first philosophy of life as a true reflection of its condition, and for over 100,000 years cultivated love to make the condition of living as prey animals, without natural contentment, tolerable.

Today, the assumption of life as a prey-predator situation in which people are only valued for their usefulness continues; but beginning with the genocide the position of man in that vision has been reversed, from prey to predator. This Great Shift has brought with it other reversals of mental orientation, and a refocusing of human attention. Humanity has disregarded the development of right hemispheric capacities in favor of those on the left. A trend was begun to look outward, with an eye for conquest, and to look away from the inward aim of cultivating love as a balm. Rage at Neanderthal forced the development of long dormant left hemispheric capacities. Speech was the secret weapon scrawny and scraggly humans used to defeat the powerful brutes that preyed upon them. Between 30,000 and 35,000 years ago, man converted from defining himself as prey to defining himself as predator in the jungle of life. We discussed in Chapter Five how speech became associated with the stimulation of power-pleasure centers in the brain. Power-pleasure became humanity's new balm for the pain of living with a constricted Schucman Corridor.

During the time of the genocide, then, human attention took its first leap to the left. But, of course, the habit of attending to right hemispheric processes was not completely lost all at once; rather, a momentum was begun. Following the Paleolithic Revolution in art and technology, there were lesser leaps and long moments of stasis in human cultural development. Still, the trend, begun then, continues today. The rise of word stock, the growth of rational learning, the spread of material wealth, go along with the proportional decline in community, love, oneness with nature, and awareness of nonverbal communication. These patterns flow from the time of the genocide, just as the universe continues to expand from the moment of its "Big Bang."

Emphatic science appreciates the development of left hemispheric capacities; indeed, it would not exist if human attention had not turned to the left. But we see as our mission, finding some way to slow the momentum of loss and begin to recover some of the inward wealth humanity once had. To this end, we believe that *scientific rationality may be used to restore feeling.* If so, then we are at the beginning of a New Age, which will witness a synthesizing of the wisdom of both right and left hemispheres for dealing with an unrelenting problem. In this chapter we will present our adaptation of a program for healing first presented by Dr. Helen Schucman. The reader will see how ancient wisdom has been combined with modern rationality to produce a program which can, if followed, increase the individual's feeling of oneness within, oneness with others, and of oneness with the surrounding world, or nature.

To begin with, one might ask why one should make the effort to work this program. Like the Zen Master we referred to earlier, we could quip facilely "is it important to put out a fire on the top of your head?" But to remain true to science requires a more elaborate explanation of why this effort is needed.

Healing the human birth defect is a biological imperative. The imperative to heal has been shaped by natural selection. It comes from the impulse towards health of every normal organism. This is not a whimsical matter of selecting from a menu of options, like one's choice to believe in The One True God, or in many gods, or in no god at all. The organism in ill-health longs to heal, and cannot do otherwise. Thus, every self-conscious human organism whose mind/brain relation is out of alignment longs for alignment. This longing is experienced by the individual as a form of acute discomfort. Most people respond to this painful sensation, not by removing its root cause, but either by distracting their attention from it, or by deadening their sensitivity to it; hence, the popularity of entertainment, drugs, etc.

Despite man's freedom for creativity, human biology determines some of humanity's basic values. Among these, as we have seen, is the natural order of values. The maxim often cited by evolutionists that "biology is destiny" finds substantiation in the human value system. Humanity's hereditary defect establishes the want of happiness as one of man's defining values. Of course, humans can, and more often than not do, live without healing. But healing is always within the realm of individual choice. As actors in the Globe Theater of Life, each of us may declare: "to heal, or not to heal? That is the question." Most choose the latter, and choose to suppress their pain.

But for those who choose the former, a second question arises as to *how to heal*. Approaches to this challenge have been proposed and bungled by religion for centuries. Here we will show how science can take its turn.[cxxiv]

How to Heal

Healing rests almost entirely upon one's willingness to heal. As Schucman often states, a little willingness is all one needs to heal. Yet, static, or noise, in the signal from one's conscious declarations of this willingness to the receiving centers in the brain prevents healing from occurring. Our program, then, consists of a set of exercises to build up that signal of willingness. We predict, as a testable hypothesis, that following this program faithfully can result in opening up one's contentment module.

However, as any healing science must, we add one precautionary note. The soft conditional "can result in" is used for several reasons. Working our program *can result in* opening the Schucman Corridor for the individual who works this program well. However, we are at the beginning of our mission. There may be unforeseen kinks. Some contentment modules may have atrophied to a point beyond redemption. As with Alzheimer's disease, plaque and decayed neuro-pathways may prevent the full use of the brain in some, perhaps older, people. Also, some humans may have inherited a genetic resistance to initiating the operation of their Schucman Corridor. These matters require further scientific research. We must also face the hard fact that there are no guarantees in life. Experience with medicine, for example, shows that nearly all remedies for illnesses have at least some failures in a wide spread application. These failures must be examined, and their causes determined. But emphatic science takes the position that this program, if applied diligently, can achieve an eventual cure rate on a par with the best of medicines.

The main obstacle to healing will generally be a fear-driven resistance to doing what needs to be done to heal. Empathic science understands how fear can complicate our lives. We suggest these exercises as ways to reduce fear and increase self-confidence enough for a person to let go of the self-created self, and release the restrictions on opening the Schucman Corridor.

Willingness, plus working the program, is a way to wear-down resistance to healing. People will vary in the amount of resistance they experience. Some need only know that such practices exist, and they will instantly begin to integrate them into their daily lives. Others, at first, may feel awkward, or find working the program artificial, inauthentic, and even downright foolish. Those with a tendency to intellectualize their resistance may draw upon Nietzsche's brilliant life-long railing against Nirvana, especially in his *Beyond Good and Evil*, and "The Genealogy of Morals." Indeed, Schucman's book, *A Course In Miracles*, can be read as a sisterly reply to Nietzsche, whose psychology is characterized there by the term "ego."[cxxv]

As we stated in Chapter Two, to initiate the operation of the Schucman Corridor, one must form the right intention. The right intention is the ultimate test of willingness. When considered as an expression of willingness, the three key elements of the right intention are: 1st) an unreserved acknowledgement that one lacks contentment; 2d) an unconditional desire for contentment;

and, 3d) an unrestricted willingness to let the natural healing processes of the brain function without any conscious effort to control the outcome; i.e., surrender. Authentic willingness and the right intention are two sides of the same coin. Let us then consider further the question "what is willingness?"

"Willingness" might best be understood in contrast to its nemesis – "willfulness." Indeed, willfulness is a mercurial and wily opponent of willingness. One obvious form of willfulness is when one demands of oneself that one "be happy, now!" This approach is unlikely to succeed. The problem is that command is a form of control, and control, in this context, is a form of fearful clinging. With every command issued, the self-created self also clings to its image of itself as a "great power." Command, then, is a sticky substance that can never result in release. The consciousness of consciousness is more likely to be attained by the surrender of control to one's subconscious healing processes than to any form of command issued from one's consciousness. Commanding oneself to "attain Nirvana," then, entails the *unwillingness* to let go of the self-created self. Such a command is issued from the very self which must be released. But one can no more achieve what one wants without doing what is required for success, than one can have one's cake and eat it too.

There is a subtler form of controlling behavior, which is far more difficult to recognize, and therefore remedy. This occurs when one compels oneself to behave as the "happy person" whom one wishes to become. Here, one is hoping that faking it will somehow turn into authentic happiness. But this is unlikely to happen. In effect, one is asserting that "I want my self-created self to act happy, without my letting go of it." This is the same old "cake" dilemma. That is just not how it works. There is an important difference between imitating a "happy me," and having "happiness." In the first case, one is actually hoping for a new jolt of power-pleasure chemicals as the brain, like a dancing bear, performs in compliance with one's commands. But "happiness" can only be had when all desire for control is given-over to the brain's natural healing processes. One must give the power to heal to the brain by releasing one's restraints on healing, rather than trying to manipulate them by pulling the leash on that bear's nose ring.

The problem here, although unique in every instance, can be stated generally. It is to learn to bring one's willingness exactly into line with the requirements of one's own brain for starting-up one's own Schucman Corridor. By listening to one's own contentment module messaging to consciousness, one can understand for oneself what is required of oneself. Gradually one will see that philosophically analyzing and talking about the problem can become a life-long distraction, if one lets it. Analysis, too, is a form of control; that is, of "getting a grip" on a problem or a conception. Talking about it keeps it an abstraction, which is useless unless fully integrated. For those who do not see this point immediately, practicing the empathic science program can help to make it clearer.

Participating in small support groups of like-minded and trusted persons may be as helpful as using a paid therapist to try to work through one's obstacles to developing sufficient willingness. In such groups, one can share one's fears, and learn about the fears of other members. Participants can share journals, if they so choose. Of course, there are risks in working with others. Among these are forming dependencies, being manipulated, or having one's fears reinforced rather than illuminated and uprooted. Aside from such hazards, working with others can speed one through blocks that would prevent progress for a lifetime in one who chose to go it alone.

Another risk of group work is that a false willingness may be used as an article of display. That is, one may shout from the mountain top, for all to hear, "I am willing!" Or, one may wear a shirt of horsehairs with "I am willing" silk-screened upon it; or, may have a scarlet "W" tattooed on one's forehead, for all to see. But none of these efforts to gain social status will bring inner success. Social status is a power-pleasure stimulant. To rework Lincoln's well-known saw, you can fool all of the people some of the time, including yourself, but you cannot fool your own brain at any time. The exact connection must be made from mind to brain through authentic, unconditional willingness, or no Door Prize. The "willingness to be seen as willing" is a self-deception.

In the process of working this program, there are some specific questions, which one may ask oneself to aid introspection, and to keep one's mind focused. Among these are: (1) What am I unwilling to give-up to become contended? In other words, what price for happiness do I regard as too high? (2) What am I afraid will become of me if I let go of my self-created self? For example, will I lose my desire for sex, or my sexual orientation? Will I make bad investments, or lose my competitive drive? Will I become a babbling idiot, wandering the streets and eating out of garbage cans? Will I start standing on street corners, tambourine in hand, singing "Hallelujah Jesus"? (3) What sense of urgency to achieve the consciousness of consciousness do I really feel? I.e., do I feel that it might be "fun to try someday"? Do I feel "it's out of reach for an ordinary person like me"? Or, do I feel "it's just a myth," and that "people were not meant to be happy"? These questions, and others like them, can be asked to help one to understand one's lack of sufficient willingness. They cannot be asked too often. They are apt for group discussion.

The development of willingness entails a process of recognizing the fears that stunt its growth. Such statements as "I am willing, but …," or "I am not willing because …" are indicators of fear. As fear is recognized and acknowledge, courage is cultivated. Courage is required because letting go of the self-created self will, indeed, result in it changing. That fear is right, it will die; the *alienated self* will be lost forever. After returning from the consciousness of consciousness, one will find a new self. One may fear the terrible torment of Everlasting Insanity; but, by letting go, one will actually melt easily into a depth of satisfaction beyond measure. Willingness can be seen, then, as entailing a balance between fear and courage. Gradually for many, rapidly for some, the scale can be tipped in favor of letting go, come what may.

The Sages of the East have said for centuries that the key to happiness is to let nature take its course – to follow the Tao. The impulse of humans to impose their will on nature is part of the legacy of genocide. While human willfulness put an end to the attacks by Neanderthals, it brought no one the contentment that was their ultimate desire. War won the relief from the threat of Neanderthal, but only surrender, and never attacking, will win the peace sought. A person with the courage to follow "the Tao of the brain" will have the reward which humanity once saw promised in the false happiness conditional of genocide.

"Surrender" is not the same as "giving-up," that phrase could imply a self-defeating despair. Rather, the intentional structure of surrender, as used here, is the same as that of asking for help. This entails the admission that one's conscious "I" can neither command, nor trick, nor cajole the results desired, and that this "I" is, in fact, in need of help.

Indeed, surrender, combined with the right intention, are sufficient elements of willingness to bring about the consciousness of consciousness. These satisfy the genetically inherited program for self-healing embedded in the tissue of the brain. Every normal organ in the body has a program for self-healing. But the enabling conditions for such processes must first be met. Just rub the magic lamp, and the Genie will appear. The "magic" of the immune system also works best when there is willingness. As we mentioned earlier, many doctors have reported witnessing sick people die simply because the sick lost the will to live, and "gave-up the ghost." Thus, willingness is an element in many forms of the body's self-healing. Here, our focus is on the alienated relationship between mind and brain. The mind with the willingness to ask for, and to receive, the brain's help, if authentic, will have the desired results.

Human alienation can be stated as a case of the will not trusting the brain. Thus, willingness entails trust. Working the program we are presenting here can develop the required trust. As Schucman often said, people tend to treasure the imagined benefits of their self-alienation more than they trust their own capacity to cure their disorder. The fear of falling into the abyss if they let go of the self-created self can blind people to the strong arms of the brain, which are ready to catch, and to save them.

Contrary to the fears of some folks, cultivating inward trust will not turn one into a social or a business patsy. Surrendering one's will to the healing processes of the brain does not require that one surrender to the will of other people in daily life. How one relates to oneself can be distinguished from how one relates to others. There is no reason why one cannot command, combat, or cooperate with other people, as needed, and through it all cultivate submissiveness to one's inner healing processes. Willfulness in relation to others does not necessarily translate into willfulness in one's self-reflective relationship. In the *Bhagavad-Gita*, Krishna advises Arjuna that healing can be had even while preparing to enter into battle. Zen originated in Japan as the religion of the Samurai. There is no contradiction in the idea of a "healed warrior."

A paradox in our presentation is that one must remember to surrender. Although needed, surrendering does not occur naturally in most people. Remembering this requirement requires a conscious effort. One must also make the effort to study about the problem sufficiently to understand what to remember, and why remembering it is important. Making such conscious efforts implies a kind of controlling of oneself. One must fix one's attention on the issue. Turn off the TV. Pick-up a book. Or, go to a meeting. Yet, controlling oneself is precisely what must be surrendered! What is our solution to this seeming contradiction? Let this be one's Zen Koan: "How can I discipline myself to let go of myself?" Seeing beyond the superficial paradoxes in verbal formulations can be a sign of one's progress. Only the fear of letting the brain heal itself makes the simple seem complex. The appropriate relationship of mind to brain is one of submission; for, ultimately, the brain is the mind's "creator," and "higher power." Thus, the way to happiness is opened to the person who can say, with the right feeling, "Brain, I cannot make it happen. I beg thee to heal thyself!" One may practice this self-reflective petition to the brain throughout the day. (However, it should be kept separate from meditation, which will be discussed shortly.) Pause a moment, if you care to, and practice it now. Just turn it over to the brain.

Did you try it? Did that work? Are you there yet? If not, perhaps the block is in the words themselves. Let us look again at the role of language in maintaining alienation.

The Great Speaker

We have said that fear is a major, and ultimately the single, obstacle to letting go of the self-created self. Yet, fear has an army of allies. We have mentioned power-pleasure. There are many stimulants that feed into the addiction to power-pleasure. One of these is speech. Speech is a problem in two ways. The first is that one learns to identify oneself as "a speaker." The second relates to the use of speech in making judgments. We will discuss what it means to be "a speaker" before we examine the self-defeating use of language in playing the judgment game.

As we have often said, semblances are created in the realm of nonverbal, preconceptual meaning making. These include the meanings, which are passed from generation to generation nonverbally. A major theme in this communication is about what it means to be "human." Since the genocide, to be "human" entails the notion of being "a speaker." To be "a speaker" is to identify oneself as among the proud victors of the genocide. A close look at the elements of this important theme in the human self-definition will reveal how such pride can be self-defeating.

Prior to the genocide, there was no organized conception or custom of "teaching speech," as there is today. Speech remained at the level of animal culture, and was causally acquired as that culture was passed on. Early humans put their special focus upon teaching nonverbal communication. This included the first philosophy of life, the ways to communicate the pain of emptiness and fear, and how to send and receive the balm of soothing, loving, emotional embraces. Oral communication was a secondary element in the means of producing the material necessities of life, which consisted of such practices as gathering, trapping, hunting, scavenging, preparing, sharing and eating food as a community. But, nonverbal communication was central to the quality of life. People then *lived for feeling*, and oral communication could only distract the human mind from feeling by drawing attention to conceptions.

After the Great Shift, mothers, and the adults around baby, began the special efforts to "teach speech." Before then, baby's vocalizations were likely just accepted as baby behavior. But, after this Shift, the practice began of rewarding baby with special attention for every utterance, which sounded like a word. Today's custom of eagerly awaiting "the big day" when baby pronounces his first "momma," or "dada," or even "wa-wa," is a legacy of genocide. This is an initial step in teaching baby to associate language with power-pleasure. Baby soon learns the thrill of having the power to command special attention for himself by his or her verbal utterances. As the child grows, the distinction of being "a speaker" increases the power connotations within his or her self-created self. This element of meaning originated in the genocide, and reached its apex with the triumph over Neanderthal. From then on, to be a speaker was to be among "the triumphant ones." People acting in accordance with this new human self-understanding spread the Age of Articulation throughout humanity, by conquest or conversion.

Emphatic science, as we said in Chapter One, follows the principle of phenomenology that consciousness is always "of" something. In the age of cultivated love, it was *of* the need for love, and *of* the loving responses that people sent to one another nonverbally. Consciousness dwelt on the feelings of the love one was sending to others, or receiving from them. However, consciousness in the Age of Articulation dwells on speech, far more so than on feeling. In its most personal form, modern consciousness is nearly always *of* one's "inner dialogue." This addiction to mental chatter is such that it must be continued, no matter what is being said, to keep the brain producing the flow of power-pleasure chemicals one needs to ease the burden of one's Hapsburg Jaw. Just consider all the time that such chatter occupies one's consciousness. Why does it go on so?

People generally act so as to fulfill their self-created semblance of themselves. Mental chatter is an "action" which fulfills the individual's self-understanding as "a speaker," and therefore as one of "the triumphant one's." Thus mental chatter constantly triggers low levels of triumphant feelings; that is, of the mix of power-pleasure chemicals needed to stave-off the dormant torment that lurks in the shadows of consciousness. Modernity's attention to this internal, some would say *infernal*, dialogue enables people to live in alienation by "keeping the motor running." During the time of cultivated love, there was no "mind chatter," as we know it today. People put their focus on feeling. Attention was centered as much on right hemispheric processes then, as it is on left hemispheric processes now.

Empathic science finds other problems with the speaker identity as an obstacle to achieving the consciousness of consciousness. In addition to being an addictive stimulant, language is always a lie. Speech is a deception both as to fact and as to value. Words are never the thing about which they speak. Instead, words create illusions in the mind, which often dupe both speaker and listener into confusing names and things, actual events and stories about them. But beyond this "General Semantics" fact, words fool people into believing that they have something *worth* saying and *worth* listening to. Every speaker proclaims by implication:

> I have something to say! My words and I are important for you. Indeed, my germy utterances are more worthy of entering your consciousness in this moment, than is your own consciousness. Now is not the time to turn your consciousness upon itself, nor to free your Schucman Corridor from constraint, nor to escape your isolation and misery. Now is the time to give your attention over to me and my words, which are far more important than those alternatives!

Thus, does every speaker deny the natural order of values. These, as we have said, put oneness, joy, and objectless love, as the most urgently needed values in life. Because it puts itself before these, every use of language is a boldface lie about its own worth. And, while creating the illusion of "communicating," speech actually desensitizes people to the oneness they could experience with each other by separating them into speaker and listener. It also ties consciousness to content, and it is incapable of ever focusing consciousness upon itself. Speech lures people into a continuous involvement with the self-created self, which it cloaks in a shroud of specialness, making that self all the more difficult to release.

These claims about what it means to the speaker to be "a speaker," can be readily verified by empathic observation in any culture, and by honest introspection. Who among the human race does not distinguish himself or herself from the animals because of his or her "superior" powers of speech? Is not such self-aggrandizing an obvious ploy for stimulating one's power-pleasure centers? The capacity for speech has been made the foundation stone for human exceptionalism. However, informed introspection reveals that for humanity's first 100,000 years the human self-image contained no feeling of superiority or specialness in nature. Humans felt so much a part of nature that no alienating left hemispheric conception of specialness ever made its mark in our ancestral memory. The notion that speech makes man special only took hold in our minds as humanity became addicted to power-pleasure stimulants during the genocide.

But this self-destructive addiction to language is not a curse which empathic science is the first to call attention to. Indeed, long before there were books about the problem, even long before there was writing at all, there was wisdom. There were seekers who found a way to follow the call of their contentment module. They felt the natural order of values, and believed them to be true. For them, objectless love, joy, and oneness had to be had at any cost. Each found his or her own way to let go of the self-created self, and let the brain heal itself. While their words of wisdom have passed into various forms of religious dogma, myth and mysticism, they have left behind a priceless heritage, part of which is the knowledge of meditation.

Meditation

Long before written records were kept by the Sumerians, beginning some 5000 years ago, ancient wise men of the East had invented techniques of meditation, which were meant to "quiet the mind, and free the spirit." These sages recognized that mental chatter was no harmless habit, but a bar to attaining enlightenment, and the life-long contentment that achievement brings. Those rare seers lacked the knowledge of humanity's pre-historical context which empathic science now provides.

William J. Kelleher, Ph.D.

Nevertheless, they intuitively grasped the problem that confronts all modern humans. That is, the heavy task of breaking the addiction to speech so as to achieve happiness.

In the healing program of empathic science, meditation has two important uses. It can be both a diagnostic tool, and a therapeutic technique. Let us examine these two aspects of meditation. Diagnostically, meditation can be used as a self-test to determine if one has the addiction to mind-chatter that we have mentioned. The hypothesis to be self-tested is this: if one is not addicted to the use of language as a power-pleasure stimulant, then one ought to be able to relax and rest with a quiet mind. But if one has the addiction, then one's mind will be unable to rest in quiet.

To begin, find a quiet place to sit comfortably. Turn off all your electronic devices so that you can concentrate without interruption upon the test. Now, just relax and quiet your mind. Try this experiment for two or three minutes. If it does not work, that is, if your mind does not cease its constant stream of chatter, try the exercise again for five minutes, or ten, or thirty. Try it again tomorrow, and the next day. If the chatter will not stop, it may be that your brain will not let it stop. Such unceasing chatter could indicate that you are addicted to the power-pleasure stimulus of speech.

If you are unable, as the Zen Masters say, to "empty your mind," you can be sure that you are not alone in this. The left brain's production of continuous chatter is a legacy of the genocide. It is "Bad Karma," which hounds people all over the world, and has done so for many thousands of years. Without this stimulant, the unbearable horror of the human birth defect would emerge in your consciousness and torment you day and night. But in the consciousness of consciousness, all chatter is silenced, and only the experience of oneness is felt. After that, the need for chatter sinks into the past and is forgotten. One's mind is then freed to think with words when necessary, or to dwell on the thought-free feeling of oneness at one's leisure.

As a therapeutic technique, meditation, when done properly, entails an effort to overcome the deleterious effects of the speaker identity, which is a variant of the body identity. As a therapy, it can help one to make the transition from chatter-dependency to quiet freedom.

Let us consider, then, how to practice the ancient therapeutic technique of meditation, hopefully with more success than we had in that self-test! For most beginners, meditation is a struggle for silence frustrated by sound. Some may slip into silence immediately, but most had better not expect to have everything all at once. Meditation is a technique which, to work well, requires regular practice. To succeed, it should be approached with an informed understanding of its original aim. That aim is to weaken the link of language to the power-pleasure centers of the brain, and to wean the meditator from using speech as a substitute for the deeper pleasure of life-long contentment.

Probably the best method of meditation for beginners is that recommended in *The Relaxation Response,* by Dr. Herbert Benson. This method was devised by a group of Harvard University Medical School researchers. While it is a contemporary and secular approach to meditation, the method is consistent with the most ancient techniques known in both East and West. As with the self-test, find a quiet place to sit comfortably. An uncomfortable, or painful, position will only distract one's mind from the aims of meditation. The positions used in some sects of

Yoga and Zen are peculiarities of their respective cultures. Indeed, a Westerner who attempts to meditate in the Lotus position is more likely to achieve sore knees than Satori!

With lights low or off if possible, close your eyes. Then focus your attention on your natural breathing pattern. As you inhale through your nose, think to yourself the prefix "re-" and as you exhale, think to yourself the suffix "-lax." So, with each cycle of breathing you will think "re-lax," "re-lax." Breathe from the lower diaphragm, rather than from the upper chest.

Are you aware of feeling more relaxed than when you started? If so, then you are meditating well. But do not let yourself go to sleep. Meditation and sleeping are two different endeavors. Some self-discipline may be required to keep them separate. One is not likely to uproot long entrenched habits of mind while dozing!

Meditation is a form of discipline in which one practices withdrawing attention from chatter, and focusing the mind upon "relaxing." This requires both patience and gentleness with oneself. Taking one's "monkey mind" off chatter seems easy enough as an idea, but in practice it can be extremely threatening. Chatter is one's lifeline to the balm that makes life in alienation tolerable.

Therefore, only tiny steps away from chatter should be attempted at first. The impulse to sleep may be a sign of panic, and an effort to escape more meditation. Drifting off into reveries may have the same meaning. In both cases, one should keep calm and gently draw attention back to the breath and "re-lax." This discipline may be thought of as a way of reparenting one's insecure inner child who thinks that he or she just cannot live without that old security blanket. Meditation is an opportunity to try to do without the reassuring chatter for a few minutes at a time. One may set aside twenty to thirty minutes a day for the practice. The time may be increased as one's self-confidence increases. Thus, meditation is a safe way to practice letting go of dependency.

We go beyond the Harvard view of meditation, and see much more meaning in it than mere physiological relaxation. There are feelings and experiences available to one in meditation that one might not otherwise encounter in one's life. These should always be positive, and if they are not, one should stop and try again later. The repetition of the word "relax" can serve as a reminder to pay attention to that feeling and its experience as one meditates.

With patience, one can experience what the ancients called "the void." In the void, one visualizes the consciousness of consciousness. With eyes closed, attending to the breath, look at the field of light within. One may then envision illuminated empty space. As the void is envisioned, chatter is relegated to background – like a reader might do with a radio softly playing behind him or her. Awareness of the chatter is not lost, but silence takes the foreground of attention. The void appears as the virtual experience of a vast distance.

Simultaneously, one may feel an aesthetic response to the presence of the void. Of course, adjectives will differ, but this feeling dimension is often described as one of awe before great beauty. One also may feel whole, some say almost bursting with fullness. Whiffs of joy and objectless love may drift into consciousness with child-like excitement as the mind anticipates the healing of enlightenment.

In meditation one can get a glimpse of what one's personal experience of happiness could be in post-consciousness of consciousness life. By visualizing the void, one can acquire some understanding of that vital difference, which we mentioned earlier, between "happiness" and a "happy me." One learns to see that happiness is not a quality of personality, but is the natural condition of being. Thinking about this distinction throughout the day can also help to reduce fear-driven clinging, and increase the courage to let go.

During meditation one attempts to simulate the consciousness of consciousness. That is, one tries to visualize consciousness purely in itself, free of all content. However, content, in the form of speech, music, or images, will be present. Indeed, the visualization of the void is itself content, until it is real. This simulation exercise may have a kindling effect on the neurons, axons, and dendrites that comprise the Schucman Corridor. Even if one undertakes meditation out of curiosity, or simply to relax, regular practice can help to realign one's values with the natural order of values. Then one may feel an increasing sense of urgency that one let go of the self-imposed constraints on the brain's healing processes. Thereafter, one may attain the true goal and meaning of one's life – a healed mind/brain relationship!

Researchers have found that meditation measurably reduces left hemispheric activity. Of course, the degree to which that is done will vary between individuals. But the ultimate aim of meditation is to go beyond mere reduction of power-pleasure stimulation by the left hemisphere. The ultimate aim is to achieve a reconfiguration of brain activity so that left hemispheric processes become deeply subordinated to the continuing experience of contentment.

This ancient therapy for the speech addiction is an excellent exercise for the development of willingness. As we have said, releasing the self-created self requires the willingness to give up all the devices one uses for self-stimulation and self-deadening. In meditation one can learn to replace these with the simulated experience of "no self," as they say in Zen. Regular meditation in a small support group with people who share an understanding of its aims and method can be quite beneficial. Verbal sharing about one's meditation experiences can be very helpful. Sharing can be an opportunity to air one's fears of letting go.

Study groups can also be helpful for the more intellectually inclined. Reading books of all sorts, related to enlightenment and healing the human birth defect, can help reduce fear and boost courage. Reading *A Course In Miracles* can be very helpful, unless one's scientific or secular prejudice against religious language is too bothersome.

Many people report that there is a carry-over effect from meditation. That is, one feels more relaxed between meditation sessions, and one's perspective on what is valuable in life changes. Those wonderful feelings from the "bright moments" of meditation can be recalled and relived, somewhat, in memory. Some people begin to develop a "hunger" for meditation, which is a positive sign that it is doing what it was originally intended to do; i.e., move one closer to a cure.

Unfortunately, even the most well practiced meditators are unable to sustain their happy state for long. The addiction to power, and the fear of letting go of the self-created self, inevitably push the simulated Nirvana out of mind, as meaningless and worthless chatter reclaims its place at the center of attention. While meditation was invented to off-set the curse of chatter, thousands of years of practice in the East show that it only leads to enlightenment, or healing, for small numbers of the most dedicated practitioners. This unhappy inevitability is another element of the Bad Karma of the genocide. Even among Buddhist monks, who meditate for several hours daily, those who actually attain enlightenment are so few and far between that they are given legendary status. Some reports say that after years of disciplined effort, only one in a thousand novitiates attain the true goal. Why meditation produces so few healed humans is a ripe subject for empathic research. Fame and a Nobel Prize may be in store for the one who can untie this Gordian Knot.

Despite its low success rate, the discipline of meditation can be useful as one exercise of willingness among many. (Chanting "aum," or engaging in other rituals, may feel more suitable to some, depending upon individual proclivities and constitutions.) There are two more exercises that we will present in the remainder of this chapter. One is to stop playing the judgment game. The other is to start cultivating compassion.

The Judgment Game

Playing the judgment game is yet another of man's addictions, and a legacy of the genocide. It is as great an obstacle to oneness as is humanity's addiction to chatter. One difference between the two is that chatter is an individual event, while judgment requires others as one's target. Another difference is that chatter acts as a continuing low level stimulant, but judgments provide immediate jolts of the power-pleasure opiates that give The Judge the thrill of victory. We will discuss the consequences of man's addiction to judging here, as well as how that addiction can be overcome.

In short, one stops playing the judgment game simply by relinquishing judgment.[cxxvi] The practice of forgoing judgment is a narrowly focused exercise of willingness. One who can muster the willingness to fully forgo judging others will have thereby developed the willingness to let go of the self-created self.

Here is something that anyone can do. One can begin today to practice refraining from judging others. Let us look carefully, then, at this "judgment game." How is it played? Why do people play it? What is the harm in it? What is the alternative, if any, to it? Assuming that one would like to stop playing the game, how can that be done?

To begin our explanation, let us consider the word "judgment." That term has numerous connotations. One may seek the judgment of a stockbroker prior to making an investment. The judge of an athletic performance may rate a diver, skater, or boxer from one to ten. A doctor will exercise his or her judgment as to whether a chest pain is indigestion or a pulmonary infection. A botanist judges whether that T-shaped plant is a mushroom or a toadstool. An umpire makes a judgment call as to whether a pitch was a ball or a strike. A judge in a trial renders numerous rulings as to whether certain evidence is admissible or inadmissible. A jury may be called upon to judge the guilt or innocence of a defendant. And, an architect makes a judgment that the materials he has selected will support the building that he has designed.

Such everyday judgments as these are inescapable elements of life. Without exercising judgments, people would not know whether to put one foot in front of the other. Each step assumes a quick judgment that our eyes do not deceive us about the existence of solid ground beneath our feet, and that our legs are strong enough to carry our weight. Here, we will focus on a distinct category of judgment. These are the judgments one makes of others, not with the dispassion of an umpire, but with a particular kind of passion – that is, the passion to attack.

Some judgments are forms of attack. Attacks may be physical, verbal, or mental. Our focus is on the latter, because it is less visible than the other two. Judgments may stem from such feelings as grievance, self-pity, jealousy, racism, sexism, social status arrogance, national pride, religious rivalry, or simply a malicious response to frustration. But if the roots are severed from this ugly weed, it will not grow again.

The propensity to launch thought attacks on others is a legacy of the genocide, which, as we have said, has since been blessed by religion. Attack judgments consist not only of those thoughts about others that would physically eliminate them, but those which would in any way condemn, damn, or otherwise reduce the person's position in the natural order of values. We have seen that in the natural order of values every human is a brother or sister who is too precious to use. But an attack judgment is the use of the imaginary power to strip away the human status of another, and to reduce him or her to the level of a "creep," an "Infidel," a "whore," a "sinner," a "nigger," a "foreigner," or a "piece of shit." Any diminishment of another is an attack.

Each judgment of this sort assumes a deadly power. In the modern mind, the power to judge is the power to destroy. Even seemingly mild judgments reserve the right to exert murderous rage the next time. Judgments replicate the genocide in several ways. They assume a separate and antagonistic relationship between The Judge and the object of His wrath. They exercise power in response to frustration. They intend to destroy. They always result in triumph.

Thus, judgments have an invariable structure.[cxxvii] First, judgments occur in a tacit self-reflective recognition of the existence and the validity of the natural order of values. As we discussed in Chapter Two, and elsewhere, in the pre-consciousness of consciousness condition the natural order of values holds the achievement of the consciousness of consciousness as the most urgent need. This is the need of a constricted organ in the brain to be free of its constraints so that it can do its job of producing and regulating the flow of contentment causing brain chemicals. Once this has begun, one recognizes, as a natural reality, one's oneness within, with others, and with the surrounding world. One also sees clearly that each human is unique, and too precious to use.

In tacit recognition of the intrinsic value of each person, fixed by nature in the human brain, judgments then engage in the fantasy act of stripping away the intrinsic value of the target. The Judge interposes an imaginary ideal of "right," or "good," or "perfection," and then condemns the target for failing to fulfill that ideal. Thus, each judgment assumes that The Judge has the power to change nature. This assumption stems from the idea of "improvement," which originated in the time of the genocide. The idea of improvement entails a rejection of acceptance, and the arrogant assertion that one "knows better than" actual reality. Attack judgments assume that one knows better than the natural evaluation of each person as too precious to use, and "improves" upon this value reality. In this way, The Judge creates the semblance of himself or herself wresting the other individual from his or her natural position as too precious to use, and forcefully reducing that person to the status of a "jerk," "square," "nerd," "sinner," an "evil one," or any other epithet which ultimately designates another human being as a target rather than a person. Part of the illusion, then, is that the disvaluation of another is an "improvement" upon the natural order of values. As Dr. Schucman often points out, judgments like these are a form of mental illness.

Because a target is an object for use, The Judge objectifies a person, and thereby "murders" his or her personhood. In such judgment, then, the triumph of the genocide is replicated. Each judgment is an analogue to God expelling Adam and Eve from Paradise, or condemning Lucifer to Everlasting Hell. Of course, every idea of "right," which is used to justify the revocation of another person's intrinsic value, is wrong. The ultimate value of every person is fixed in the neuro-connections of the neocortex in conjunction with the plain fact of being a person; that is, personhood and preciousness are coterminous in the healthy human mind/brain. Thoughts, fantasies, daydreams, and other delusions of grandeur cannot change that fact/value relationship any more than a moving picture can change the screen on to which it is projected. (The pompous deeming of corporations as "persons" in US law is an institutionalized attack on humanity.)

But if thought attacks, or judgments, are such self-deceptive illusions, why would anyone engage in them? Because, in practice, judgments are a form of self-stimulation. They operate as a semblance of great power in the lower regions of the brain. These semblances stimulate the same pleasure centers that are activated when an animal predator captures and kills its prey; indeed, every attack judgment entails those very acts. Judgments, then, enable the most frail and puny human to feel as powerful as a lion, or as a Judge at the Bench of Law.

Condemning is a form of controlling. With each damning of another person, one controls the fate of the target. "That object is no longer human!" Thus speaketh

The Judge, who controls all! However, this fantasy attack changes nothing but the type of chemicals surging through The Judge's brain. The precise chemical compounds used when judging have yet to be identified. In response to coded instructions from the semblance of great power one conjures up when judging, such invigorating brain chemicals as testosterone and dopamine are likely combined. This cocktail is experienced in consciousness as a boost in one's sense of power and well being. Thus, each judgment shows that The Judge would rather engage in a moment of mental masturbation than enjoy the real thing for life.

Judging is a strategy for adapting to the human birth defect, devised in the wake of the genocide. This practice has been handed down and built upon by each generation since that time. Very little introspection is needed to determine the extent to which one engages in judging others throughout the day. Also, everyone has observed others as they imbibe the sweet nectar of judgment. Indeed, people often select as "friends," or allies, those Judges with whom they agree on the rules of engagement. The act of judging enjoys widespread popularity. One reason for this is, as we have said, each judgment triggers a surge of the power-pleasure chemicals in the brain. Secondly, even "killer judgments" can be fired at another without risk to The Judge. The mere thought, kept to oneself, will spark a little thrill of victory. Thirdly, provided they are not acted upon, thought attacks seem to present no threat to the social order, making them acceptable to the ruling authorities. A fourth reason for the popularity of judgmental thinking is that it is encouraged by religions.

Finally, judgments are readily available to everyone. Philosopher Bertrand Russell comments about the "moral superiority" of the victim in his book *Unpopular Essays*.

Even while politically suppressed, or otherwise wronged, exploited, or abused, people can safely turn their situation into an opportunity for self-stimulation. The victim can find solace, even triumph, in condemning the wrongdoer. Ironically, the victim's feeling of "moral superiority" stimulates the same power-pleasure centers stimulated in the brain of his wrongdoer!

Many people nurture grievances as a way to feel morally superior. Nurturing grievances entails the judgment that one has been "wronged." Such grievances may be held by adults against their parents for the "wrongs" the parents committed against these adults when they were children. Unless a way is found to let go of these grievances, however justifiable they may be, one who nurtures them only denies himself or herself the contentment he or she could have. Nurturing grievances against one's parents, and others, is contrary to the natural order of values because doing so keeps one in the alienated mode of "look at what they did to me." But continuous sitting on the "pity pot" only distracts one from the organic based feeling of oneness with all people that lays dormant in the neocortex. Unfortunately, this indulgence in nurturing grievances is so widespread that there are even nations, which socialize their youth into nurturing grievances against other nations based on events in ancient history. This is a continuation of the "them vs. us" thinking, and the idea of an "enemy," which originated in the period of the genocide so long ago. Indeed, one prerequisite of organized war is the demonization and dehumanization of the persons labeled "the enemy."

That we call attention to the element of self-stimulation in judgments does not mean that we are being cavalier about the terrible reality that people can express their murderous rage in real acts of terror, murder, torture, rape, and mayhem. Indeed, all crimes against humanity are very serious matters. The horrible acts of terror on September 11, 2001, for example, cut innocent lives short, and inflicted deep wounds in those who had loving relations with the deceased. Such wounds may never fully heal. "911" has been repeated in various forms all over the world, and throughout recorded history. But nurturing grievances can only prolong the pain.

An important distinction is to be made here between the acts committed and the persons who perpetrated those acts. Nurturing grievances against persons desensitizes The Judge to the feeling of oneness with others that he or she could have. But feeling one with others does not blind a person to reality. Some brothers and sisters can be extraordinarily cruel, and even murderous. There are times when measures must be taken to protect oneself and others from dangerous members of the human family. As the "father" of the United States Constitution, James Madison, wrote, in *Federalist Paper* number Ten, "if all men were angles, governments would not be necessary."

In the case of violent offenders, government is fully justified in removing them from society, both for the protection of others, and in the hope that the wrongdoer may be rehabilitated. Where the convicted are likely to repeat their crimes, or when their crimes are so terrible that society can take no chance on their repetition, such as with the Al Qaeda terrorists, a life-time in humane confinement would be proper, as an act of self-defense. However, the idea of "retribution," born of genocide, is a false happiness conditional. No one is made happy by hurting or executing a wrongdoer. "Getting even" boosts the production of power-pleasure opiates temporarily, but it never restores the victim to the way he or she felt before the crime. The genuine pain of the victim is best overcome by learning to forgo judgment of the offender.[cxxviii]

Contrary to the common assumption, there are numerous harms to society that are caused by judging, even when the attacks are confined to imagination. First, each Judge keeps the culture of judgment alive. One who judges also fears the judgment of others, and often attacks as a preemptive strike. On the theory that the best defense is an offense, many people are constantly on the lookout for opportunities to attack. Second, while some Judges can keep their thoughts to themselves, in this cultural atmosphere other Judges will inevitably allow their judgments to erupt into overt expression.

The judgment-ready frame of mind is disclosed both by verbal demonstration and nonverbally. Facial expression, body language, and right hemispheric communication broadcast one's predisposition for judgment attack. Each person communicates his commitment to the first philosophy of life by his or her readiness to judge or to defend against a judgment. These collectively reinforced attitudes create a judgment jungle in which each person is the potential target of the other – a Hobbesian "war of all against all." As one struggles to stop playing the judgment game, the fear and rage in oneself, and others, becomes as palpable as the pistol in a gunslinger's holster. If one could view social interactions with special lenses that highlight judgments, like night vision lenses highlight heat, daily life would look like an extended shoot-out at the OK Corral. A little self-reflection would verify this empathic observation.

Think, for example, of a person who, first thing in the morning picks up the newspaper, goes online, or turns on the TV or radio news to judge the "bad people" for all the terrible things they did during the night. The electronic media broadcast such targets hourly, to provide viewers with plenty of opportunities for self-stimulation. Then it's on to the road for the morning commute, where there is an ample supply of "idiots" and "dumb bells" to judge. The workplace always provides opportunities for imaginary attacks, and, if you are the boss, perhaps you can indulge in some verbal abuse to boost your feelings of well being. If you are not the boss, you can always get away with verbal abuse by using the "just kidding" defense. "Joking attacks" have the virtue of stimulating oneself while disarming those who could counter-attack. "Attack artists" practice their skills to sooth the pain of an unhealed brain, and they attempt to keep other attackers at bay with their first strike strategy.

Then its on to the commute home. Along the way, and in the privacy of one's mind, one may demonize and condemn a fellow motorist of whose driving one disapproves. Perhaps one will take a mental pot shot at a pedestrian in the street who happens to have an expanded waistline, or scorn a person whose way of dressing one disapproves of, or put down a member of a racial group or religion with which one finds fault, or the citizen of another nation who may lack papers, or a person of a different age, gender, or sexual orientation. Any pretext will do, and none have to be true. Once home, one can eat dinner while judging the "bad guys," politicians, and all the "evil ones" who are paraded across the TV screen for your target practice and self-stimulation between commercials.

Another potential harm of this cultural pattern is that it not only keeps everyone living in defensive fear, but it also keeps people susceptible to the kind of demonizing and condemning of "the enemy" which governments use to mobilize the public for war. Thus, private judging has the potential to result in catastrophic public consequences.

Additionally, judging does continuing harm to The Judge. People do not see the harm they are causing themselves by their repeated use of power-pleasure stimulants. The price for that pleasure is very high. Primarily, as we have said, judging desensitizes The Judge to the natural order of values and the signals for attention from the Schucman Corridor. Thus desensitized, one has no source of inner guidance, which is absolutely essential to achieving the consciousness of consciousness. The first philosophy of life, and the attack-defense mode, become one's bearings in life simply because that is all one knows. Alienated from one's internal navigation system, one follows the familiar path of attack as a way to feel better.

As we have said, judgments are the exercise of the imaginary power to diminish the intrinsic worth of another person. While such attacks objectify others as targets, they also validate oneself as a player in the judgment game. This also diminishes oneself to the status of a "target" that must be defended. Every condemnation of another is, then, in actual practice, a self-condemnation. As the comedian Groucho Marx once quipped, "I would never join a club that would have someone like me as a member."

That "club" is, of course, the human race. By judging others, one refuses to join the "club" of persons who are too precious to use. One might as well cut-off one's nose to spite one's face! That every judgment is mutually diminishing – for both the target and The Judge – shows that each attack is an ignorant and misguided expression of the natural desire to feel oneness with others. In other words, judgments are an expression in the negative of one's longing to feel the mutuality that is latent potential in the neocortex. An attack is a form of negative relating, of satisfying a need in the negative. Like Groucho's remark, attacks mirror one's negative self-evaluation as much as they reflect a negative evaluation of others.

This rejection of oneness with others is a denial of value reality in favor of living in a Wizard of Oz fantasy. By giving highest priority to stimulating one's power-pleasure centers, attack also denies the value of striving for the consciousness of consciousness. With each judgment, one chooses to dwell angrily and arrogantly in alienating fantasies of superior power over others, rather than to dwell joyously in the factual feeling of one's oneness with them.

The problem we are analyzing here can be stated simply as "how does one get from Point A – playing the judgment game, to Point B – where one has stopped playing it?" Dr. Schucman's writings suggest that there are two ways to choose from. One can just step out of judgment and into oneness with a little pure willingness. Or, one can take some time and work on purifying one's willingness. Because there is no order of difficulty to achieving the consciousness of consciousness, one can take the first step mentioned at any time along the way of the second step.

Cultivating Compassion

Judging is a habit that can be broken. Since it was learned, it can be unlearned. Forgoing judgment is a specific antidote for all the harmful effects of the judgment addiction. A companion exercise is to try to cultivate compassion.

Besides making the deliberate effort to refrain from damning another, one can try to see the other with compassion. To see another person with compassion requires that one see each individual as a unique instance of a self-reflective consciousness in pain. That pain comes from the person's frustrated desire for pure self-reflection; that is, the achievement of the consciousness of consciousness. The final cause of this frustration is, of course, that person's fearful clinging to his or her self-created self. This self currently mediates that person's self-reflection, and thereby obstructs the immediate realization of the longed for unmediated, pure self-reflection. Cultivating compassion is a specific program for replacing the habitual negation of the intrinsic value of others with the habit of honoring that value. This honoring will, then, reflect back upon oneself. This change of value will gradually reposition one's divisive self-image, as that of a Judge and a target to be defended, to that of one who naturally deserves oneness.

As with any program that requires self-monitoring and self-control, forgoing judgment and cultivating compassion are parts of a discipline. While there are immediate rewards for working the program well, especially an increase in relaxation, this is not an exercise in hedonistic self-indulgence. This practice requires taking a stoic stance towards oneself. The more one is a gentle, kind, but firm parent to one's childish self-centered desire for power-pleasure, the more progress one will make. The line of progression is from painful alienation to a more fulfilling feeling of all around oneness.

Compassion increases as one learns to see the pain in others, and comes to understand its causes. One never feels the pain of another, but only one's interpretation of another person's pain. This empathy can be educated by self-parenting, study, and practice. The day when one has learned to empathize with the suffering of others, rather than judging them, will stand as a milestone of one's progress. Thus, this progress can be measured. As one sees with increasing clarity the psychology of judging operating within others, one will experience the shock of recognition as one sees, also with increasing clarity, the same psychology in oneself. Let us, then, take another look at that psychology.

An attacker superficially experiences himself or herself as enjoying the pleasure of exercising power. But this superficial self-awareness requires a denial of the syndrome operating below the surface of his or her shallow self-knowledge. Compassion includes the understanding that, in most cases, an attack, whether mental, verbal, or physical, is driven by the convergence of several painful feelings. These include fear, rage, and an *urgent* desire to do something to bring relief from one's own pain. Each of these feelings desensitizes one to one's own Schucman Corridor signaling. Because these messages are filtered through the first philosophy of life, they become distorted. With the world defined as a predatory jungle, signals to release the self-created self are turned into unspecified mortal threats coming from an unidentified source. Frustration follows from the inability to find the cause of the threat and eliminate it.

Rage is humanity's learned response to frustration; yet another legacy of genocide. We noted in Chapter Two that the contentment module's signals to consciousness contain coded instructions both as to how to let go of the self-created self so that the brain may heal itself, and as to the urgency of doing so – as urgent a need as is putting out a fire on one's head. But through self-ignorance, and the filter of the first philosophy of life, these signals, which are meant to rush one home, are turned against oneself by oneself. Fearing imminent attack, one devises strategies for self-defense. Each attack one fires off, then, contains within itself a sense of urgency that the fortress be defended. These two senses of urgency are in conflict. One urges letting go of the very thing that the other urges defending!

Fear driven urgency is the louder one in consciousness. It overrides all rational calculations, and erupts in attacks, as well as in various forms of other compulsive behavior. The obese "cake straightened," the "one more drop" drunk, the "this time I'm hitting the jackpot" gambler, the kleptomaniac, the sex addict, and so on, all act under a sudden sense of urgency in common with the urgency that drives attack judgments. In part, this feeling that "something must be done right now" is appropriate. But the choice of action is almost always self-defeating, rather than self-assisting. Attacks, and other forms of compulsive behavior, can be seen as desperate and misguided attempts to make the actor feel better. The desire to feel better is right, but the chosen means for satisfying it are wrong.

Compassion recognizes that the attacker is desperately trying to reduce his or her own pain. The Judge's involvement with the targeted person is not what it seems to be. An attack, then, can be seen as an expression of despair, frustration, and a self-ignorant, impotent plea to the target for help. As in a set of Chinese boxes, the attacker wants to experience the triumph over the other, and wants relief from his own painful alienation, *and* wants to be one with the other. The anger underlying attack always entails agony. In this sense, an attack is as shortsighted and self-defeating as is the heroin addict giving himself another injection. His sense of urgent need is relieved, but not for long.

Gradually, one can learn to see these painful conflicts operating in the minds of oneself and of others. Then, attacks become depersonalized actions that one can view with emotional detachment. As one realizes that people need to attack each other as a way of injecting themselves with a brain opiate to calm their fear and ease their pain, one gradually learns to see that the attacks are really not "malicious," but are ignorant expressions of a deep personal crisis. Following Schucman's advice, when one encounters a frustrating or aggravating fellow human, and the old tapes start playing the judgment tune, one can ask oneself "how can I see this person differently?" Or, "how can I see this person as expressing his or her longing to feel one with me, rather than as trying to inflict pain in me?" The struggle to see attackers differently pays for itself as defensiveness fades with an increasing understanding that the challenge is not merely to protect oneself, but to do so and feel as one with the attacker. Gradually, attacks can be seen as a form of service, providing an opportunity for which one may be grateful.

By working this program, one begins to see that the personality, which one defends from attack, is already causing one more pain than any attack by another ever could. In this case, defense is futile because no "killer judgment" by an outside attacker can increase the pain in which one is already dwelling in daily, albeit suppressed from awareness.

Forgoing judgment and cultivating compassion, then, are not simply the act of denying oneself a treat, they are ways of opening a window on oneself and others. As one learns to see the syndrome of self-inflicted pain operating in others, one becomes more sensitive to that same process carrying-on in oneself. Seeing just how much others are pursuing the illusions of false happiness conditionals, one finds it easier to acknowledge the same error in oneself. By observing with increasing clarity the petty power games played by others, one becomes more aware of the same self-protective fear, which drives those games, in oneself.

The view into one's interior, and that of one's fellows, becomes clearer with experience. One of the well-established lessons of science is that knowledge can reduce fear. Natural science has eliminated the fear, in most educated people, that evil spirits control natural forces, such as the weather. It has also eradicated the fear, in such people, that health is subject to the balance of "good" and "evil" spirits, which do battle within one's body. Empathic science seeks to help reduce the fears that entrap people in the syndrome of self-inflicted pain. By forgoing judgment and cultivating compassion, one can acquire new insights, which are the building blocks of fear-reducing knowledge.

One pitfall to be avoided in the practice is guilt. As one observes oneself casting condemning judgments at another, one can accept this as a part of one's social conditioning that one now seeks to correct. To attack oneself with guilt or self-flagellation for judging others is to stay within a vicious cycle of error, which will obstruct progress. Because judging is based on fear, it always causes tension. So, when one catches oneself in the act of attack, take a deep breath and try to relax, rather than being self-accusatory. To attack oneself for attacking another is to stay in the attack mode. Being a kind parent to oneself can produce more progress. Gently, but firmly, remind yourself that judging is not in your best interest.

Plan, Act, Enjoy

One who understands that the need to attack is based on a desire to make oneself feel better can then reason out which means to that end would likely be more effective and enduring. Do attacks make one feel as well as one would like to feel? Does the pleasure of attack last as long as one would like it to last? One may ask oneself whether one really prefers to see oneself and others as objectified targets, useful for self-stimulation, or if there might be more profit in learning to value oneself and others intrinsically.

Of course, these questions require engaging in more introspection, and with more self-honesty, than most people have ever dared to undertake. But Schucman's writings assure us that people who pursue such introspection improve the quality of their lives far more so than do people, like behavioralists, who shrink from looking within. The basic question that each person can ask himself or herself is "what do I really want more, the intermittent pleasure of exercising imaginary power, or the continuous flow of real objectless love?" We offer here a program which, if practiced, can result in the desired experience of life.

For most people, this program can work, at first, as a confidence builder. One will gradually develop enough trust in oneself to distinguish between the noise of false happiness conditionals and the çlear homing signals of the Schucman Corridor. An increasing desire to follow the latter is one measure of progress. This is a process of correcting illusions about one's values. How in-line with the natural order of values are the actual values by which one lives? As one calls forth the wisdom inherent in the natural order of values, one will grow the courage one needs to take the final step of relaxing one's grip on the self-created self, and easing into enlightenment.

Self-deception is another pitfall of the practice. Faking the relinquishment of judgment is a self-defeating self-deception. This consists of such thoughts as "I'll overlook that 'sinner's' behavior this time!" But that is not the idea. The aim of forgoing judgment is to learn to step out of the judgment game altogether. One who reserves the right to judge has not authentically forgone judgment. Thus, to stop playing the judgment game demands complete authenticity. The struggles one is experiencing in correcting the habit of judging are, as we mentioned earlier, an excellent subject for journaling, or for sharing in an appropriate small group.

Authenticity requires that one be true to oneself. But when one is unsure, or conflicted, the question arises as to which part of oneself should one be true? Attending inwardly to decipher the signals of the Schucman Corridor can be understood as a process of learning to feel. But this notion must be carefully qualified. Feeling alone may not be one's best guide. When one is responding to frustration with rage, for example, feeling may lead to one's ruin, rather than to one's salvation. Charlie Manson and his "family" followed their bliss as they indulged in torture and murder. Our ancestors followed their happiest feelings as they slaughtered Neanderthals and a host of other large animals.

One can measure one's progress by the way one feels, but one must learn to discriminate carefully between feelings. One's knowledge of the natural order of values is the best reference point for checking whether feelings should be acted upon. In our program, impulses that tend to continue one's addiction to power-pleasure stimulants must be tamed through self-discipline. Feelings must be overseen by scientific principles, if true progress is to be made. Thus, forgoing attacks may require some inner struggle with feelings of frustration, as the desire to condemn is restrained by one's commitment to the principle that such judging is ultimately self-destructive. The confusion involved in learning to discern feelings may not be easily resolved. With 30,000 years or so of left hemispheric momentum behind us, learning to shift attention back over to the feelings of oneness on the right will surely entail some inner struggle.

In working our program, one will also wean oneself from dependence upon authorities as a source of reassurance that one is "in the right." One will find a new center of values based squarely on one's own self-awareness. Increasing sensitivity to the natural order of values within oneself will erase all doubts about the universality and/or relativity of ultimate values. The natural order of values is relative to each human neocortex, and is a universal among human beings. The individual's urgent need of happiness, and his or her intrinsic worth, are not selections from cultural menus, but values which are fixed in human nature by the human genome.

The extent to which one is willing to forgo judgment is an exact measure of the degree to which one is willing to let go of the self-created self. Here is a quantifiable test of willingness. As the number and intensity of one's judgments per day decreases, one's willingness to let the brain heal itself rises. If one carried a counter in one's hand, the size of a stopwatch, one could theoretically count and record the number of one's judgments per day, or per hour. One could draw a graph of the peaks and valleys over a month's time, and look into the causes and conditions for the highs and lows. This could help focus introspection on problem areas. These areas could be studied, and their knots untied, so that one's total number of daily judgments could be reduced, perhaps someday to nil. At that point, letting go would be a cinch.

In conclusion, then, we have presented the empathic science plan for reducing one's addiction to power-pleasure stimuli, and for increasing one's willingness to really heal. This program is derived from the giants of empathic science, and from ancient wisdom. Because willingness is the key to oneness, the causes of unwillingness must be uncovered and exposed to the light of reason. Willingness will come of itself, as the weight of resistance is lifted. Fear and the addiction to power-pleasure stimulants are the chief causes of unwillingness. We stated that meditation, if done well, could loosen the bonds of language as a power-pleasure stimulant. The teaching of language to children entails the nonverbal transference of the entire configuration of assumptions that were originally attached to language in the time of the genocide. At the core of this set of meanings is the connection of language to power. The increase of an authentic willingness to heal requires a corresponding reduction of our dependency on language as a power-pleasure stimulant.

Humanity needs to learn to see language differently. Of course, we cannot all suddenly shut-up and try to live in silence. Nor can we turn-off the inner dialogue, like water from a tap. We need writers, poets, scholars, public speakers, and philosophers to show us how to value speech as an instrument of communication without being addicted to its power.

We can be thankful that the ancient sages of the East have given us meditation. But, frankly, Eastern religions have been a stupefying failure at producing enlightened people. As in the West, these religions have been little more than divisive alliances against opposition, providing members with ammo for judging outsiders and rivals. This is one reason why meditation, of itself, is not enough to "free the spirit" of most people. To remedy the inadequacy of meditation, we have presented the two steps of forgoing judgments and cultivating compassion. We have also suggested participation in small groups, taking inventories of fears and obstacles to willingness, journaling, asking questions to aid introspection, self-tests, and a self-reflective petition to one's brain. We are mindful of Schucman's epigram that "you need do nothing;" however, on the assumption that all progress would be stalled by just sitting and "waiting for willingness," we have offered this plan for action. To conclude this book, we will look at one more obstacle to oneness that Schucman calls our attention to.

Conclusion:

Some Observations on Specialness

We have seen that baby's formation of the body identity engenders a belief in the adult that "I" am separate from others and the world. This idea of separation alters perception so as to reinforce its own validity. Those who believe in their separation see the world that way. As baby's mind/brain relationship matures, the belief in separation as a fact also becomes enveloped in the self-evaluation of specialness. The socialization into the "Speaker identity" further reinforces this self-evaluation.

The idea that "I am special" is a way of relating to oneself, others, and the natural world; indeed, the universe. Specialness is an imaginary self-separation of oneself from the rest, of which one is actually a part.

Specialness, as a value, implies a hierarchy of values. That is, some people become more or less special than others. Immediately, the way for attack is opened, and says Schucman, "cannot be escaped." Also, the fear of being attacked is ignited, as one's specialness, being untrue, must be defended.

In the adult, the assumption of one's specialness signifies a triumph over others. In this, it is a legacy of the genocide. To regard oneself as special is to dwell in the semblance of triumph over everyone else. The lower brain, which does not distinguish between truth and illusion, unless the effort to do so is made, produces a small measure of power pleasure chemicals for as long as specialness is preserved.

Preserving one's specialness becomes an end in itself. Ultimately, according to Schucman, this unnatural and egoistic goal is the final obstacle to realizing one's natural desire to heal. Although an illusion of high self-evaluation, specialness is actually the ultimate in self-degradation because it functions as a denial to oneself of one's awareness of oneness.

The myth of specialness has numerous supporting derivatives. One is the false doctrine of "human exceptionalism." Religions thrive, and profit, from this mistaken belief by casting man as god's special creation. Pioneers of science were once persecuted for teaching that the universe does not revolve around humans and "their" planet Earth. Resistance is still strong against the notion that humans are a product of evolution, like every other living organism. The idea that our much vaunted capacity for reason is a birth defect of our inbreeding hominid progenitors, whose instincts and contentment we lack, will surely be rejected by those who seek to protect their own specialness. Indeed, the suggestion that those animals had a higher quality of life than we do will also be seen as a threat to human exceptionalism, or specialness.

Our pride in the supposed "achievements" of our materialistic societies is yet another form of specialness. The great mass of mankind is poor, while only a relative few have wealth. For we privileged few, does our over-abundance of things compensate us for the loss of the sense of community that once filled the hearts of folks living in primitive communism? Our bodies live longer, but our wars kill more people *per year* than primitive communists ever killed. For our first *100,000 years*, there is no evidence of humans killing other humans in mass. This did not happen until after the genocide.

Consumer society, of course, thrives on the illusion of specialness. Ads encourage people to treat themselves as special, to indulge and pamper themselves by spending money on the advertiser's product. The infantile materialism of the body identity, and its accompanying sense of specialness, renders everyone easy objects of such manipulation. Because the body is a thing, to value oneself as special through the body identity is to value oneself as a thing. The cost of this illusion is the denial of awareness of one's natural value as too precious to be used.

The old adage to "look out for number one," is given validity by the first philosophy of life, which defines life instrumentally as a prey-predator situation. Yet, within the natural order of values, this is the worst advice that can be given. This teaching reinforces the assumptions that one is special, that *as such* one has something to defend, and that the specialness of others is the most vulnerable target for one to go after.

There are still other variants of specialness. These include tribalism, sexism, racism, ageism, nationalism, you name the ism … Any conception that separates people and elevates in value one person over others, or one group over other groups, sustains specialness. Also, the very act of categorizing people *uses* them for a conceptual purpose. Thus, specialness is a concept that preserves the use-value of people, and obscures the sense of each individual's intrinsic value.

To value another as unique and too precious to use is not to value them as special. Specialness is always a relational evaluation. It requires comparing differences in fact and value. The intrinsic valuation of another person has its own form of perception. Intrinsic value marvels at uniqueness; that is, the one-of-a-kind quality of each human being. The other person is seen as one with oneself, but unique as well – a singular expression of oneness. Specialness separates people from oneness. Intrinsic valuation is made possible by the experience of our unity as factual.

This new point of view can only be grasped individually. But as more folks do so, consequences for social organization, and the content of our culture, will surely follow. A true vision of what those consequences will be cannot be known in our time. We are too steeped in our own illusions. Yet, if a turning point is ever reached for the human race, the articulating of that vision will become humanity's goal.

Finally, specialness, too, is subject to the hold-release mechanism of the mind/brain relationship. This gives everyone a choice. What will *you* choose to do?

Endnotes

Introduction
[i] *The Study of Man,* page 27.
[ii] *Personal Knowledge*, page 387.
[iii] Nature PBS "The Cheetah Orphans," at

http://www.pbs.org/wnet/nature/episodes/the-cheetah-orphans/what-makes-a-rehabilitation-program-work/24/

Chapter Two
[iv] Houghton Mifflin, NY 1951.
[v] Houghton Mifflin, NY 1961.
[vi] MIT Press, MA 1998.
[vii] William Morrow, NY 1998.
[viii] Ballantine Books, NY 2001.
[ix] *The World's Religions* (Harper, San Francisco 1991), footnote 53.
[x] Allen Watts often acknowledges his debt to D. T. Suzuki. Also see Christmas Humphreys, *Concentration and Meditation* (Penguin, MD 1968) at page 194.
[xi] Grove Press, NY 1964.
[xii] ibid, page 95.
[xiii] id., page 96.
[xiv] id., page 92.
[xv] id., page 93.
[xvi] id., pages 93 and 97 respectively.
[xvii] id., page 97.
[xviii] Quoted in *The Tao of Physics*, Fritjof Capra (Shambhala, Boulder 1975), at page 99.
[xix] Van Nostrand, NJ 1962, page 78.
[xx] *An Introduction to Zen*, ibid, page 98.
[xxi] "The Eastern Buddhist," May, 1921, pp. 12-13.
[xxii] *Zen Mind, Beginner's Mind* (Weatherhill, NY 1999), Shunryu Suzuki.

Chapter Three
[xxiii] *Genetics*, 4th ed. Susan Elrod, Ph.D., and William Stansfield, Ph.D. McGraw-Hill, NY 2002.

xxiv ibid, p. 301.

xxv ibid, p. 300 passim.

xxvi See Richard Leakey, *The People of the Lake.* Avon Books, NY 1978, esp. Chapter Ten; and, *The Origins of Humankind.* Basic Books, NY 1994.

xxvii *Origins,* id., p. 28 passim.

xxviii *People,* id., p. 145.

xxix ibid, pp. 174 ff.

xxx ibid, pp. 178 ff.; *Origins,* id., pp. 121 ff, 132 ff.

xxxi *People*, id., p. 50 passim.

xxxii ibid, pp. 111, 113 passim.

xxxiii ibid, p. 202.

xxxiv *Origins*, id., p. 97 passim.

xxxv *The Human Brain*, Marian C. Diamond, Ph.D., Arnold B. Scheibel, M.D., Lawrence M. Elson, Ph.D. Harper Perennial, NY 1985. Quotes taken from plates 5-26 and 5-21 respectively.

xxxvi *People*, p. 120 passim.

xxxvii This is D.T.Suzuki's message quoted earlier, at page 48.

xxxviii ibid, page 120. Indeed, the hominid way of life provides a historical example of the "gift economy" in action. Out of this came the mode of production of the first true humans; that is, the "primitive communism" that we describe in Chapter Four.

xxxix ibid., page 118.

xl ibid., page 120.

xli ibid., page 137. Also see, Franz De Waal, *Good Natured* (Harvard University Press, Cambridge 1996).

xlii ibid., page 183.

xliii ibid., page 203.

xliv Of course the Human Genome Project has some critics. One of them is Horace Freeland Judson. He writes, in *The Eight Days of Creation* (Cold Spring Harbor Press, 1996), that this Project assumes a single genome, and that this assumption is "both false and pernicious," because, in part, "it perpetuates the deep error called essentialism." pp. 606-607. In our view, however, Judson's implication that a plurality of human genomes exists rests upon a confusion of the particular with the general. That is, a plurality of *gene pools* exists in the world today, which contain the formulas for the ethnic diversity that appears between people. But the fecundity of inter-ethnic relations strongly suggests that we are one species, and that our superficial differences are variations on a common theme. "Multiregionalism," the notion that the peoples of the world evolved in place, separately, and simultaneously, commits the same error of logic. It is too improbable to accept, and invites inferences of racial superiority.

Chapter Four

[xlv] *Language,* Virginia P. Clark, et al, eds. (St. Martin's Press, NY 1977. All quotes of the Halls are taken from page 454. The reader will see, after reading our Chapter Five, that the Great Shift has created a situation in world culture in which, following a "three monkeys" strategy, the left brain does not know what the right brain is doing. Further research on this "bisected-brain syndrome" could begin with Dr. Michael S. Gazzaniga's essay, at Ch. 7, "The Spilt Brain in Man," *Language,* ibid. This condition is perpetuated, in part, because our schools subliminally instruct trusting and naïve students in the practice of "auto-commissurotomy." Cf. the essay by Roger W. Sperry at the conclusion of *The Encyclopedia of Ignorance*, Ronald Duncan and Miranda Weston-Smith, eds. (Pocket Books, NY 1977).

[xlvi] Alan W. Watts, *The Book* (Collier Books, NY 1966).

xlvii See Gore, Richard. National Geographic, July 2000, page 91, ff; and, Shreeve, James. *The Neandertal Enigma.* William Morrow, NY. 1995

[xlviii] All quotes regarding the Tasaday are taken from page 146.
[xlix] See the website of Thomas N. Headland, at www.sil.org/~headlandt/caveppl.htm (accessed 12-8-11)

Chapter Five

[l] Constable, George. *The Neanderthals.* Time-Life Books, NY. 1973, page 26.

[li] Trinkaus and Shipman. *The Neandertals.* Alfred A. Knoph, NY. 1992, page 174.
[lii] Trinkaus and Shipman, page 177.

[liii] Trinkaus and Shipman, page 254.

[liv] Trinkaus and Shipman, page 259.

[lv] Trinkaus and Shipman, page 335 f.

[lvi] Shreeve, James. *The Neandertal Enigma.* William Morrow, NY. 1995, page 90 f; cf. Tattersall Ian. *The Last Neanderthal.* Macmillan, NY. 1995, page 96 f.

[lvii] Trinkaus and Shipman, page 178.

[lviii] Trinkaus and Shipman, page 174.

[lix] Tattersall, page 130.

[lx] Tattersall, page 170.

[lxi] Tattersall, page 167, Shreeve page 54.

[lxii] Tattersall, page 169.

[lxiii] Tattersall, page 170.

[lxiv] Tattersall, page 170.

[lxv] Shreeve, page 36-38.

[lxvi] Shreeve, page 91 f.

[lxvii] Leakey, Richard. *The Origins of Humankind.* Basic Books, NY. 1994, page 145.

[lxviii] Tattersall, pages 170, 171, 391, T-S 353 f, 391 f, Shreeve pages 120, 273, Time N page 82. Recent studies of Neanderthal DNA show that they had the FOXP2gene associated with some speech functions in humans and some primates. But the presence of this gene does not support the inference that they developed complex speech, or even had an anatomical capacity for speech.

[lxix] Tattersall, pages 95-97, 167.

[lxx] Shreeve, pages 21, 134-137.

[lxxi] Tattersall, page 17; Shreeve, page 92.

[lxxii] Shreeve, page 21, 52 f.

[lxxiii] Constable, page 128 f.

[lxxiv] Shreeve, page 154.

[lxxv] Tattersall, page 63, cf. Shreeve, page 161.

[lxxvi] Tattersall, page 148 f.

[lxxvii] While hominids, Neanderthal evolution separated from their common ancestor with humans long ago. According to the July 11, 1997 issue of the journal Cell, DNA analysis of Neanderthal bone fragments now show that Neanderthals "probably diverged

from the lineage leading to modern humans about 550,000 to 690,000 years ago." Source: Encarta Yearbook, Microsoft Corp., July 1997. Cf. note 104.

[lxxviii] Trinkaus and Shipman, page 241.

[lxxix] Tattersall, page 15.

[lxxx] Tattersall, page 156.

[lxxxi] Tattersall, page 157.

[lxxxii] Tattersall, page 15, Trinkaus and Shipman, page 417.

[lxxxiii] Shreeve, page 5.

[lxxxiv] Trinkaus and Shipman, page 367.

[lxxxv] Trinkaus and Shipman, page 381.

[lxxxvi] Trinkaus and Shipman, page 417.

[lxxxvii] Tattersall, page 14, Trinkaus and Shipman, page 356.

[lxxxviii] Constable, page 104.

[lxxxix] Smithsonian June '03, page 84.

[xc] Shreeve, pages 210-239.

[xci] Leakey, page 125 passim.

[xcii] Trinkaus and Shipman, page 245, quoting Dorothy Garrod.

[xciii] Shreeve, page 182, Tattersall accord, page 103.

[xciv] Trinkaus and Shipman, page 393.

[xcv] Tattersall, pages 104, 106.

[xcvi] Shreeve, page 179.

[xcvii] Leakey, page 86.

[xcviii] Tattersall, page 116, Shreeve, page 182.

[xcix] Trinkaus and Shipman, pages 248, 271, 287.

[c] Leakey, page 98; cf. Trinkaus and Shipman, page 415; Shreeve page 196; and Tattersall, page 198.

[ci] Shreeve, page 196, quoting John Shea; accord, Trinkaus and Shipman, page 415.

[cii] Constable, page 23.

[ciii] Trinkaus and Shipman, pages 393, 415; and, Shreeve, page 193.

[civ] One effort at decoding the Neanderthal genome is "A Draft Sequence of the Neandertal Genome," by Richard E. Green, et al, in Science, 7 May 2010: Vol. 328 no. 5979 pp. 710-722 http://www.sciencemag.org/content/328/5979/710.full

Green et al suggest that some gene flow between true humans and Neanderthals did occur, probably in the Levant more than

30,000 years ago. They base their claim on their analysis of nuclear DNA taken from Neanderthal bone fragments. Unfortunately, contamination of the bone specimens from a variety of sources, including bacteria and human contact, undermine the hypothesis of the authors that interbreeding resulting in fertile off-spring occurred.

The authors acknowledge that "The only part of the genome that has been examined from multiple Neandertals, the mitochondrial DNA (mtDNA) genome, consistently falls outside the variation found in present-day humans and thus provides no evidence for interbreeding" (15–19). In other words, no mtDNA evidence exists of any line of "mixed breed" descendents from a common mother.

In another study, Noonan et al. found no evidence of Neanderthal admixture to the modern human genome, hence no descendents of interbreeding. For a discussion of the controversy see the "Neanderthal Genome Project," in http://en.wikipedia.org/wiki/Neanderthal_Genome_Project

[cv] Tattersall, page 143.

[cvi] Tattersall, page 17.

[cvii] Leakey, page 94.

[cviii] Shreeve, page 122, Tattersall accord, page 186. Also, as said in note 104, whether man-Neanderthal mating in the Levant produced fertile off-spring is still a debated matter.

[cix] Constable, page 38.

[cx] Tattersall, page 179.

[cxi] Leakey, page 99; Tattersall accord, page 179.

[cxii] Leakey, page 99.

[cxiii] Shreeve, page 36. Also, whether man-Neanderthal mating in the Levant produced fertile off-spring is still a debated matter.

[cxiv] Tattersall, pages 161-162, 201.

[cxv] Trinkaus and Shipman, pages 382, 386.

[cxvi] Aristotle, page 17.

[cxvii] National Geographic, vol. 147, no. 1, Jan. 1975, pages 66-67.

[cxviii] Constable, page 115.
[cxix] ibid. page 115.
[cxx] id. page 117.
[cxxi] id. page 117.
[cxxii] id. page 119.
[cxxiii] id. page 119.

Chapter Six

[cxxiv] Empathic science is a "science" precisely because it follows its own formal system. That is the system of Hartman's formal axiology. Just as natural science consists of an empirical-mathematical system of thought, so empathic science consists of what Hartman terms an "interpretational-axiological" framework. Laws of the physical world are discovered by the natural science interpretive framework. One law of chemistry is, for example, that two parts of hydrogen added to one part oxygen will make water: or, H^2O. In the same way, laws of the universe of human meaning can be discovered by empathic science.

One of these we call "Gardner's Law," because he was the first to show clearly how this law applies to human experience. The formal expression of Gardner's Law is: $S^E=I$. In the terms of formal axiology this can be read as: "the extrinsic valuation of a systemic value can produce an intrinsic value." These, of course, are the three dimensions of value. More commonly put, the formula means: "a realistic plan, well executed, can result in satisfaction;" or, plan, act, enjoy.

This law has unlimited application, from individual, to couple, to small group, to large organization, to nation, to international system. The future of empathic science will entail the articulation of its paradigm. In turn, that will include the application of Gardner's Law to a myriad set of events in human relations. New laws will surely be discovered. In this Chapter we will confine our discussion to one very narrow, yet extremely important, demonstration of Gardner's Law. That is, we will present empathic science's program by which the individual may heal his or her case of the human birth defect; a specific version of plan, act, enjoy.

[cxxv] As if in dialogue with Nietzsche, *A Course in Miracles* also goes "beyond good and evil." But while he only finds "the will to power" there, Dr. Schucman, like Buddha (whom Nietzsche defies), finds compassion, and a way out of the power-pleasure addiction.

[cxxvi] Dr. Schucman gives a special meaning to the term "forgiveness." In her sense, forgiveness is a letting go of judgment altogether, as opposed to a one time waiver of judgment while reserving the right to judge on other occasions. In this sense, "forgiveness" can be used as a scientific term, another instance of the hold-release mechanism.

[cxxvii] There is a formal structure of such judgments. Because judgments are thoughts, or ideas, they are systemic values. A person, as we have said, is an intrinsic value. Hence, an attack judgment has the formal structure of Is, or the systemic disvaluation of an intrinsic value. The act of a judgment attack also has a formal structure: $[Is]^E=I$. I.e., engaging in the systemic disvaluation of an intrinsic value can result in a malicious pleasure. The techniques of reducing complex value patterns to their formal representation have yet to be developed due to the tragic disregard of Hartman's formal axiology; here is the repetition of Gregor Mendel's treatment by the fools who should know better.

[cxxviii] A reorganization of the criminal justice system, to better reflect the natural order of values, is possible. See this author's *Progressive Logic*, Chapter Four.

INDEX

A

D

Dalai Lama 48

Dance 147

Darwinian theory 95

Dinosaurs 27-29, 47, contentment 46f

Discontent as the product of alienation, or misalignment, of mind and brain 58, 108, 139

DNA 93, 203

double helix model by Watson and Clark 93

dualism 3, 83

E

Eastern religions, failure at producing enlightened people 270

Education 77, for body image 57, 159f, 17, 90 (also see public education)

Ego 34, 232, animal and human 34

Elrod and Stansfield 96

Empathic observation 8, 78, 111

Empathic Science

Fear, of the subjective 15, 157, 172, as obstacle to healing 232, reduced by scientific knowledge 79, 140f, 266, and Zen 86

Felix 30, 44

Ferguson, Marilyn, The Aquarian Conspiracy 11

Fetus 59

field theory of consciousness 22, 32

filtering function in reptilian and mammalian brain 21, 30f

first human tots 126

First Philosophy of Life

> defines the world as a jungle129f, desensitizes people to the natural order of values 138, learned from animal elders 129, replicated the animal worldview 130f, oldest human artifact 134, still operative philosophy 134, 228, no teaching about contentment 132, 138

Foraging apes 118-120

Four Fs 132

free loading 121

Freud, Sigmund 5

Fromm, Eric 201

G

Galileo 13, 168

gatherer-hunter 117

healing as humanity's life-task 91, 230, 248, no order of difficulty 261

healthy mind 54

Heart 55, disease 56

Heisenberg 173

higher power 19, 95

Hinduism 80

hippocampal-dentate complex 114

Hobbes 258

hold-and-release mechanism 70, 77, 88, 275

Holmes, Oliver Wendell, jr. 133

Hominid, defined by genome 97f, brain growth 103, politics 105f, instinctive altruism 118-124, gracile 99f

Hominidae 97

Homo erectus 103, "tear drop" hand held axe 190

Homo habilis 103

Homo sapiens 97

Hotel Neanderthal 185

Human, first 47, children with animal parents 129, culture101, discontent 36, 50, 103, essence 102, 124, exceptionalism 243, 273, stone work 189

Intersubjective agreement 12, 66, of Schucman with Buddha's teachings 64

Intersubjective consultation 2, 12, 92

Intrinsic value 134, 137, 275, values oneself and others as too precious to use 130, 253, and Hartman 51

Introspection 1-9, 13, 30, 69, 115, follows the logic of inclusion 62, self-healing 56, as method attempts to look from the inside 92, microscope 65, 67, read memory 224

Inventiveness 100f, 119

J

Jitters 142

Joe 8, 10

Joselito and Billy 158

Judge keeps the culture of judgment alive 258

Judgment game 250f, 298

Judgments

> as attack always resulting in triumph 252, as self-stimulation 259, as self-harming 260-265, as mental illness 254, invariable structure of 300, as a semblance of great power in the lower regions of the brain 254, provide immediate jolts of the power-pleasure opiates 250

Jung, Carl 165

differences in animal and human learning 33, on creative leaps of evolution 34f, contemporary amoeba hunts for food 26, Personal Knowledge 11-12, 25, The Study of Man 15, evolution of mind/brain relationship 25f

Politics for the early humans 105f, 147f, 197

Pooh-pooh 87

pop psychology 5, **8**

positive regard in body image 61

Power-pleasure7, the rise of 220, 229

practical judgment 29f

pragmatic instrumentalism 132

preconceptual memories 4

primitive communism 152, 174, 273

Private languages 42, 74f, 87-89

program for self-healing 62, 229

Projection 9

public education 87f, teach self-caring 61, lessons about how to form the right intention 90f, and behavioralism 77, Zen 87, health 57

punctuated equilibrium 96, 126

Q

ABOUT THE AUTHOR

Born in Chicago in 1946, Dr. Kelleher drove Route 66 to Los Angeles in 1966. In college he read his first books on Zen; Alan Watts's *This Is It*, and D.T. Suzuki's *Introduction to Zen*. His study of Zen has never ended. After experimenting with marijuana and LSD, he decided to drop out of materialistic society and hitch-hiked to San Francisco. He lived in the Haight-Ashbury area of that city for several months. Then he joined the Morning Star Ranch commune in northern California. When local health authorities closed down the commune (which was the right to do!), Dr. Kelleher became determined to continue his spiritual seeking despite living in a society hostile to higher values.

In 1969 he was given a mantra by a TM leader in Berkeley, CA. Although he practiced this form of meditation faithfully, the experience was unsatisfying. Then in the mid-1980s, while living in Santa Barbara, California, he learned to meditate from guru Maharaj Ji. Dr. Kelleher reports that he instantly slipped into a state of deep relaxation. Gradually his meditation practice came to center on the use of the techniques discussed in Chapter Six. Meditating twice a day, each time, for him, is like the experience of first walking into a grand cathedral and feeling awe, wonder, joy, and a profound sense of the sacred.

The Sunday Morning Meditators met weekly in the Pasadena area for about 10 years, between 1995 and 2005. Economic dislocations and the tragic deaths of some members, including one of the founders, Avery Clayton, due to health problems, caused the group to disband.

www.ingramcontent.com/pod-product-compliance
Lightning Source LLC
Chambersburg PA
CBHW060236290526
45789CB00001B/65

9 781470 007287